TORPEDOES IN THE GULF

Number 40: Williams-Ford
Texas A&M University Military History Series

TORPEDOES IN THE GULF GALVESTON

AND THE U-BOATS, 1942–1943

MELANIE WIGGINS

Texas A&M University Press
College Station

The paper used in this book meets the minimum requirements
of the American National Standard for Permanence
of paper for Printed Library Materials, Z39.48-1984.
Binding materials have been chosen for durability.

∞

Library of Congress Cataloging-in-Publication Data

Wiggins, Melanie, 1934–
    Torpedoes in the Gulf : Galveston and the U-boats, 1942–1943 by
Melanie Wiggins — 1st ed.
        p.   cm. — (Texas A&M University military history series ; #40)
    Includes bibliographical references and index.
    ISBN 978-0-89096-627-3 (cloth);   ISBN 978-0-89096-648-8 (pbk.)
    1. World War, 1939–1945 — Naval operations — Submarine. 2. World
War, 1939–1945 — Naval operations, German. 3. World War, 1939–1945 —
Campaings — Mexico, Gulf of. 4. Galveston (Tex.) — History.
I. Title. II. Series.
D781.D54 1995   94-31861
940.54'51 — dc20   CIP

To Herbert Uhlig and his son Ralph,
Peter Petersen, and Günther Reibhorn,
for helping me tell the German side of the story.

We called it the "If and Goodbye" era:
all our sentences started with "If . . ."
and we were always saying "Goodbye."

—SARA ELLEN STUBBS

Contents

Illustrations

MAP

Preface

"WHAT DO YOU REMEMBER about the war years in Galveston?" I asked several local women. "Were you terrified about the U-boats sinking so many ships?"

"Oh no," they would answer. "We were too busy partying and having a good time."

Their attitude puzzled me at first, but later I understood. In early 1942, at the beginning of America's war involvement, Galveston Island became a recreation center for all area servicemen. Fresh-faced recruits wearing crisp new uniforms flocked to Galveston by the thousands, arriving in buses, trucks, trains, and cars. They joyfully burst into town seeking relief from rigorous military training, which the United States had begun too late. They were eighteen years old and had never fired a gun in their lives, and both the government and the populace, knowing that many would be killed, tried to provide diversions while there was time. "Eat, drink, and be merry," everyone said, "for tomorrow we die."

Throngs of soldiers, sailors, and marines strolled along the seawall enjoying the warm sun, soft gulf breezes, and pretty girls. Red, pink, and white oleanders bloomed in all their glory, sea gulls squawked overhead, and gentle waves swished up and down the sand. At Twenty-fifth Street an enormous carousel with life-sized racing horses whirled, its music blending with the racket of shooting galleries and games next door. The Mountain Speedway roller coaster roared up and down, a giant Ferris wheel swung riders into the sky, the glittering Balinese Room offered Hollywood entertainers and gambling, seafood restaurants abounded, every shop and bar offered slot machines and tip books, and Murdoch's Pier had swimming, refreshments, and beauty contests. It was paradise on earth.

Small wonder that Galvestonians had difficulty envisioning the horrors of war, especially on their island. The entire country had refused to think about commitment to Europe until that fatal December 7, 1941. Even as U.S. troops massed and went into training, an air of festivity and excitement prevailed in Galveston. New York mayor Fiorello La Guardia, national leader of civil defense efforts, and his assistant, Eleanor Roosevelt, failed to lead the nation into action. Instead, they put their thoughts to designing uniforms for workers, debating whether to put pleats on the skirts.

Amid total disorganization in America the German navy struck, and with great success. As soon as the U-boats had polished off the East Coast shipping early in 1942, they turned their sights to the Gulf of Mexico. Galvestonians, along with the rest of the nation, were convinced that their sparkling blue gulf waters would be safe from the undersea sharks of steel. But they were wrong. And so begins our story.

Many friends assisted with the book, all with much enthusiasm and encouragement, and I wish to acknowledge and thank them for their efforts.

For their trust and friendship, I am forever indebted to the U-boat commanders, officers, and friends I met in Germany and to the many people in Galveston and nearby towns who cooperated and gave suggestions and leads. It would be impossible to list them all, but I would like to especially thank the following: Yvonne Sutherlin, Robert Scheina, Charles Lloyd (U.S. Navy Armed Guard World War II Veterans), E. J. Heins (Merchant Marine World War II Veterans), Mary Lou Featherstone, Jim Airey, Fletcher Harris, Hetta Jockusch Towler, Peaches Kempner, Ruth Kempner, Nonie Thompson, Lyda Ann Thomas, the Rosenberg Library of Galveston, the New Orleans Public Library, Dr. Howard Williams (Orange County Historical Commission), Dr. Norman Black (Gregg County Historical Commission), Carol Nelson (U.S. Army Corps of Engineers), Charles Stubbs, Sara Stubbs, Senator Lloyd Bentsen, and Patrick H. Butler III.

Others are Bernard Cavalcante and Kathy Lloyd (the Navy Historical Center), Commander Herbert Uhlig, Ralph Uhlig, Commander Reinhard Hardegen (U-123), Erich Gimpel, Wilhelm Grap (U-506), Horst Bredow (the U-Boot-Archiv), Harry Cooper and the Sharkhunters, John Taylor, Harry Reilly and Bill Sherman (the National Archives), Commander Hans-Georg Hess (U-995), Commander Gerd Thäter (U-466 and U-3506), Günther Reibhorn, Alfred Nuesser, the Bundesarchiv in Koblenz, Allen Meyer, Christian Reuleaux, Ute Carson, Hans Esken, Captain James E. Wise, Jr., USN (Ret.), and Mancel Halverson.

Editor Noel Parsons buoyed my spirits with his friendship and confidence, and Thad White, Henry Duke, and Wade Anderson solved technical difficulties with computer and printer equipment.

Special thanks go to the ones who patiently endured my interminable interrogations, and they are as follows: Jack Dodendorf, Jim McKaig, Alfred Plaschke, John Naumczik, John Kinietz, George Hamilton, Glenn Cudd, Ballinger Mills, Gene Hosey, Captain Glenn Tronstad, H. A. Suhler, Adolph Johnson, Victor Messina, Irene Rice Johnson, Lyda Kempner Quinn, Emmy Lou Whitridge, Diane Hansen, James Handy, and Harry Brown.

Last of all, I want to say that Peter Petersen answered at least ten thousand questions about how U-boats work, translated many pages of war diaries and German correspondence, and kindly related his own incredible experiences. His help was invaluable.

TORPEDOES IN THE GULF

1

The Spies

COLORFUL NATIONAL FLAGS OF CUBA, Denmark, France, Japan, and other countries fluttered from balconies and windows of consulates along Galveston's Strand Street in 1940. The German banner, with its bold red, white, and black design with swastika, caught the eye of John Focke, a native Galvestonian who had seen the flag for years but could no longer stand the sight of it. Focke stormed back to his office and phoned his friend Julius Jockusch, honorary consul of Germany, and bellowed a warning that if Jockusch didn't remove that symbol of Hitler immediately, he would never speak to him again.

Jockusch, shocked at Focke's fierce attack, told him that he felt it would not be possible to close the consulate and that he had an obligation to continue representing the Germans in America.[1]

Focke hung up and never again spoke to Jockusch, ending their lifelong friendship. Shortly after their conversation, Jockusch went to see his friend Karl Tidemann and told him that things were getting difficult for him and his family. He said they were being harassed and insulted constantly and feared that if he kept his consular position, it would get worse. They discussed the matter at length, and Tidemann advised him to quit.[2]

A few days later, on May 11, 1940, an announcement appeared in the Galveston paper: "Jockusch Resigns Post as German Consul for Texas." Jockusch said, "I prefer not to make any extended statement concerning my resignation except, according to the attitude of the U.S. government . . . I feel my position as consul of Germany is inconsistent with loyal American citizenship."[3]

Friends of the Jockusch family understood and sympathized with his resignation. They all suffered from the anti-German sentiment sweeping the country and tried to ignore it as best they could, but Hitler's campaign to suppress the Jews and conquer Europe had created fear and loathing in America for anyone remotely connected with the fatherland.

Hitler had taken Poland in 1939, invaded Czechoslovakia and seized Norway in early 1940, and in May of that year was marching on Holland, Belgium, and France. Headlines on May 22 described French civilians fleeing as Nazi planes machine-gunned them down.

Martin Dies, fiery Texas congressman and chairman of the Un-American Activities Committee, began his probes for "fifth columnists," Communists, and other "subversives" throughout the country, frequently making the news with his accusations, many of which later proved unjustified. "I have had unconfirmed reports that a number of camouflaged air bases have been built in Mexico immediately south of the Rio Grande," he announced in May, 1940. This, of course, had no basis in fact.[4]

For the next year the Un-American Activities Committee searched for suspicious persons and reported that German consuls throughout the country were collecting vital information and passing it on to the Third Reich. Some of this may have been true, for on May 2, 1941, a small news item appeared in the *New York Times*: "Nazi Consul's Telescope Scans San Francisco Bay." The article quoted W. W. Chapin, chairman of the Golden Gate Planning Commission: "The German Consulate has installed a six-inch telescope in its quarters to keep an eye on everything that goes on in the Golden Gate." He claimed that Captain Fritz Wiedemann, consul general, and his staff were moving into an old mansion on Pacific Heights above the forts and army posts flanking the entrance to San Francisco Bay. "The telescope would make the army's gun batteries at Fort Baker, Fort Barry, and Fort Wiley appear just across the street," Chapin said.[5]

Wiedemann, Hitler's handsome World War I company commander and personal adjutant after the war, had gained a reputation for being the number one Nazi in the United States. The new German consulate with its huge telescope overlooking vital military installations must have caught Congressman Dies's attention.

Baron Edgar von Spiegel, also well known as consul general of the

Gulf Coast, had been conducting his business at 3029 Saint Charles Avenue, New Orleans, since 1937. His eight-state domain included Texas, Louisiana, Mississippi, Alabama, Florida, Georgia, South Carolina, and North Carolina, plus Puerto Rico and the Virgin Islands. Von Spiegel had decorated Julius Jockusch with the Order of Service of the German Eagle in 1938 and knew all the Gulf Coast consuls well.

The baron's name became familiar throughout the United States in 1928 when Lowell Thomas's book, *Raiders of the Deep*, was published. This collection of dramatic and hair-raising tales of World War I U-boats included that of von Spiegel, commander of U-93, whose bravery and assistance of enemy sailors had won him a reputation as the most chivalrous U-boat captain in the German navy.

In June, 1919, the baron, who had been captured and sent to prison in England, was repatriated. He then went into the shipping trade, where he enjoyed great success until the German financial collapse, which destroyed his business. In 1928 he became a representative of the American Graham-Paige car company and made frequent visits to the United States. In October, 1936, the government of the Third Reich sent him to work in the German embassy in Washington and in June of the following year appointed him consul general of the gulf states.[6]

Adolf Karl Georg Edgar, Baron Spiegel von und zu Peckelsheim, a slender man with aristocratic bearing, believed strongly in Hitler's ability to bring the fatherland out of its severe depression, and he made it a point to express his views on the subject as often as possible. "There has not been any other revolution so modest or without bloodshed," he said. "The present German government is the most popular with the people of any I can remember."[7]

In 1937 he toured the states in his consular territory, speaking to various groups. "There is a man in Germany named Hitler," he said in Atlanta, "who is very much hated in other countries but who is greatly loved there. The German people do not fear the chance of another world war because they have confidence in Hitler's common sense." He went on to say that Hitler was a man of many surprises and that as soon as Germany had restored some of her colonies, lost in World War I, there would be no chance of war in Europe for many years.[8]

In 1938 von Spiegel spoke to the Young Men's Business Club at the Roosevelt Hotel in New Orleans, where he lamented that propaganda was breeding international hatred of Germany. At the end of his speech, Dr. Joseph Cohen, a member of the club, stood up. "You can take your remarks back to the head of the German government," he said. The chairman of the entertainment committee, John Ryan, asked him to sit back down and keep quiet out of deference to von Spiegel.[9]

In August, 1939, the Dies committee investigated a letter from the president of the University of Florida, saying that von Spiegel had questioned him on the status of the school's German professor, a Viennese refugee opposed to Nazi theories. He reported that the consul had also attempted to give the school free books about Germany, which von Spiegel denied were propaganda material. "The books were four or five fairy tales," he said.[10]

On June 15, 1940, about a month after Julius Jockusch resigned, Baron von Spiegel commented that he thought Germany would have an early victory over France and that his government "would not forget that when she was fighting bitterly for her very life, the United States gave every material aid to her enemies." Later, when the remark was published, he said that he had spoken in private and never intended it for the news. He also expressed his confidence that the German government would be satisfied with regaining her possessions in Africa—and possibly a little more. "The new Germany will be self-sufficient, with oil from Holland and Rumania . . . wheat and wool from her friend Russia and countless other supplies from other European countries." He predicted that Spain would soon join Germany against France and that France would capitulate in a matter of days. "For the past twenty years we have been preparing," he said with a smile, "while France and England have been sleeping, expecting that they were safe."[11]

The next day Senator Lloyd Hendrick of the Louisiana legislature said he would introduce a resolution asking President Roosevelt and Congress to demand that Germany recall its consul general in New Orleans. Referring to von Spiegel's statement, he said: "This . . . is contrary to the overwhelmingly expressed sentiment of the American people favoring the Allies. It only tends to add to the general hysteria of these troubled times. The Baron's words create a condition of unrest in our nation, as evidenced by the fact that a police guard was placed around his house after he made his statement."[12]

The following day the governor of Louisiana, Sam Jones, called upon Secretary of State Cordell Hull to investigate Baron von Spiegel, saying that the baron had an "openly unfriendly attitude toward the United States."[13]

The next morning a smiling, unperturbed von Spiegel flew to the nation's capital. "I am going to Washington on business," he told the press. "It's just a regular trip. I go there often."[14]

On June 23 the New Orleans paper announced that an investigation into the activities of von Spiegel had been submitted to the State Department. There was speculation that it might lead to a demand for his recall, but no action was taken.[15]

Nothing more was heard from the baron until September. G. F. Neuhauser, editor of the *San Antonio Freie Presse,* a German newspaper, announced to the Dies committee that he had received a threatening letter from von Spiegel. He said that the baron had told him his reporting was "hostile" and that Hitler was upset about it.[16]

The Dies committee in November accused the German consuls in New Orleans and Mobile, Alabama, of "spreading the work" of the German-founded Transocean News Service. Their report described the news service as an "agency for the dissemination of propaganda in foreign countries and utilized by Hitler as an organization that could, with a minimum of suspicion, engage in espionage activities."[17]

A letter signed by von Spiegel to the Transocean News Service in New York explained that because of excessive work, his office would no longer be able to handle incoming reading matter to the previous extent, and that therefore he requested "merely the pink sheets, summary of today's news." The Mobile consul's letter said he wanted to cancel the paper for July and August and ended, "Heil Hitler!"[18]

One wonders what all this had to do with espionage, since there was nothing secret about the newsletters. Senator Dies was convinced, however, that he was on the right track. His committee released a "white paper" describing widespread Nazi activities in the United States. "I have a list of suspects who I have every reason to believe are Gestapo [German secret police] agents in the United States," he announced. "As fast as possible we will move in on them

... but we are not going to move against innocents." Dies said he believed his report would "effectively smash" the plans of all Nazi organizations at work in this country.[19]

During all these investigations Baron von Spiegel continued his consular duties and made frequent fishing trips into the Gulf of Mexico. He often invited friends to go with him on excursions down the Mississippi River, through the river delta, and along the southern shores of Louisiana around Grand Isle, south of Houma, where fishing was excellent. The baron, lover of the sea and expert navigator, steered his luxurious mahogany yacht with ease. Many of his friends had large boats, and they frequently traveled together into the gulf trolling for mackerel, tarpon, and ling.

Reverend Harry Brown, von Spiegel's close friend and frequent fishing partner, directed the German retirement home in New Orleans, at that time called the Protestant Home for the Aged. Every February the residents of the big two-story house on Magazine Street held an outdoor festival that featured dark beer, sausages, crocks of sauerkraut, accordion playing, and singing. "It was quite an important event for them," recalled Brown's son Harry. "They spent months getting ready for it, preparing the food and practicing songs." The baron and his wife mixed with the festival guests and on other occasions visited the Browns and their retirement home residents.[20]

Suddenly, in June, 1941, President Roosevelt ordered Germany and Italy to close all U.S. consulates as well as the German Library of Information in New York, the German Railway and Tourist agencies, and the Transocean News Service. This order did not affect the embassy, the official Nazi news agency, or correspondents of German newspapers, however. The president said the action was taken based on investigations by the Justice Department. These were not made public but were understood to include much evidence of Nazi espionage, sabotage, and propaganda within the consulates.[21] "These consulates were spread all over the country and generally staffed by fanatical party members who did a lot of political propaganda," said Erich Gimpel, former German intelligence agent and electronics expert. "President Roosevelt did right in closing them."[22]

Of the twenty-four German consulates ordered closed, eighteen were located in seaport cities, which may have caused concern that shipping information could be obtained by the consuls there. Some said that the government's action was a joke, because it had no effect on German military and naval intelligence units—the Nazi military attaché had been left in place at the embassy. Actually, in 1939 the German military attaché in Washington, General von Boetticher, had advised his superiors in Berlin not to worry about American aggression in Europe, that U.S. armament was inadequate for intervention, and that Charles Lindbergh and Eddie Rickenbacker advocated keeping America out of the war.[23]

On September 18, 1939, Hans Thomsen, German chargé d'affaires in Washington, tried to warn his foreign minister in Berlin that "the sympathies of the American people are with our enemies." He further noted that there would be dire consequences if any agents tried to carry out sabotage activities in the United States and requested that there be none. His message must have gone unheeded, for in January, 1940, he wrote to Berlin saying that two German *Abwehr* (the high command for espionage) agents had reported to the embassy, ready to plant bombs in armament industries. Thomsen requested that this project be canceled. "There is no surer way of driving America into the war than resorting again to a course of action which drove America into the ranks of our enemies . . . in the World War, and . . . did not in the least impede the war industries of the United States."[24]

Hitler was conducting intelligence operations as early as 1935, according to Erich Gimpel, who lived at that time in Lima, Peru, and worked for Telefunken. The military attaché at the German embassy ordered Gimpel to get information regarding ships, crews, and cargoes in port and to pass on the information regularly. As time progressed, the attaché requested that Gimpel build a shortwave radio to send Morse code messages to Germany. "A transmitter wasn't very big. You could build it, if you had all the pieces, in a couple of hours. It was very simple," he said. So the agent began sending messages from Lima to Berlin, telling them what kinds of ships were entering and leaving the port.[25]

"Our whole network of agents [in the United States] . . . had been hastily contrived after the war had actually started," Gimpel recalled. "When we were at peace and preparations could have been handled with comparative ease, the Foreign Ministry had declined to do so for political reasons. It was only shortly before the outbreak of war that they intensified espionage activities in the States, but even then they were working too much with amateurs and not enough with experts." Various German clubs were requested to give information to their former fatherland, and the ones who did gave nothing of value. The FBI broke up a twenty-nine-member spy network (mostly ships' stewards) in the United States in July, 1941, and the news hit the papers the same day that all Italian and German consuls sailed for Lisbon. "We suddenly found ourselves with no secret agents in the country of our principal enemies," Gimpel went on.[26]

Gimpel, trained by the *Abwehr* in 1944, said that the German military knew nothing about America, had no production figures or armament information, and lacked any knowledge of standards of army training, reserves, or morale. "The Foreign Ministry . . . hustled Germany into war with the richest country in the world. We had no idea how rich until afterward," he wrote.[27]

If the American people had known how few real spies were in this country, they would have laughed Chairman Dies right off his podium. In any event, he convinced the State Department that the consuls were aiding and abetting the enemy and that they should go.

In the San Francisco consulate a swarm of reporters interviewed Captain Fritz Wiedemann. A small American flag sat on his desk. "The times here have not been very easy," he said. "All I can say is that when I came here two and a quarter years ago, full of hope and good intentions, I by no means realized this as the desirable end. I don't think I will have to join the [German] army. I am very curious, too, and very interested in where I will have to go."

"Did the order of the State Department come as a shock?" asked a newsman.

"I would say no," he replied.[28]

The *New York Times* carried portraits of a smiling Wiedemann; Dr. Herbert Scholz, consul at Boston; and Baron Edgar von Spiegel with his narrow face, piercing eyes, and black eyebrows.[29]

In New Orleans a few days later, someone played a small joke on Baron von Spiegel. An ad appeared in the *Times-Picayune* announcing a six-piece white porch or garden set for sale and on display at 3029 Saint Charles Avenue. "Will be sold highest offer. Proceeds British war relief." The address and phone number listed were those of the baron. He probably did not notice it, being busy preparing to leave the country. He and his wife were stuffing their clothes into suitcases and boxing up all papers and personal effects for shipment to New York. Assistants stripped the consulate building of furniture, china, silver, and other household items—including the swastika over the front door—and put them into crates for storage in New Orleans. By this time crowds surrounded the house, yelling and screaming insults. Von Spiegel and his wife left by the back door and were driven to the Italian consulate nearby, where they spent five hours with Consul Marquis Gian Gerolamo Chiavari. From there a chauffeur took them all to the train station.[30]

Harry Brown, concerned about the safety of the baron and his wife, drove to the Saint Charles Avenue house to tell them good-bye, but he was unable to get near the place, now surrounded by police and the National Guard. Brown left and never saw his friends again.[31]

The von Spiegels arrived in New York on July 14, 1941. Their taxi joined a stream of vehicles carrying German and Italian consuls, their families, and baggage onto the pier, while a crowd of thirty-five hundred friends and relatives, held back by police lines, tried to get a glimpse of departing loved ones. No one shouted, waved, or cheered, and a few held wilted bouquets. Detectives, FBI men, immigration officers, and customs agents watched as the line of diplomats boarded the *West Point*, a former luxury liner converted into a drab gray troop transport. Most of the four hundred fifty passengers were assigned to triple-deck steel bunks, and seventy-five lucky ones had cabins with beds.[32]

A crowd stood at the ship's rail as the vessel slowly drew away from the pier, into the Hudson, and past the Statue of Liberty. The *West Point* stopped momentarily to pick up Consuls General Fritz Wiedemann and Johannes Borchers and their families, who had arrived at the last minute with ninety-eight pieces of luggage weighing five tons. (Wiedemann brought along the entire confidential file of the San Francisco consulate.)[33]

The ship, armed with four five-inch guns, several antiaircraft guns, searchlights, and a degaussing system, sailed across the U-boat–infested Atlantic, with safe passage guaranteed by the warring nations. Baron Edgar von Spiegel had gone, but he was not to be forgotten.[34]

2

Preparing for War

As CONSULAR OFFICIALS sailed back to Europe in the summer of 1941, Galveston made the first attempts to prepare for air and sea attacks. Mayor Brantly Harris called a meeting of city and county groups to discuss activities and plans. Galvestonians feared that as an important oil tanker port they would be a likely enemy target, and they began to mobilize the Red Cross, install sirens, and recruit volunteers.[1]

The army conducted its first field training programs for soldiers of nearby camps, and in July a troop of twenty-five hundred artillerymen arrived in town for a four-day practice session. They came with four hundred vehicles, 37-millimeter antitank guns, 155-millimeter howitzers, and various other artillery and equipment and set up twelve hundred pup tents on the east beach for maneuvers. To alleviate possible boredom, Galveston women planned dances for them at Kempner Park and the city auditorium, erected a recreation tent, and announced that loans of sofas, chairs, and rugs would be appreciated.

No sooner had the tent camp been established than a monsoon-like storm blew in from the gulf with blasts of wind and torrential rains. The troops steadfastly remained in their flapping canvas shelters, but after two sleepless nights, those in command decided to cancel the operation. The drenched soldiers packed up their soggy pup tents, antitank guns, and other paraphernalia and drove off to Camp Wallace in nearby Texas City to seek refuge.[2]

The island of Galveston, extending across the entry to Galveston

Bay, had been fortified since the time of Jean Laffite and other pirates in 1816. When Congress declared war on Spain in late April, 1898, the Army Corps of Engineers added searchlights to the harbor entrance and installed gun batteries in all three local forts. Fort San Jacinto, dating from 1836, on the eastern tip of the island overlooking the channel into Galveston harbor, now had four batteries, a mining casemate, and a few other buildings; Fort Crockett (1897), on 125 acres at the western edge of town on the seawall at Thirty-ninth Street, had three huge guns facing the gulf; and across the channel, behind a seventeen-foot seawall on Bolivar Peninsula, sat Fort Travis (1898) with two gun batteries.[3]

In all this time, the big artillery had never been fired at an enemy, because invaders had not entered the Gulf of Mexico since the Yankees sailed up in 1862 and captured Galveston. But the guns were there—just in case. What worried everybody was the thought that Germany would send over a massive wave of bombers or an armada of warships and blast Galveston off the face of the earth.[4]

The commanders of Fort Crockett and Fort San Jacinto announced that they would begin practice firing in September and warned swimmers and campers to stay off the east beach on weekdays. They said the guns would make tremendously loud booms and that people living near the forts should open their windows six inches, remove any pictures and mirrors not securely hung, and pack away delicate objects that might fall off tables and shelves. All vessels were warned to stay out of the gulf in front of the forts, where target practice would take place. The roaring blasts did begin in September, rattling windows and breaking china dishes and bric-a-brac. Housewives took it for a few days and then boxed up all their breakables and put them in the closet.

The United States, as part of the Lend-Lease Act, was sending oil and gasoline to Great Britain, causing a shortage of fuel on the East Coast. The demand was so great that Texas suppliers could not keep up with it, having an insufficiency of ships. Finally Erle Halliburton, president of Halliburton Oil Company, came up with an idea for a radical new petroleum carrier. He proposed to Secretary of the Interior Harold Ickes the building of "trailer tankers," which could be hooked onto merchant ships or other vessels plying between the Gulf of Mexico and eastern ports.[5]

Socony-Vacuum Oil Company announced that they had just carried the first extra load of gasoline on a tanker, with 108,000 barrels instead of the previously allowed 104,000. The new federal law permitting greater amounts of petroleum products to be transported on tankers meant that a daily increase of 30,000 to 40,000 barrels could get to the East Coast. Little did anyone dream that these greater loads of tanker oil would merely cause bigger explosions when the U-boats came on the scene.[6]

Ickes requested that citizens in the East try to use one-third less gasoline and at the same time urged petroleum industry leaders to immediately build an $80 million pipeline system and fifty high-speed tankers. (The government had transferred one-fifth of all tankers to British service.) He warned of additional gasoline shortages in the East and asked for construction of the world's largest pipeline to transport 250,000 barrels of crude oil a day from Texas refineries to those in Philadelphia and New York. Ickes's proposal came shortly after Congress authorized certain public and private companies to build interstate pipelines by use of condemnation.[7]

Roosevelt okayed the plans for a smaller pipeline to run from Louisiana to North Carolina for gasoline. Even though Texas produced almost half the petroleum in the country, Rear Admiral Emory Land, chairman of the Maritime Commission, said he was adamantly opposed to building the huge new pipeline proposed by Ickes. "I'd rather build tankers than pipelines. If that's not satisfactory, I'd rather build barges. I don't know where they can get 750,000 tons of steel, but if it's coming from the navy or our ships, I'm against it."[8]

In Congress a bitter dispute arose over the proposed world's largest pipeline, with Admiral Land reiterating his stance that too much steel would be taken away from the navy. He prevailed, with the result that the Supply Priorities and Allocations Board refused to grant the necessary steel plates. The pipeline, to be built and paid for by eleven oil companies, was put on hold.

In April, 1941, the navy began to train armed guards to help protect merchant ships. Many of the young navy men picked to go through training for duty aboard a merchant vessel had never before been to sea or even been near a ship. "When I joined the navy, I didn't know I was going to be in the armed guard," said Jim McKaig of Texas City. "I had finished boot camp, and they called out all the names of the different ships and the people going on them, and when they got through, my name hadn't been called. So they said, 'Now these are the "submarine bait"'—and they called my name. I didn't know what to think." He said that the presence of a retired navy man from his hometown who was going along as an instructor gave him courage.[9]

In those days merchant ships were small, defenseless, and completely at the mercy of German submarines. The navy launched an armament program, but because of a severe shortage of suitable weapons, they simply added life rafts to the ships in addition to the standard four lifeboats, and so the armament program creaked along like a Conestoga wagon. The government, having no stores of heavy weapons, procured World War I–era guns from parks and museums, and the first merchant ship to be armed was given an obsolete four-incher in Hoboken, New Jersey, on November 26. Several vessels went to sea sporting telephone poles to fool the U-boat commanders. Cargo carriers without poles or cannons were lucky to have a couple of World War I .30-caliber Lewis machine guns for defense against U-boats.[10]

On December 7 the Japanese bombed Pearl Harbor, and Galvestonians went wild trying to register for the service. At the same time the Galveston Junior Chamber of Commerce announced its theme for the fourth annual Christmas lighting contest: "No Blackout in America." The chamber urged citizens to display brilliant lighting that could easily be seen from sidewalks and to have as many lights as possible burning between six and nine o'clock on Christmas Eve. Its aim was to make the city "a blaze of lights during the Christmas season." No one realized that coastal illumination would become a critical factor in the U-boats' success. A few days later navy officials in Washington advised shipping companies that navigational lights along the American coast and its territories might be extinguished and radio beacons discontinued without notice, but nothing was done.[11]

On December 12 Germany declared war on the United States, and the army asked that all key cities in the danger zone—within three hundred miles of the Gulf Coast—conduct test blackouts as soon as possible. The next day Galveston Jaycees reported that they needed seven more entries in the Christmas lighting contest. The city fathers decided to go ahead with a test blackout, and on January 7, 1942, the city went into inky darkness except for a few dimmed headlights. The event was pronounced a big success.

One week later, headlines announced the sinking of a Panamanian tanker sixty miles off the coast of Long Island. Reinhard Hardegen, audacious commander of U-123, with no charts of U.S. waters, had followed the shore lights of Long Island and dispatched the *Norness* to a watery grave. More sinkings by Hardegen and other U-boats followed, making a total of thirteen vessels in two weeks. The war had reached U.S. shores.[12]

America was poorly armed—defenses were practically nonexistent, and shipping enjoyed the protection of six blimps along the East Coast. Large numbers of single vessels plied the waters between New York and Cape Hatteras, running at night with lights on. The German navy realized it had to take advantage of the situation before convoys came into use, and the submarines' success was phenomenal. U-boats blew up tankers and freighters just off Nova Scotia, North Carolina, South Carolina, New Jersey, and New York with the greatest of ease.[13]

On January 28 the American navy caused consternation in Texas with a report that one of its patrol planes had sighted a submarine, "doubtlessly German," about fifteen miles from Port Aransas. Officials thought the U-boat had "sneaked in during the night with the intention of attacking oil tankers" and had come up to recharge its batteries. All towns along the south Texas coast from Rockport to Corpus Christi turned out their lights that evening, creating the first real blackout in U.S. history.[14]

Galvestonians took the news as though they expected it. "If an enemy submarine sneaked into the Gulf of Mexico, there is reason to hope that it has sneaked out again or better still been sent to Davy Jones' locker," observed an editorial in the local paper. "Preparations were made for a blackout but none was ordered Wednesday night. The city is standing by for a possible alert."[15]

The mayor ordered air raid wardens to wait for orders and all citizens to listen for sirens and whistles, in case a German U-boat appeared off Galveston. He told everyone to be on guard and notified doctors at the hospitals to be ready in case of emergency. "There is no more time for test blackouts or alerts," Harris said. "It's the real thing now and Galvestonians must understand that they have to put their shoulders to the wheel and be ready for action on call."[16]

All this stir had to have been a false alarm. German U-boat war diaries indicated that the first U-boat to enter the gulf arrived at the end of April, 1942. In January, Admiral Dönitz was using all five of the navy's big type-IX submarines off the U.S. East Coast, and these boats were the only ones thought to be capable of operating near America. Also, the U.S. navy said, "We have reason to believe that there were no . . . U-boats operating within this [Gulf Sea] command throughout . . . January 1942."[17]

On February 6 the Gulf Sea Frontier came into being, first under the Seventh Naval District and later the Eighth. There were two officers and four boats to protect the Florida Straits, most of the Bahamas, all of the Gulf of Mexico, the Yucatán Channel, and most of Cuba. For emergencies a few Fleet Sound School boats at Key West were available; air forces comprised fourteen P-47 observation planes at Miami with .30-caliber machine guns, nineteen unarmed Coast Guard planes, and two decrepit B-18 bombers at Miami.[18]

The Gulf Sea Frontier, which included the lower east coast of Florida, felt the first attacks in February when U-128 and U-504 sank three ships off Cape Canaveral. The experts held opinions from one extreme to the other, ranging from beliefs that subs would never enter the Gulf of Mexico to expectations that U-boats filled with big groups of saboteurs would land in a gulf port. The frontier headquarters at Key West was in a risky location, because the small island was connected to the mainland by a bridge and causeway road that could be blown up. Communications were almost nonexistent: if Florida lookouts spotted a U-boat off Palm Beach, they notified Key West, who called—on a civilian telephone—the Third Army Bomber Commission at Charleston, South Carolina, to request that the army's Miami planes start a search.

While Americans frantically prepared for war, a German U-boat maneuvered up to within three miles of the tiny island of Aruba, close to the coast of Venezuela. It torpedoed seven tankers in the harbor and fired at the big oil refinery and storage tanks. The shells missed the refinery and whistled through the U.S. army bachelor quarters and library but did not explode. A shell hit one of the oil tanks and dented it, and one torpedo landed on the beach. The next day four Dutchmen were trying to dismantle the "dud" torpedo when it exploded, killing all of them. U.S. army bombers on a dawn patrol saw the U-boat and dropped a heavy load of explosives as the commander took his ship under.[19]

The surprise U-boat raid off Venezuela produced quite an uproar. President Roosevelt warned that New York and Detroit could be bombed, and Secretary of War Henry Stimson said that forays such as the German attack on Aruba "were to be expected along our coasts."[20]

Readers of the *Galveston Daily News* learned on February 23 that Galvestonian Alexander Korb, a merchant mariner, had survived the sinking of his freighter, *Delplata,* in the eastern Caribbean. Korb told reporters that they were attacked by two U-boats and that the first torpedo hit on the starboard side just under the bridge, causing the ship to list and fouling the whistle cord. The whistle started to blow constantly, causing thirty-six of the crew to think it was a warning to abandon ship, and they left as fast as possible in three lifeboats. A second torpedo exploded, flooding the engine room and two or three holds. Soon afterward the captain, chief engineer, and navy gun crew escaped on the last lifeboat, and a navy rescue ship picked up all fifty-two survivors a few hours later.[21]

With the specter of enemy invasion growing closer, the National Civilian Defense Office announced on March 11 that it would distribute vital war items to coastal target areas and vulnerable inland industrial centers. Galveston's allotment, based on a population of 60,862, included surgical equipment, stretchers, body identification tags, steel helmets, firemen's hip boots, coats and pants, gas protective clothing, and fire-fighting equipment. No decision had been made about the problem of who was to get the gas masks.[22]

Americans, with memories of horrible World War I stories of mustard and chlorine gas, had no doubt that history could repeat itself, and they tried to make ready. Two days later a gas defense class brought in a thousand people, who learned from Dr. Bernard Demaratsky how to become familiar with and best use a gas mask. "It is wise," he advised, "to put on the gas mask at the first sign of an attack and not take it off until all traces of gas have gone." He said that one way of avoiding the effects of gas was walking diagonally upwind, either to the right or left of the gassed area.[23]

The United States was now losing ships faster than it could build them, with tankers the biggest problem. Gasoline rationing had begun in the eastern states because of oil shortages, and fuel was badly needed for the war effort in Europe and the Pacific.

Sinkings continued off Florida and throughout the Caribbean, while Galveston's mayor struggled to get the town ready for war. Harris explained to his Washington liaison, Bob Nesbitt, that new government regulations required city officials to certify that they had trucks to transport fire-fighting equipment. "I understand that the reason the Government did not put these fire pumps on trailers is because they did not want to waste tires and . . . metal," he said. Harris asked Nesbitt to go to the Civilian Defense Office at once and see if its bureaucrats expected Galveston to buy fifteen or sixteen trucks, put them in garages, tie them up, and never use them except after an air raid. "Or," he went on, "do they expect us to be able to throw the pumpers on regular city trucks when the emergency arises, when we can stop using them for gathering garbage and whatnot?" The mayor ended his letter with an appeal to "go around and have a thorough discussion with somebody whose brainchild it was to do away with the trailers that could be hitched on to the back of a wagon or pushed by the men themselves and find out just how the hell this thing is going to work."[24]

In early April the navy began to prepare a mine field north of Key West to protect the Smith Shoal anchorage, planning to use the area as a gathering spot for merchant vessels awaiting the formation of convoys. The navy ordered several minelayers to report for duty, and in anticipation of their arrival the Eighth Naval District began construction of a mine depot at Boca Grande, about sixty-five miles south of Tampa, on the gulf. This was accomplished in short order, after which the first minelayer, the USS *Keokuk,* arrived, later joined by the *Miantonomah* and the *Monadnock,* the last two 1890s-vintage monitors. On April 24 the three vessels began placing mines near Smith Shoal while aircraft patrolled overhead.

Two days later, when all 3,460 mines were in place, the U.S. destroyer *Sturdevant,* unaware of the mine field, hit one of the sunken bombs and sank, killing seventeen crew members and wounding twenty-three, with thirteen missing and subsequently declared dead. When the ship was hit, most of the crew ran to the lifeboats, but the torpedomen stayed at their posts disarming depth charges to protect the survivors after the ship sank. Some of them drowned because they waited until too late to leave. The next day, April 27, the secretary of the navy conducted a court of inquiry to study the disaster, but the decision was made to leave the field in place.

About six weeks later, on June 15, the merchant ship *Gunvor* ran into a mine, blew up, and sank; then, on June 19, the SS *Bosilijka* met the same fate. On July 2 the *Edward Luckenbach* went down, making a total of three more sunk. The U.S. navy claimed no responsibility for them, saying that it had not been notified that the ships were seeking entrance into the mined area. The navy believed that the mine field's benefits outweighed its drawbacks and left it there until May, 1944. Besides causing four Allied ships to be demolished, it forced vessels coming through the Florida Straits to travel an extra eighteen or twenty hours to get to the anchorage, but naval higher-ups were convinced that they had the U-boats fooled. As it turned out, not a single U-boat ran into a mine—the commanders must have known about it.[25]

While the navy was preparing the convoy anchorage near Key West in April, a number of U-boat commanders blasted merchant ships from New York to southern Florida close to shore, so close that people on the beaches could see the smoke and flames. These included Reinhard Hardegen, commander of U-123; Georg Lassen, of U-160; Erich Topp, of U-552; Rolf Mützelburg, of U-203; Johannes Östermann, of U-754; Helmut Möhllmann, of U-571; Heinz Hirsacker, of U-572; Heinrich Zimmerman, of U-136; Horst Uphoff, of U-84; Adalbert Schnee, of U-201; Karl-Ernst Schroeter, of U-752; Hans-Dieter Heinicke, of U-576; and Siegfried von Forstner, of U-402.[26]

"One of the most reprehensible failures on our part," wrote Samuel Eliot Morison, "was the neglect of local communities to dim their waterfront lights, or of military authorities to require them to do so, until three months after the submarine offensive started." U-boat commanders could scarcely believe their eyes when they entered U.S. coastal waters, expecting to see the same darkness that had been ordered in Europe. "The towns were a blaze of bright lights. The lights, both in lighthouses and on buoys, shone forth, though perhaps a little less brightly than usual," wrote Admiral Karl Dönitz in his memoirs. Tourism boosted the economies of all coastal towns, where amusement parks, hotels, and restaurants crowded the water's edge and advertised with colorful, sparkling signs. Submarines heading south could follow the glow of coastal highways and towns until the Eastern Sea Frontier commander ordered all lighting turned off on April 18.[27]

During the assault on the East Coast, Admiral Adolphus Andrews, who considered convoys inadvisable because there were so few escort boats and planes, began a system whereby groups of ships moved from one anchorage to another escorted by sundry local craft. Thus began the "Bucket Brigade," with ships steaming in daylight hours as close to shore as possible and taking shelter at night in mined anchorages. These precautions, however, deterred the enemy about as much as throwing a thimbleful of water on a forest fire. The U-boats continued their work unscathed, and the German navy fixed its sights on southern waters.[28]

3

Enter U-507

ON APRIL 30, 1942, *Korvettenkapitän* Harro Schacht, commander of U-507, had just crossed the Atlantic and arrived in grid square DM, the German navy's secret mapping code for the area surrounding Cuba.[1] Saving his torpedoes for later use, he fired his deck guns to sink the small tanker *Federal* off the western tip of Cuba near the entry into the Yucatán Channel. Four days later, on May 4, he wrote in his *Kriegstagebuch* (war diary): "At the Florida Straits. I'm going to get to my area of operations via Tortugas Bank [just off Key West]. The Tortugas navigational lights burn as though it were peacetime." As we will see, his operational area turned out to be the exact place where Baron von Spiegel usually fished.

At 8:18 A.M. he spotted a nine-thousand-ton tanker and estimated that the earliest he could be in attack position would be in the Florida Straits, where swift currents made maneuvering difficult. Schacht decided the amount of fuel needed for the chase would be too great, so he let it pass. "I hope for better opportunities in the area of my assigned operation," he noted.

Two hours later Schacht entered the Gulf of Mexico, near the west end of Cuba, where he spied the twenty-five-hundred-ton freighter *Norlindo*. He fired one torpedo and hit the ship at the waterline. "The steamer goes down right away at the stern, and in three minutes stands vertical . . . sinks," reported Schacht. He immediately saw two other ships and pursued at full speed. The chase was short, for the nearer one turned to go into the Florida Straits.

At 12:45 P.M. Schacht went back to the place where he sank the

Harro Schacht, commander of U-507, the first U-boat in the Gulf of Mexico.
Photo courtesy of U-Boot-Archiv, Cuxhaven, Germany.

Norlindo and found the shipwrecked crew floating on three rafts. He went up on the deck and yelled to the men in English, asking the name of their vessel, for no radio message had been sent from the *Norlindo*. They did not tell him, but he nevertheless supplied them with cigarettes, tobacco, crackers, and drinking water before leaving the scene.

The next day, at 6:00 P.M., Schacht chased a ninety-nine-hundred-ton tanker, got within five hundred yards, and fired a torpedo—a hit. The tanker exploded and burst immediately into bright flames. The submarine surfaced and Schacht saw part of the tanker still floating, but it sank quickly. The entire sea around the ship was burning, and above rose "a gigantic mushroom cloud of smoke."

Schacht now heard on his radio: "SSS of tanker *Joseph M. Cudahy.* A tanker hit by a torpedo nine nautical miles from us is burning. Position sixty-five nautical miles northwest Tortugas [U-boats could decipher Allied coded messages]." The message was repeated by the Coast Guard radio stations, and the German commander assumed that the vessel that sent the SSS (attack by submarine) must have been within sighting distance. He therefore scanned the horizon with great care and saw a tanker to starboard. "This should be the one that reported us," he wrote. Schacht moved into attack position at high speed, but the tanker had turned away from the flaming waters and went off on a zigzag course.

After chasing the tanker for over two hours, he fired his first torpedo and missed. The second one hit, and the ship exploded. "It went up at once in bright flames from bow to stern," he wrote. "The sea is burning around, and above a huge smoke cloud is rising." During the attack he heard on his radio band "SSS from tanker *Joseph Cudahy,*" with the ship's position. The radio operator did not have time to finish his message because the tanker blew up. U.S. coastal radio stations issued a warning: "Urgent. U-boat attack in 25.30 north, 83.45 west. All ships in gulf have to operate completely darkened."

Near the shipwreck area Schacht saw a search flare, and after it went out he saw the lights of an airplane circling around the burning site. He took off to the east and used the darkness to transfer torpedoes from his U-boat deck into the firing tubes.

At 2:00 A.M., as they were lowering a torpedo, the winch block and tackle broke, and the torpedo snapped loose and slid on its gliding rails into the boat. While this was happening, a crewman caught his left forearm between the torpedo and the gliding ring and suffered a multiple open forearm fracture. Schacht dispatched a radiogram to U-boat headquarters: "Radio petty officer Haas multiple open arm fracture while getting caught in a slipping torpedo. Requesting instructions. No pain relieving drugs on board. Stand by at grid square DL 33 [west of south Florida]."

At 7:00 A.M. they had finished loading the torpedoes and made a test dive to see if the balance was correct. An incoming radio message directed: "Lay down injured. Arm to be put up by splints and dressing. Danger of infection high, therefore put sterile dressing and cod-liver ointment. If no morphine on board give cognac. Report condition in two days."

"We have already done some of the procedures," Schacht wrote. "In addition, luminal [sleeping medication] has been used." He said the patient was lying in a bunk in the officers' mess and being cared for by a constant sick watch.

Three hours later another radiogram came for Schacht and Erich Würdemann (a second U-boat commander in the gulf): "To all boats. Unreported successes should be reported before May 7 morning." Schacht wrote that his report was late because he had been attacked several times, was busy receiving radio messages and reloading torpedoes, and was dealing with several cases of seasickness.

Another message arrived five hours later for Schacht and Würdemann: "For delivery of pain relieving drugs, on May 6 at 1500 be on grid square DL 31. . . . In case of late arrival Würdemann report by short signal. . . . Medical corpsman of 2nd U-Flotilla back at the base claims that morphine, according to U-507's radio mate, should be on board."

By midnight of May 5, Schacht had not heard any short signal from Würdemann in U-506. He then received a radiogram saying that Würdemann was one day late coming to the rendezvous point, so he started traveling to grid square DL 31.

Schacht next sent a message to headquarters telling them that he had sunk four ships. At 5:00 A.M. the sea was calm and visibility good, with single clouds in the sky. He saw a fully loaded freighter "of modern make" of about eight thousand tons at a distance of nine nautical miles. The U-boat submerged for attack and fired one torpedo—a miss. Schacht reckoned he had estimated the distance wrong and said the trail of the torpedo was seen by the steamer, according to the ship's radio messages.

The U-boat surfaced and began to fire the deck guns. This stopped the freighter, which radioed: "SOS-SSS *Alcoa Puritan.* Submarine on surface position 28.40 north, 88.22 west . . . submarine still shoots, torpedo did not hit."

With that, Schacht fired another "eel" (torpedo) for the coup de grâce, and the vessel went below the water. He sped away from the sinking on a false course, watching until the lifeboats were out of sight; then started toward his rendezvous point with Würdemann, south of Mobile in the middle of the gulf.

The commander spotted a small, older freighter and submerged for attack, but the ship zigzagged away from him, making a torpedo shot impossible. As he approached the port side of the ship, he rose to the surface and approached at high speed. The sub's deck guns began firing and blew off the foremast, at which point the crew began to lower the lifeboats. The freighter's radio sent a message, "SSS from HREN [code name for *Ontario*]," with location. This message was then repeated by coastal radio stations as a submarine warning.

As soon as Shacht's artillery had set the *Ontario* on fire, he discovered he was out of ammunition. An airplane appeared, and the submarine crash-dived. Soon the U-boat surfaced again, getting ready for the coup de grâce, but the tanker was burning fiercely and sinking fast. Schacht decided that no more torpedoes were necessary and drew away, where he watched the ship, in flames along its entire length. An airplane approached and the submarine dove, then surfaced again. "Again airplane comes quite close but does not see us," Schacht reported.

A radio message arrived for Schacht, saying that because of air attacks, the rendezvous with Würdemann would not be possible until May 8 at 1500, the next day. Meanwhile, the commander decided to travel north to the sea lanes connecting New Orleans–Mobile with Tampa–Key West and the Tortugas. He radioed a message that navigational lights on the north coast of Cuba and the Tortugas were burning just as if it were peacetime and that ship traffic was heavy west of the Tortugas. He reported that he still had twelve torpedoes and 130 cubic meters of fuel.

The next day Schacht went to the rendezvous place—no Würde-mann. As he waited around he saw a freighter traveling at eight knots. He submerged and fired a torpedo, hitting in front of the bridge, and the ship began to sag at the bow end. "I have to retract my periscope because there is a lot of ship debris flying through the air," wrote the commander. "After surfacing we found on our deck a piece of our own torpedo. After I looked through the periscope again, the ship had already sunk." From a radio message he heard the name, *Torny*, a Norwegian vessel "probably headed for the Mississippi."

Schacht now returned to the rendezvous point and still found no Würdemann. He began to steer a search course and had to crash-dive when an airplane came into sight. "It looks like a Martin B-26," he said. (Because of the constant hissing of the sea, it was difficult for U-boat crews to hear an approaching aircraft.) Schacht traveled at periscope depth and heard two detonations a long way away. "Proba-bly torpedo hits from Würdemann," he surmised. The airplane was still circling far behind, and the U-boat surfaced again. The crew heard four more detonations in quick succession "like from bombs. . . . Maybe Würdemann torpedoed a ship and is now getting bombed. We can still hear the engines of the airplane although we can see nothing because it is hazy." Schacht decided for safety reasons to move about ten nautical miles to the west. (A nautical mile is around 6,080 feet.)

A radio message went out from the U-boat: "Sank armed Norwe-gian ship *Torny*. Würdemann has not arrived at the rendezvous point." Schacht began to search for his fellow captain. In the haze the crewmen thought they saw the conning tower of a submarine, but upon closer inspection they discovered that it was part of the wreck-age of the *Torny*. Then they came upon a floating lifeboat and searched it for a first aid kit but found none. They did, however, cap-ture a set of sea charts. Schacht spent the rest of the night looking for U-506.

It was May 9, and the commander sent another message: "Have not found Würdemann. However, we heard at around 1800 [German time] far distant detonations like from a torpedo. At 1833 four quick detonations like from airplane bombs. I am about ten miles to the west from rendezvous point." An airplane appeared, and Schacht took the boat down. "Possibly a patrol plane going from Key West to Galveston. I remained submerged for a while in order to redress Haas's wounds," he reported. Then the search for Würdemann continued.

Suddenly a plane dropped two depth charges on U-507, causing tremendous explosions, but they were too far away to damage the boat. Schacht resubmerged as fast as possible and stayed down to work on his port diesel engine, "a repair which was long overdue." He then left the rendezvous point because he had spent the whole day trying to find U-506.

On May 10 Schacht ran to the north "to cross as many shipping lanes as possible, such as the New Orleans–Florida Straits, etc. After arriving at the 200 meter line I will turn toward the west so I can steer toward the mouth of the Mississippi." He radioed headquarters that he was leaving the meeting place because of haze and bombs. "The injured has 39 C degrees fever and his wound is festering. So far no blood poisoning," he noted.

"Don't move the patient," said an incoming message. "Keep the patient absolutely quiet. Several times daily put damp dressings of hydrogen peroxide . . . or similar solutions." The instructions went on to advise giving various medications and ended, "If getting worse, send new message."

The chief engineer of U-507 then reported that some fuel was missing from one of the storage tanks, and Schacht thought it was because of the air attack the day before. He also found out that a steel cable from the starboard hydroplane had been torn loose and was wrapped around it. Reaching down from the upper deck, the crewmen cut the cable as far down as they could. Schacht now realized that this loose cable accounted for the banging noise they had been hearing and could not identify.

Over the radio they intercepted a message: "Urgent. U-boat at 28.35 north, 90 west. Commander of Eighth Naval District. The sub position lies on the western side of the Mississippi on the way to Galveston." Schacht thought they were talking about Würdemann, who might be trying to get to the meeting point.

"Until now the water has been clear and deep blue, but now it becomes dark green and slightly milky. This color promises a good cover against sight from above," Schacht wrote. He estimated the distance to the Mississippi River and the coast as about eighty nautical miles (about ninety-two miles).

May 10 at 7:00 P.M., U-507 turned toward the mouth of the Mississippi. "I want to be there at dawn in order to be able to operate in front of the entrance," said Schacht. "According to navigational data, I should reach the 200 meter line in one hour, but soundings now are already fifty meters."

A U.S. Coast Guard plane appeared, saw U-507, and dropped four bombs, but none did any serious damage. The U-boat submerged and headed for deeper water. The hydrophone picked up a propeller sound, and they surfaced into a hazy atmosphere. Nothing was to be seen, so Schacht headed back toward the Mississippi delta. He then heard Würdemann sending a message to headquarters: "Did not find Schacht. On first rendezvous point was forced under water by subchaser. . . . Will be on May 11, 1500, grid square DB 77, left upper corner" (south of Mobile).

Schacht wrote in his log that he could not make it in time and that the state of the patient had improved, so he did not need to meet with U-506. At 5:00 A.M. dawn was breaking and the coast was in sight, so the commander could not send an outgoing message about his intentions for fear of being heard by land-based listening stations, which could pinpoint his location. "The light and sound buoy and the South Pass light are in sight, so I haven't come as far as I wanted," he reported. Shortly before, "we passed the sweet water line [border between fresh and salt water]. . . . The water is dirty yellow and covers well against being detected by planes. Furthermore, many pieces of lumber, etc. are floating around, so that a periscope can hardly be recognized."

He saw a small fifteen-hundred-ton tanker but considered it too little to bother with; then a twenty-five-hundred-ton loaded tanker, still "not rewarding." At 9:56 A.M. he fired at a freighter and missed. Three hours later he left the yellow-dirty river water and entered dark-green brackish water, noting that "the mainstream of ship traffic has to come according to the *Segel Handbuch* [sailing manual] shortly before dusk." He reasoned that steamers should be leaving New Orleans before noon in order to have good visibility for the river journey, because the mist rose around 6:00 P.M.

A patrol plane buzzed in toward U-507, and Schacht withdrew his periscope. Then he saw a red and white barrel buoy marking the right side of South Pass. At 7:00 P.M. he reentered the yellow Mississippi water and saw navigational lights burning. "We noticed a strong fuel oil smell at the bridge, but a trail of oil cannot be detected," Schacht reported. He took a course toward the Southwest Pass on the west side of the river delta and sent a message: "Do not need aid any more. Rendezvous point cancelled." U-507 was now hunting but couldn't see any traffic. He spotted a PC (patrol corvette) boat in the distance and said visibility was good, with occasional heat lightning. The commander noted that the PC boat was heading south and apparently patrolling the entrance to Southwest Pass. He saw another one. "There are at least two of this type here," he concluded.

At dawn on May 12 Schacht surfaced to reconnoiter the existing conditions at Southwest Pass. "After looking through the periscope I see a stream of steamers pouring out of the Mississippi. Most of them turn sharply around the west jetty and the west shallow water warning buoy. I am too far away to get into position to make an accurate shot," he reported. He saw a minesweeper with its engines stopped about a thousand meters away and fired a torpedo—a miss. The minesweeper turned and came straight at the U-boat, which crashed under the water. According to a message Schacht heard later, his torpedo detonated on the western jetty of the southwest entrance to the Mississippi.

"All day long single steamers and tankers are running from west, south, and east, in and out," Schacht wrote. "In spite of all efforts I don't get a chance for a shot. Unpredictable currents, shallow areas and changing courses of ships do not let me get into a favorable firing position." He said that when things seemed lucky, a PC boat showed up and that he was having difficulty steering depthwise as well as sideways because of the changing water density and currents at the mouth of the river. Nevertheless, he would have been able to shoot several times if he had had an electric torpedo for the longer distances. An airplane passed by, "apparently the usual afternoon patrol."

Schacht saw a tanker coming out of the river and noted, "I will wait for it at the head of the jetty." But the PC boat came between U-

507 and the ship, forcing him to lower his periscope and go deeper. The PC boat passed him astern.

When Schacht raised the periscope he saw a big, modern ten-thousand-ton tanker lying stopped at the river entrance. He thought the ship must be waiting for another vessel to come out of the river. Schacht fired a torpedo and hit, causing a big brown cloud to rise. "As nothing more happens, I shoot from tube 5. At the moment of firing the second shot, the tanker explodes, and two parts of it are burning," he observed. The sea was aflame in a wide circle, and overhead an enormous mushroom-shaped cloud billowed upward. The other tankers made off as fast as possible. One that was close by was protected by a PC boat, so that Schacht was unable to do anything "in daytime and in shallow water" (with only eight meters under his keel), because his A-torpedoes would leave a wake. He submerged, withdrew to a distance, and recharged his batteries during the night.

At 8:48 P.M. Schacht surfaced and saw the tanker still burning. He wrote, "No wind and swell, individual clouds, heat lightning from north to east, brightly illuminating the sea in several areas." He intended to steer toward the light and sound buoy south of Ship Shoal because "all ships operating between Galveston as well as Sabine and the mouth of the Mississippi River have to pass by there." (This information had to come from intelligence sources—Baron von Spiegel?) He reported that he was traveling at half speed so as to recharge the batteries while he got away from the sinking ship. He could thereby "meet the ships which should stand at early dawn in front of the Southwest Pass as well as the ones two hours later that are leaving the pass at dawn going west."

In Schacht's next radiogram he stated that Southwest Pass at night had no traffic; early morning saw the great majority of outgoing and incoming vessels, all of larger tonnage. He said that all day long there were "single runners" and that the east and west traffic turned off shortly after the ends of the jetties. The first morning group of ships to the west was escorted by a minesweeper, and in addition there was air cover on the main sea routes.

At 1:00 A.M. the commander saw a light and headed toward it, but it was only a fishing boat. Again he steered toward Ship Shoal light buoy, just south of Houma, and on his right he spotted a great number of fishing boat lights. U-507 headed south to arrive at daybreak in deeper water.

At 6:00 A.M. he spied a tanker, submerged, and pursued it for fifteen minutes. The ship was zigzagging as Schacht fired the first torpedo, but the tanker stopped just as he fired. The torpedo missed, and Schacht thought the captain had seen him. Again Schacht sent a torpedo and again missed as the tanker slowly steamed ahead. The third torpedo missed and the tanker turned to starboard, sending a message, "SSS *Gulfprince* 38.38 north 91.05 west." The tanker moved off, wildly zigzagging in an easterly direction. Schacht said he couldn't do anything about it: underwater he couldn't catch him because the sub's speed was too slow, and on the surface it would be no good because he was out of artillery ammunition. Besides, the whole area was alarmed and other tankers were turning off. For several hours he tried to attack another one but could not get into firing position.

He went south and waited, planning to operate that night in the Ship Shoal–Trinity Shoal sector, which paralleled the Louisiana coast and was von Spiegel's favorite fishing area. At 8:00 P.M. the U-boat surfaced, and Schacht spied a freighter on the left that was going too fast for him to catch. He followed it anyway and fired a torpedo— missed. "Torpedo track can be clearly seen in the fluorescent water. While he was turning off, the steamer saw it and shot at us with his stern gun," he reported. Schacht took the boat down with a crash dive to avoid getting hit. (Submarine hulls were highly vulnerable to being punctured by artillery shells.) He could hear the freighter, *Eastern Sun,* sending a message giving the longitude and latitude of the U-boat.

Schacht came close to a tanker and attacked—the first shot missed, and the ship slowed down. He turned the sub around to fire from the stern tubes, because he had no more torpedoes in the bow. Then he shot another "eel." This one started running in circles, but it went away without coming back to blow up the U-boat. The tanker sent an emergency message and reported that two torpedoes passed close by. "I can't get at the tanker to attack him with my 3.7 and 2 cm. antiaircraft guns, for that would mean foolishly risking the boat, knowing that the tanker is armed and alarmed. According to the previous experiences, I have no more confidence in the last torpedo, which I still have aboard," Schacht wrote. He believed he must "inevitably check it through before firing." There was no doubt in his mind that to use it immediately would be futile, and he therefore let the tanker go, "bitter as it is."

At the rising moon, the commander turned his U-boat south to reach deeper water and stayed submerged at twenty-four meters. At dawn he remained underwater to give the crew a chance to rest and to avoid the intensified air patrolling that was likely after his attacks of the previous night. Schacht reported that the crew checked out the last torpedo and found it met all requirements.

Early that afternoon the injured crew member had his wounds dressed again and was returning to a state of good health. Schacht surfaced and went south toward the Tortugas, hoping to find on the way an opportunity to fire his sole remaining torpedo. He saw on the port side a vessel, turned on high speed, and tried to get ahead of the steamer but couldn't make headway. "I am running full speed on the surface," he said. The ship saw him and radioed: "SSS from *Amapala*, 26.10 north, 89.10 west. A submarine is chasing me." Because Schacht was out of artillery ammunition, he started shooting his smaller guns. The freighter sped up, sending another message, "U-boat is shooting at me." In order to get close quickly, Schacht steered directly toward the *Amapala* and used his electric motor for extra speed. Because his smaller guns were behind the bridge, he could not shoot them; he then ordered the light machine gun to be brought up to the bridge and raked the ship with machine-gun fire.

The distance stayed the same between the traveling U-boat and the freighter, and the ship continuously radioed his position and gave signals for radio direction finders. "I am not giving up the chase, since there seems to be a front approaching with very dark rain clouds, and I hope that the U.S. airplanes that are probably already airborne will not find us. I'm gaining on the ship noticeably now," wrote Schacht. The *Amapala* radioed to New Orleans: "Airplane, hurry up. I'm being shot at."

U-507 changed course so that Schacht could use his 3.7- and 2-centimeter weapons. After a few shots with the larger one, he noticed that the steamer was stopping, and he quit firing. "I let the crew get into the lifeboats and maneuvered for the coup de grâce abeam of the steamer," he reported. He fired the last torpedo from tube 5; it misfired and became a circle-runner. Schacht was mystified.

He headed over to one of the ship's lifeboats and took it in tow in order to get aboard the *Amapala,* because the sea was too rough to use his own dinghy. The lifeboat had two leaks, however, and the men had to abandon the effort. Schacht took his U-boat up close to the ship, so that the second watch officer, Lieutenant Scherraus, and control room machinist Tornow could swim across to the vessel, open the seacocks, and sink it.

The time was 6:41 P.M. A bomber—a Douglas DB-380—came from nowhere, and Schacht crash-dived. When the submarine reached forty meters, the plane dropped four bombs; the crew felt great jolts but discovered no damage. They returned to periscope depth and saw the ship still floating, the airplane still circling. The commander wrote: "I remain fairly close to the ship, and here's how I figure it. Based on past experience, the airplane will probably fly home at dusk. I hope that my two men will sink the vessel and then board a raft and remain in the area of the sinking, so I will surface on the lee side of the steamer and pick them up."

The airplane kept circling after dusk. After a while it turned on its position lights, started firing machine guns at the two crewmen, and suddenly vanished. Shortly afterward, the deck lights of the ship came on. "I interpreted this as a signal from my men that everything was okay," he said, "but in reality it was an automatic switch that turned on the emergency lighting because by now the electric generators of the sinking vessel were under water."

Schacht surfaced in front of the bow of the steamer, because he was completely in the ship's shadow, and then moved to the lee side. After a short search he located his men drifting in a raft and took them on board. They brought with them the steamer's papers, among which was a zigzag scheme. Schacht learned that the *Amapala* was a freighter of the Standard Fruit and Steamship Company sailing under the flag of Honduras. The ship's captain rowed up alongside the U-boat and yelled to Schacht, "I didn't know that Honduras was at war with Germany. Why did you sink my ship?"

"You radioed for help from American airplanes to be used against me," Schacht called back.

"Those were my orders."

U-507 at U-boat base, Lorient, France, March 25, 1942. Photo courtesy of Bundesarchiv, Koblenz, Germany.

"In a case like that my orders were to sink your ship," Schacht yelled. In the meantime the steamer had sunk to the top of the upper deck, and it looked as though the end was in sight.

Schacht set course for the Florida Straits. "Further lingering at this area did not seem advisable to me," he noted. "All of a sudden the lights of the steamer disappeared. It probably sank." Schacht sent a message to headquarters: "May 16 . . . *Amapala* after two hour chase stopped by machine gun fire. A coup de grâce torpedo shot resulted in a circle runner. Sank ship by opening the seacocks. I am out of ammunition and proceed with return trip. Total score, 50,001 tons. . . . Condition of the injured man is good."

4

Is It the Baron?

"BRAVE SUBMARINERS IN THE GULF OF MEXICO," the story of
U-507's springtime exploits, appeared in a Hamburg daily paper on
June 15, 1942. War correspondent Hans Kreis related some of the
details (without mentioning the sub's identifying number) in the exaggerated and glowing terms of that day. "The submarine arrived in
port June 15 after patrolling in the hunting ground of the Gulf of
Mexico," he wrote. "The little flags attached to the periscope happily
fluttered in the fresh morning wind—they announced that the boat
had sunk a number of merchant vessels with a gross tonnage of
49,995 in total. This included four tankers." (Schacht's total was
eight ships.)

"Quite a good result," he went on, "especially as this was the first
patrol of the commander and the crew." (Meaning that this was
Schacht's initial mission as a submarine commanding officer.)

Kreis said that the boat operated "right under the noses of the
guards at the strongly fortified Mississippi Delta and torpedoed a fat
and loaded tanker of at least 10,000 gross tons." The crew had a
great laugh when they heard the U.S. radio message later in the day
reporting "an unexplainable large blowup in the gulf."

The U-boat sank ship after ship, "aiming their torpedoes and guns
well," he continued. "A lieutenant, petty officer and a mate did the
final execution of a fully loaded freighter virtually by hand." (Schacht
said there were two men, not three.)

In the article, a young, blond petty officer described his experiences. He related that they had had to cruise for quite a while chasing

the freighter (*Amapala*) before they stopped it by "blasting a machine gun salute" in front of its bow as a warning. The lifeboats were lowered, and the crew climbed down rope ladders and boarded the boats. "They were mostly colored people," he said. "As we did not have any torpedoes left and as such a big fish could not be sent to the bottom of the sea by a light machine gun, the commander ordered us to board the freighter and sink it by opening the sea valves inside." The three men tried to leave the submarine in a rubber raft, but high waves forced them to return. At this point they took off their clothes, jumped into the water, swam over to the freighter, and climbed up the rope ladder still hanging over the side.

Once on board, the German officers realized that they were on a fairly new and modern ship with a cargo of fresh fruits and chemicals. They found some dry clothing, put it on, and went to work opening the sea valves and watertight doors. "All of a sudden we heard the thunder of heavy detonations," the petty officer recalled. "We rushed upstairs and looked carefully around for our sub. It was not there any more!" They heard airplane engines and realized that the sub had just been bombed because they could see the ripples in the water. More explosions went off nearby, but the U-boat had already submerged.

The three men now faced a strange situation. Dressed in civilian clothing, they stood on the deck of an enemy freighter, with an airplane circling overhead, the lifeboats in the water filled with black crewmen, and their U-boat nowhere to be seen. "We had no weapons with us, and the situation looked rather precarious at first. We decided to wait and see, and to calm down and pass the time, we ate some of the excellent fruit we had found," the officer said. Evening came on and still the plane hummed around overhead.

Because there was no sign of help coming, the crewmen hurriedly built a makeshift raft and had it ready to board. The three then pulled the plug. "With a thundering bang and crash the lid of the bottom valve flew up because of the pressure of the water shooting in," the narrative continued. They ran back to the deck where the raft was waiting, carefully lowered it into the water, loaded it with provisions, and climbed aboard. "Then we anxiously awaited the slow sinking of the freighter with a little panic because of a possible explosion of the boilers, still under pressure," the officer recounted.

Suddenly the lights of the bridge switched on, a completely mysterious phenomenon. "The shine lighted the night around us, for heaven's sake!" he exclaimed. "And that was good luck for us." The plane, obviously for lack of fuel, had turned off. Shortly afterward, their U-boat surfaced close by, and they knew they could be seen in the ship's lights. Their commander sent a raft to pick them up, and they made it safely back to their submarine.

"The only thing we regretted was that we could not bring a box of the wonderful fruit to our comrades. The fruit went down with the ship," the petty officer concluded.[1]

When the crewmen and captain of the *Amapala* made it to the navy base at Burrwood, Louisiana, they gave their side of the story. Their ship had been en route from New Orleans to Cristóbal, Canal Zone, with a full cargo of supplies for the army and navy at the Panama Canal. The *Amapala* did not sink immediately and was later taken in tow by a Coast Guard cutter, but sank while being towed the next day.

The vessel was traveling along at fifteen knots and zigzagging. Three lookouts were posted, the weather was overcast with some rain squalls, and visibility was poor. No other ships were in sight.

The lookout first saw the U-boat on the surface about four miles astern bearing west and south, making around fifteen knots. The captain maneuvered the ship in order to place the submarine dead astern, and the sub immediately opened fire with a four-inch gun mounted forward. The ship sent an SSS requesting a plane, and immediately afterward the U-boat started shelling and machine-gunning the radio room. At this time the captain threw the confidential code books over the side in a cardboard box weighted with a chunk of concrete.

U-507 overtook the unarmed vessel, and the captain ordered the crew to abandon ship. Fifty-seven men climbed into three lifeboats. The U-boat pulled up alongside the number one lifeboat, put a line aboard the boat, and asked the ship's second officer to take members of the submarine crew over to the *Amapala* so that they could place explosives aboard and sink her. At this point the story became confused, but evidently the *Amapala*'s second officer went aboard the U-boat, refused to comply with the request, got back into the lifeboat, and cut the towline. The submarine then started away. When the sub drew close to the ship, a bomber appeared, and the sub crash-dived.

The bomber dropped several explosives and, in the opinion of the ship's crew, "destroyed the submarine." The U.S. second officer said that the submarine was apparently of Italian make but that the crew was "undoubtedly German." He described the vessel as "light blue-gray, the deck painted red, with a four-inch gun forward and a three-inch mounted aft, length about 250–260 feet."[2]

A deeply tanned, shorts-clad Harro Schacht stood on the bridge after torpedoing his first gulf ship on May 4 (the *Norlindo*) and called out to the survivors, "Sorry we can't help you. Hope you get ashore okay." The crewmen later reported that Schacht had asked the name of their ship, its tonnage, and whether they needed medical assistance. They said the commander gave them German cigarettes, French cookies, French matches, and ten gallons of lime pulp made from fresh limes. When interviewed by the press, crew members told reporters that the captain was speaking "perfect American," and the story they related of his courteous behavior immediately caused a rumor in New Orleans that the commander was Baron Edgar von Spiegel.[3]

"Former Nazi Consul General for Gulf Coast Believed Sub Chief," announced the Galveston paper. The story said that von Spiegel, who had commanded a U-boat in the First World War, never sank a ship with loss of lives and that he had been "Germany's most chivalrous U-boat captain." The paper explained that during the baron's four-year stay in New Orleans he had traveled widely around the gulf, making frequent trips to the mouth of the Mississippi.[4]

In New Orleans a similar news item appeared: "Former Nazi Consul Here Knows Tropical Waters." The story described the baron as a "hard-bitten Nazi who had returned to fight the United States in the waters he knows best." Remembering his statement of June 14, 1940, a few days before Paris fell, that "Germany would not forget when she was struggling for her life that the United States did everything in its power to aid her enemies," and recalling reports that he had directed Nazi activities in Central and South America, many believed that von Spiegel was now orchestrating the U-boat attacks in his old fishing waters.[5]

"Wake Up, Galveston," warned an editorial on May 11. "We had heard rumors of enemy submarines in the gulf before. But this time there is no doubt of it. Two merchant ships were sunk . . . last

Wednesday," wrote the editor. He said it was significant that a passenger on one of the ships (the *Joseph M. Cudahy*) reported that a general alarm was sounded after the first torpedo missed, but because there had been frequent practice alarms, the response was not immediate. The U-boat then surfaced, stopped the ship with gunfire, and sank her with a torpedo.

"Those people on the doomed ship were slow in responding to the real alarm because enemy submarines were not supposed to be in the gulf," he went on. "They thought it was just another practice alarm."

The editor admonished Galvestonians to take civil defense seriously and not to believe the city was beyond the reach of enemy attack. Many still condemned defense equipment purchases as a waste of money. "How," they asked, "could enemy warplanes or ships get into the gulf?"

"We don't know how the German subs got into the gulf, but there they are," he wrote. "The navy did not say exactly where the ships were sunk, but it couldn't have been more than a few hundred miles from Galveston." He pointed out that the two ships sunk so far had been traveling alone when attacked. "Our armed forces can't be everywhere at once," he commented.[6]

Three days later an additional disaster story appeared on the front page of the Galveston paper, saying that U-boats had sunk another small freighter (the Norwegian *Torny*). The vessel, inbound from Central America and hurrying to port in response to the warning to clear the gulf, was hit by a single torpedo and sank in three minutes. Two crewmen were killed, and when the other twenty-four had escaped in a life raft and motorboat, the submarine surfaced about ninety feet away. The captain (Schacht) called out in English, asking the ship's name, tonnage, and destination, but the crew refused to answer. They said that the U-boat was freshly painted a light gray and had no identifying marks. It stayed on the surface from about 7:40 until 8:30 in the morning.

At noon a couple of navy planes from Pensacola picked up the survivors and took them to shore. Naval officers at the base refused to comment when reporters asked if one or more submarines were operating in the gulf, where two ships had sunk on May 5 in daylight, with the crews getting away in lifeboats.

"The gulf subs . . . might be under the direction of Baron Edgar von Spiegel," speculated the paper. "During his four-year tenure . . . he had ample opportunity to gather much information on the gulf, as his district ranged from Texas to Florida and he traveled through it extensively."[7]

The baron, born in 1885, had reached the age of fifty-seven in 1942, far too old to be in charge of a U-boat. Nevertheless, people along the Gulf Coast believed he had returned to wreak vengeance on the United States. German foreign service records do not say what the former consul was doing in Germany between his eviction from New Orleans in 1941 and his appointment as consul general first class in Marseille, France, in 1943, but he definitely did not go back to U-boat service.[8]

On May 8, 1942, Commander Erich Würdemann in U-506 had gone to meet Schacht to give medical supplies to U-507's injured crewman. At 8:00 A.M. he reported that he arrived at the first rendezvous place west of Florida, saw a subchaser, and crash-dived. "They had no depth charges or searching equipment," he wrote, "so I departed by sneaking away on low speed."

At around 11:00 A.M. he heard four depth charges off in the distance. Schacht, looking for U-506 at periscope depth, could not find her, so he surfaced and then heard the explosions. He naturally thought Würdemann was getting bombed by an airplane. Neither U-boat was being attacked, however—apparently a plane was dropping depth charges where its crew thought a U-boat had submerged.

At 4:02 that afternoon a message came for Würdemann: Schacht had radioed to headquarters that he was unable to locate his fellow U-boat and was moving west to avoid air patrols. Würdemann went north toward the Mississippi delta that night and heard another message from Schacht that the latter was afraid Würdemann had been hit by depth charges. (The boats did not communicate with each other but could hear messages being sent to headquarters.)

Schacht spent the entire next day looking for U-506 while Würdemann headed on toward the Mississippi delta, having given up on Schacht. At ten o'clock on May 10 Würdemann saw the navigational lights at Southwest Pass as if it were peacetime and traveled toward

Erich Würdemann, commander of U-506, the second U-boat in the Gulf of Mexico. Photo courtesy of U-Boot-Archiv, Cuxhaven, Germany.

them. He soon saw an empty tanker heading west and accelerated to get ahead of it. Just before attacking, a message came in: "Würdemann, immediately report position."

The commander at this point fired his two stern tubes and hit the ship in the center. "The tanker shows only a small effect and continues to run with slightly reduced speed," he reported. "It radios having been torpedoed with exact position, whereupon the commander 8th Naval District gives submarine warning to all ships." Würdemann moved again into firing position and shot two bow torpedoes, which hit the aft edge of the bridge and engine room. The tanker stopped and started listing to starboard while the crew climbed into lifeboats. As soon as they were off, the U-boat commander commenced blasting the ship with incendiary ammunition, starting a fire on the forecastle.

"Due to the beginning of dusk, I left the burning tanker in a state of sinking. According to the code name KERX given, this is the U.S. tanker *Aurora*," he said. He then sent a "short signal" giving his position, but confirmation did not come back.

That night (May 10), U-506 made a surface run to the rendezvous point (not given). An hour later the commander sent a message saying that up until May 9 he had seen nothing in the gulf and had not found Schacht. He reported that at the first meeting point he had been forced underwater by a subchaser, had sunk the *Aurora*, and still had eight torpedoes left. (Schacht at this time was cruising around the Mississippi delta looking for ships.)

The next morning, U-506 went to the rendezvous point, giving its location as DA 9690, southeast of the delta. An hour later Würdemann crash-dived, because his bridge watch had not seen an approaching airplane. The plane dropped a bomb very close to the boat, making a thunderous detonation. "The boat was really lifted by the explosion and caused various defects," Würdemann wrote in his log. Upon inspection, however, he found that he had only one serious problem—the nonoperation of tube 5.

The next day he stayed a bit west of the rendezvous area and saw no action. That night the sub headed up toward the Mississippi and received a message that Schacht had "settled" their meeting, meaning that he canceled it. At midnight he saw a glow of fire in the distance and surmised that this was the tanker hit by Schacht two hours earlier (the *Virginia*). "The glow could be seen for thirty nautical miles," he noted.

Würdemann traveled along submerged near the Southwest Pass and just after lunchtime spotted several freighters and tankers. "Most of them are in an unfavorable position," he wrote. An hour and a half later he fired two torpedoes at a loaded tanker going east and hit the engine room. The ship started going down fast and in seven minutes had disappeared.

At 9:00 that evening he chased after another loaded tanker headed east, moved in front of it, and fired two "eels." After forty seconds they hit the bow and amidships "with a ruinous glow of fire." The commander reported that after heavy detonations, "burning oil with raging speed poured into the sea."

Because of the bright illumination reflecting on the U-boat, Würdemann moved off underwater and watched. "The tanker is one great torch," he commented. "The glow of the fire is visible at more than twenty-five sea miles. . . . Sinking of tanker is sure."

Under cover of darkness U-506 moved away from the Louisiana coast and reloaded six torpedoes from the deck into the tubes. "No disturbances," the captain reported.

A radio message came in the next day asking Würdemann to give a short situation report. He sent one back immediately, saying that his situation was the "same as Schacht" and that he had left a loaded tanker "as a torch with sinking assured."

At square DA 9288, very close to the Mississippi delta, he spotted two ships with westerly courses. The commander sped up to get into firing position ahead of the first one and fired two torpedoes—both missed. He then fired two "eels" at the second one (a tanker) and both hit, causing the ship to stop, list to starboard, and burn at the stern. Würdemann took U-506 up closer and fired twenty-four shots from his artillery gun at the tanker, hitting the superstructure and waterline. Because dawn was breaking, he left the scene with the tanker sinking at the stern in "an inferno of flames." Shortly afterward, he said that there was nothing more to be seen of the ship.[9]

On one of the nights when Würdemann was stationed near the coast, he saw a ship passing with its position lights on and started following it through the delta and up into the Mississippi River. "The tower of 506 was full of the guys who were off duty, and we were

U-506 at Lorient, France, March 25, 1942. U-506 and U-507 were the first two U-boats in the Gulf of Mexico. Photo courtesy of Bundesarchiv, Koblenz, Germany.

watching the steamer," said Wilhelm Grap, at that time an oiler on the submarine. The U-boat was traveling on the surface, and suddenly Würdemann called for someone to check the water depth. "It was the commander's sixth sense that saved the boat," recalled Grap. "We only had three feet of water under the keel, so we turned around right away and left the river." [10]

At 8:30 P.M. on May 16, U-506 sank another loaded tanker south of the Mississippi delta, making a total of four ships sunk since it came into the gulf on May 8. Würdemann noted that the light on Ship Shoal light buoy, to the west of Southwest Pass, was "obviously turned off."

At 1:00 A.M. on the nineteenth he torpedoed a freighter (the *Heredia*), hitting amidships and astern. He reported that the ship was sagging fast and that the stern hit bottom at a depth of seventy-five or so feet. "The forecastle up to the bridge for the moment is still sticking up out of the water but going down, too," he commented. "Several brightly illuminated lifeboats and rafts were lowered."

That night at 11:20 Würdemann spotted a loaded tanker and hit it at the bridge and amidships. "The tanker started burning and became a torch within minutes," he reported. "A strong inboard explosion followed." He said that obviously the tanker had been torn apart in the middle. The forecastle turned over and sank, and the glare of the fire was so bright he could not see anything more, so he turned away and submerged.

After watching the victim for an hour and a half, the German commander saw it sink and observed that oil burned on the surface for some time. (This was the tanker *Halo*.)

The next morning at 9:20 he fired a single torpedo at an unarmed freighter and missed. He saw another freighter with camouflage paint and a gun and shot two "eels"—both missed. "All torpedoes used up," he said, "so I started my trip home."

Würdemann sent a message to headquarters: "In front of the Mississippi there is permanent heavy single traffic. For sure, this is rewarding for U-boats. There is frequent air cover but no naval cover. . . . Altogether I sank eight ships with 52,700 tons as well as hitting a tanker of 8,000 tons."

U-506 traveled back out of the gulf with no major problems—just a few crash dives to avoid airplanes. Würdemann had sunk all eight vessels within a few degrees of latitude twenty-eight north and longitude eighty to eighty-one west.[11]

Slightly over a year later, Erich Würdemann's boat was depth-charged on the surface by a diving Liberator. The attack had come as a surprise, and the six men on the bridge, who were wearing life jackets, jumped into the water. The commander was knocked unconscious and fell overboard as the boat went down. First Lieutenant Hans Schult, one of the six, ordered two new seamen to hold the commander up out of the water; then he and three others swam over to where they had seen a yellow spot, thinking it was a life raft. They did find a raft, dropped by the Liberator, with food and medical supplies. When the four rowed back to their comrades, Würdemann was nowhere to be seen. Schult asked them where the commander was, and they replied that the "old man" had ordered them to let him go. Being inexperienced seamen, they obeyed, and Würdemann swam away and disappeared. He was lost forever.

"Our commander was one of the best in the German submarine forces," said Wilhelm Grap. "He was careful but not afraid to do something. He was our father and our friend, and we always thought of him with honor." [12]

Erich Würdemann was captain of U-506 throughout her career. In March, 1943, he was awarded the Knight's Cross for sinking a claimed one hundred thousand tons. Hans Schult, who was twenty-three and six years younger than Würdemann, served under him the entire length of his command. He recalled that the captain had a habit of keeping things to himself and seldom spoke to his junior officers. On one occasion, however, Würdemann did ask for advice during a long depth-charge attack when he was getting desperate.

U-506 had been plagued by trouble since she was commissioned in the fall of 1941. Once she rammed a destroyer at anchor; another time she ran aground in the Elbe River at the beginning of an air raid on Hamburg. Early in 1942, in a final overhaul at the Deutsche Werft, she was frozen in, and it took five tugs and a small floating dock to get her out of the ice; she was so battered that she had to go to Heligoland for repairs. U-506 sailed from there in early March to North America but was called back and put into Lorient after being at sea only eighteen days.

On U-506's second patrol she shared with U-507 the distinction of being the first sub to enter the Gulf of Mexico early in May, 1942. The crewmen said the temperature was extremely high and that no cooking was done during the daytime, when she stayed submerged: the heat of the engines was trapped in the boat, making cooking unbearable. Meals usually consisted of cold rice and gruel that had been prepared the night before. The crew considered itself luckier on that patrol than those who came after them, because at that time antisubmarine forces were weak. After the commander had exited the gulf, he sank two merchantmen with gunfire off the east Florida coast, one of them costing him one hundred rounds of ammunition. He refueled from a seven-hundred-fifty-ton "milk cow" submarine and reached

Lorient on June 15, where he was proclaimed the "tanker-cracker of the 10th Flotilla."

On the third patrol of U-506, Würdemann went to the west coast of Africa and sank five merchant ships, totaling thirty thousand tons. In September, 1942, his boat participated in the rescue of survivors from the SS *Laconia*, a British troop transport that was sunk by a U-boat about three hundred miles off Ascension Island on the twelfth. The ship had about two thousand Italian prisoners on board, and many were killed when torpedoes exploded in their quarters. Some British service personnel were also aboard, as well as some British women and children. Four or five U-boats were sent in to rescue the Italians, but their captains, seeing women and children in the overcrowded lifeboats, took care of them along with the Italians, keeping them fed and letting them come on board to sleep.

After five days of aiding the survivors, U-506 and the U-boat that had torpedoed the *Laconia* were attacked by two U.S. aircraft, but 506 had prepared for this contingency and crash-dived. Würdemann later handed over the survivors to rescue ships and left the scene.[13]

On September 17, 1942, Admiral Dönitz issued orders to all his U-boat commanders: "All attempts to rescue members of ships sunk . . . fishing out swimmers and putting them into lifeboats, righting capsized lifeboats, handing out provisions and water, have to cease. Rescue contradicts the most fundamental demands of war for the annihilation of enemy ships and crews. . . . Only save shipwrecked survivors if [their] statements are of importance for the boat. . . . Be hard. Think of the fact that the enemy in his bombing attacks on German towns has no regard for women and children."[14]

In any case, in spring and summer of 1942, when U-506 and others scored victories in the Gulf of Mexico, the commanders did the best they could to allow the escape of merchant ship crews, although many perished. The U-boat men did not hate the Americans. They were just doing their job.

5

Danger Zone

MAY — THE BIG MONTH IN GALVESTON. Every year the town celebrated the opening of swimming season with Splash Day, attracting fun lovers from all over the Southwest. Thousands gathered at Murdoch's Pier to enjoy the sun and watch the "Glamburger Girl Number One" carhop queen contest.

At midmorning on Splash Day, Harro Schacht in U-507 sank his first ship, the *Norlindo,* and the next day destroyed two more tankers. His fourth, the *Alcoa Puritan,* received no notice in the local papers, probably because no one was killed. The ship had been heading toward Mobile with ten thousand tons of bauxite, and the captain was holding a straight course without zigzagging. Schacht's first torpedo passed fifteen feet astern, and the chief officer rushed to the bridge yelling, "Submarine torpedo!" The captain ordered full speed ahead (about sixteen knots) and turned the ship to try to keep a small profile toward the U-boat. Schacht's sub came to the surface, started chasing the ship at eighteen to twenty knots, and began to overtake her, approaching on the starboard side. Schacht opened fire with both guns from a distance of one mile and fired for the next forty minutes, scoring fifty hits, one of them breaking the *Alcoa Puritan's* steering mechanism. With the vessel out of control, the captain gave orders to stop and abandon ship.

The crew lowered the lifeboats and rafts and all escaped as the U-boat waited. As soon as they were out of harm's way, Schacht fired another torpedo into the ship, and it sank seventeen minutes later.

The captain said that his vessel was unarmed and that the British and American navy codes went down in the sinking.

The ship's third mate told his superiors that once he was in a lifeboat, he discovered that there were many holes in it needing immediate repair. He found a canvas sack with some wooden plugs for fixing holes "which might be caused by machine gun bullets." The plugs were useless in the irregular, jagged openings caused by shrapnel, so he tried to find some toggle bolts, washers, and nuts he had placed in the boat earlier, but they were not there. A couple of sailors then carved out some larger plugs from debris, wrapped them with strips of cloth, and stuffed them into the holes, which were leaking badly. "The boat was not taking on much water then," the mate said, "and Captain Kranz decided to allow the men on the raft to come into the lifeboat, which they did all at once." Now the small craft had fifty men with no dry clothing and six blankets, but they made it in good shape until they were picked up four hours later by the Coast Guard cutter *Boutwell*.[1]

The crew members described the attacking submarine as about seven hundred fifty tons, painted sea green with no stripes or streaks, having one gun forward and one after the conning tower, and with a wire from bow to stern. They believed it to be German. The commanding officer of the sub—blond, about twenty-five, and "obviously German"—called through a megaphone in excellent English saying, "Sorry I had to do it. Hope you make it in."[2]

At midnight that night Naval Radio in Washington proclaimed the entire Gulf of Mexico and Florida Straits a danger zone. They advised all unescorted merchant ships in that area to make for the nearest port. Four ships had been attacked by U-boats in three days. The first was the *Norlindo,* the next two were the tankers *Munger T. Ball* and *Joseph M. Cudahy* (Schacht disposed of them on the same day within sixty miles of each other three hours apart), and the last was the *Alcoa Puritan*.[3]

About a month before Schacht showed up, Gulf Sea Frontier defenses had increased slightly with the addition of two more converted yachts; two 125-foot cutters, *Boutwell* and *Woodbury;* four 165-foot cutters, *Triton, Pandora, Thetis,* and *Galatea;* two destroyers, *Semmes* and *Dahlgren;* one Fleet Air Detachment at Miami; and a few more army aircraft. In May and June, when U-boat attacks reached a climax in the gulf, more small Coast Guard cutters, two minesweepers, another yacht, and some converted motorboats came into the picture, but the submarines clearly had the upper hand.[4]

On May 4, Admiral Ernest J. King requested that the Coast Guard Auxiliary get cracking and put together a fleet of private patrol boats to do "offensive action or rescue work." Owners of large yachts had been begging the navy since 1941 to let them participate in the fight against German U-boats, and until the fourth month of 1942, when eighty-two ships had been lost in the Eastern Sea Frontier, the navy had turned a deaf ear to their pleas. Now things were getting desperate. In May, 1942, Congress amended the Coast Guard Auxiliary Act to authorize enlistment of suitable members of the auxiliary, even though they had minor physical defects and were too old for any other duty. And so a fleet of yachtsmen sailed out in the last week of May from Galveston, New Orleans, Miami, and other ports, each equipped with four depth charges, a .50-caliber machine gun, and a radio to patrol off the Atlantic and Gulf coasts.[5]

On May 10, Würdemann's first gulf torpedo victim, the *Aurora* (a 1920 tanker headed to Beaumont, Texas), did not sink. The U-boat commander apparently was unconcerned that the ship was in ballast (empty of cargo and carrying water for ballast). His first "eel" hit the tanker with "little effect and [it] continued to run with slightly reduced speed on previous course," wrote Würdemann in his war diary. The *Aurora* was not zigzagging, a normal wartime procedure to avoid torpedoes, and the captain did not change direction after the attack, another mistake. The ship's radio operator sent a distress call, and the gun crew started to try to fire their five-inch gun, but the submarine was traveling submerged and they could not see it. Two more torpedoes smashed into the starboard tanks; then U-506 surfaced and began to shell the *Aurora* from three- and five-inch guns. The crew abandoned ship, and the captain made no effort to dispose of the confidential papers scattered about in a locked bureau drawer, the radio room, and inside a safe. (All ship captains carried secret codebooks to send and receive radio messages in coded language; they were supposed to make sure the books did not get into enemy hands.) A Coast Guard vessel and a tugboat rescued all the crewmen except one, who had died in the lifeboat, and the tug towed the *Aurora* to

Burrwood, Louisiana, where the navy had a small base and hospital.

None of the crew members or armed guards could give an accurate description of the submarine. They said they saw "a dark shape" that looked like a "large green wave," and none could draw a silhouette, but several said they heard orders being given in German. The navy report stated that the vessel's master, Captain William H. Sheldon, was "very lax in his handling of confidential British and American codes" and that another breaking of rules occurred when one of the pump men walked around the deck with a flashlight at 2:30 A.M., about half an hour before the attack.[6]

The Coast Guard wrote in the May 5 summary of operations: "Squadron VP-81, Key West, reported two ships burning. . . . No help at hand. Survivors in boats. Both ships are burning and will sink." Out of a crew of thirty-seven on the *Joseph M. Cudahy,* twenty-seven died in fire, and the remaining ten, including three injured, were rescued by an Allied plane. On the unarmed *Munger T. Ball,* loaded with gasoline, thirty-seven died and four lived to tell about it. The commandant of the Eighth Naval District notified the commander of the Gulf Sea Frontier that two patrol corvettes were leaving Galveston for Key West and should arrive on May 8.[7]

"It should be noticed," wrote navy historians in 1945, "that the enemy was acting openly in daylight as well as in morning and evening twilight. At least two of the areas where sinking occurred were under constant patrol."[8]

In the first week of May, U-boat activity was just beginning near the Mississippi Passes and in the Florida Straits as well, where the Gulf Stream flows into the Atlantic. The passage, relatively narrow and deep and dark blue in color, had a maximum velocity of four knots, a thousand times swifter than the Mississippi. Many experts had figured the straits would be too tricky for U-boats, but they were wrong.[9]

"The [Gulf Sea] Frontier seemed alive with submarines," the navy wrote. The Germans were busily torpedoing merchant ships to the south of Cuba, off the east coast of Florida, and in the northern Gulf of Mexico. From May 1 to May 6, seven U-boats revealed their presence in or near the Gulf Sea Frontier: U-108 (Scholtz), U-333 (Cremer), U-109 (Bleichrodt), U-506 (Würdemann), U-564 (Suhren),

U-125 (Folkers), and U-507 (Schacht). That week the few available forces in the gulf were searching everywhere for U-boats, trying to pick up survivors, and having hell.[10]

Three days after the *Aurora* attack, Würdemann went after the *Gulfpenn,* a tanker in the same vicinity, and news of his activity made the front page of the Galveston paper: "Two More U.S. Ships Sunk in Gulf; 33 Seamen Reported Lost." The story said the ships were the sixth and seventh sunk in the gulf, but in truth they were the ninth and tenth.[11]

The unarmed *Gulfpenn,* headed to Philadelphia from Port Arthur, Texas, carried ninety thousand barrels of fuel oil and was traveling in "irregular patterns," with the radio silent and four lookouts on the bridge. The weather was clear, the sea moderate, and the wind light. At 4:50 in the afternoon the first torpedo blasted into the engine room, killing all twelve men there and stopping the engines. An automatic alarm sounded, but the captain sent no distress signals. He immediately placed the secret codebooks in a weighted bag and left it to sink with the ship. Twenty-six of the crew made it into lifeboats, where one of the men died. A Honduran vessel, the *Telde,* picked up the survivors and brought them to Pilottown, Louisiana.

None of the crew saw the torpedo, and a U.S. navy bomber had been patrolling the area where the ship was traveling for almost two hours before the attack. The plane completed its last circle over the *Gulfpenn* ten minutes before the U-boat sent its deadly missile. The pilot said that the water in the ship's path looked patchy with scattered muddy and clear areas, and he conjectured that the submarine must have been lying in one of the dark brown spots.[12]

The next day (May 14), the tanker *David McKelvy,* loaded with eighty thousand barrels of crude oil, encountered Erich Würdemann thirty or forty miles off the mouth of the Mississippi. The time was 11:45 P.M.; the lone tanker was completely blacked out, had five lookouts, and traveled on a zigzag course going east, about thirty miles south of the Mississippi Passes. The sea had a slight swell, the wind was light, the night moonless, and no other ships were in sight. The U-boat spotted the *McKelvy* and sped up, maneuvered into firing position ahead of the ship, and then released two torpedoes. One hit amidships, causing an immediate earth-shattering explosion; seconds later, the *McKelvy* burst into flames. As Würdemann put it, "Burning oil with raging speed poured into the sea," and the water around the ship became a brilliant inferno. The radioman sent an SSS signal.

Two of the four life rafts were launched and one lifeboat with seven men in it. Some of those in the water climbed onto the rafts, one of which drifted into the flames, and all aboard had to dive off. The men in the lifeboat had had no emergency training, and in a panic they allowed their boat to drift into the fiery waves, where they perished. A Coast Guard report said that "while the ship was burning furiously the crew was calm and showed extreme bravery helping each other."

"I saw the raft we had thrown overboard catch on fire," said Chief Engineer Petro Waldermarsen. "I knew that way was too risky, and I told the boys still on deck not to jump, that we could go below to the water tank, but [Helmar] Martin was the only one who remained with me." The chief had remembered a friend's story from thirty years back about saving his own life by staying in the ship's water tank for three days.

The two men found the forty-by-fifty-foot tank about half full and only about four feet deep, so they were able to stand in it comfortably. They stayed in the water, afraid to leave, for twelve hours, and when it seemed safe they made their way across the hot decks to the gun platform and waved to a navy plane circling overhead. The *Boutwell* came to pick them up a couple of hours later, but seventeen crewmen had lost their lives.[13]

One of the survivors said he saw the U-boat through the smoke and flames and that it was painted light green. He could make out just the hull and conning tower. The sub went under the water between his lifeboat and the ship as he watched.[14]

Navy historians commented that "fifteen minutes before midnight still another tanker, the *David McKelvy*, was sunk in the very same area [Mississippi Passes] . . . despite the concentration of surface craft in the area." The situation seemed hopeless. Lack of radar on U.S. planes precluded night detection of U-boats, and during the day the Germans were staying submerged. Besides, freshly recruited American pilots, Coast Guard, and navy crews were inexperienced in war activities, not to mention dealing with German submarines manned by experts.[15]

On May 11, one day after the news that Baron von Spiegel had come back to the Gulf of Mexico in a U-boat, the city announced it was setting up a civilian defense control center but gave few details for fear of sabotage. "It will be a nerve center . . . for protection from air raids," said R. E. Fristoe, in charge of the project. The location was not given, but a general description said that about a hundred female workers had been trained to serve as telephone operators handling calls and dispatching various services. "The women have been checked for calmness, clear thinking, handwriting, availability for service, and their extreme patriotic willingness and desire to do their bit in community service," Fristoe explained. "They will be subject to call at any time." He went on to say that the list of names could not be revealed because the women had been pledged to secrecy concerning their work. "Everything is being done in the way of comfortable appointments such as chairs, adequate lights, fans, and good reading material," he said. Coffee and toast were to be provided for the workers as they waited for an incident.[16]

At this time the pipeline dispute started up again. Oil coordinator Harold Ickes in April had recommended that the Texas Railroad Commission slash state petroleum production to 960,000 barrels a day in May because of transportation problems. The state replied that they had not complied with the request because this curtailment could force small operators into bankruptcy. "The oil transportation system has undergone violent displacement," said E. DeGolyer in Ickes's office. "The OPC knows Texas is suffering and believes the solution is a pipeline job." He said that currently only 800,000 barrels of oil a day were reaching the East, leaving a shortage of 520,000 barrels. "The OPC has applied to the War Production Board for priorties to make steel available for construction of a twenty-four-inch pipeline. . . . We believe it is absolutely essential that a 24-inch line be constructed."[17]

Headlines blared the news on May 17: "27 Killed in Bold Torpedoing in Gulf: Four Galveston Men Reported As Casualties." The story said that the vessel (the *Virginia*) had been attacked only a mile and a half from the mouth of the Mississippi. The Eighth Naval District claimed it was one of the greatest marine tragedies in the history of the Gulf of Mexico. Twenty-seven of the forty-one crew members died in flames, and the rest were all critically burned. "The attack was by a German submarine, which apparently was lying on the shallow bottom waiting for the ship to enter the river," the navy reported.[18]

The *Virginia* was carrying 180,000 barrels of gasoline to Baton Rouge, Louisiana, and the tanker had stopped at a buoy to pick up a pilot when it was attacked. It was 3:06 in the afternoon, the weather was fair, the sea calm, a light breeze was blowing, and the visibility was excellent. No one saw the submerged U-boat, and when the first torpedo hit, the captain was unable to get the ship underway because two more torpedoes blasted into it, causing immediate explosions and fire. Roaring flames enveloped the ship and burning gasoline blazed up in scattered areas on both sides, making it almost impossible for the crew to get off the ship. All eight lifeboats and rafts were unused because there was no time for launching. Within four minutes, fourteen men jumped off the vessel and swam for about thirty minutes before a PT (patrol torpedo) 157 boat picked them up. "Great courage and bravery were exhibited by certain crew members who saved the lives of two or three men who were able to get off the ship but were so badly burned that they could not swim," according to a Coast Guard report.[19]

Two survivors recommended to the navy that cork life preservers be discarded and that the lifeboats and rafts be easier to launch. "They had the rafts tied with one-and-a-quarter-inch rope and if you didn't happen to have a knife, you couldn't get them overboard," said the oiler.[20]

The navy could only muster its feeble forces and watch the devastation. "The Americans, apparently, had not anticipated the appearance of U-boats in such far distant part of the Caribbean as the Gulf of Mexico," wrote German admiral Dönitz in his memoirs. "Once again we had struck them in a soft spot."[21]

The mayor of Galveston, thoroughly worn out with the frustrations and endless problems of war and construction of a huge "Pleasure Pier," announced that he was planning to take a ten-day trip to Chicago, leaving immediately. He told reporters that this would be his first vacation since becoming mayor and that he needed a rest.[22]

As soon as the mayor was back, W. J. Aicklen, head of the local civilian defense, announced that because of submarine attacks on gulf shipping, all volunteers were to stand by for "any emergency" and be ready for action. Workers for the central control room and air raid wardens had to rush to their posts in a test drill. "There was some confusion, but the test was generally satisfactory," reported Aicklen. The city sounded its five air raid warning sirens for ten seconds and found out that some parts of town received no wailing noise. "I was directly back of Seawall Cafe at 17th and Avenue O at twelve o'clock, and I couldn't hear anything," said Julius Blackman.[23]

The Fort Crockett guns boomed and roared at the gulf horizon while sentries in concrete boxes stared out at the water, expecting to see periscopes among the waves.

6

Adventures of U-106 and U-753

GALVESTONIANS BEGAN TO ENJOY the bright sun and pleasures of summer, while shipping in the Gulf of Mexico continued at a frantic pace, despite the U-boat presence. Merchant mariners, well paid for their services, faced terrible hazards when they set out to sea, and navy armed guard crews tried to be brave.

"When I finished armed guard training, I was barely sixteen and had never been on a ship before in my life," said Jim McKaig. "Our ship was the SS *Kewanee,* and it was outfitted in February of '42 with a four-inch, .50-caliber gun on the stern. That's all we had on the ship."

The *Kewanee,* an old tanker that held forty-two thousand barrels, traveled from Texas City, Texas, to Tampa and Port Saint Joe, Florida, delivering gasoline. "We made trips from February until about May by ourselves, back and forth across the Gulf," recalled Jim. "We didn't zigzag, we went straight across." He said that when the submarines began to get "hot" the tanker had to anchor at night in various places along the coast. "We got as close to shore as we could, mostly around inlets like Pilottown, off the Southwest Pass. We stayed there overnight, then come back out."

There were six men including Jim on the gun crew, and they started to notice huge fires at night off in the distance. "We didn't know what was happening to the ships, but we figured it must be torpedoes. We couldn't get anywhere near 'em because we would have been a target. We just had to keep trucking through the gulf," he said.

One day the *Kewanee* was moving along about twenty miles from the entrance to Mobile. It was noon. "The reason I know it was noon is because the clock in the galley stopped when we fired the gun," Jim went on. "It interfered with our lunch." The radio operator received a message that a submarine was somewhere in the vicinity, and the gun crew manned the gun. "Suddenly this conning tower started coming up out of the water about three or four hundred yards away," said Jim. "I was the pointer, so I got the U-boat into the gun cross hairs and fired off a couple of shots at it. By the time we got off the second shot they were on their way down." As to why the U-boat commander did not attack, Jim believed that the tanker was "too small for them to waste a torpedo on."

After the submarine encounter, the tanker headed into Mobile and anchored overnight. "As soon as we arrived, a Coast Guard officer and his assistant came aboard and wanted to know what we were shooting at," related Jim. "We weren't very happy with the Coast Guard because they weren't doing much to prevent attacks, but we told them what was going on."[1]

Mayor Fiorello La Guardia, who had been relieved of his job as director of national civil defense in January, 1942, took the drastic step of regulating New York's night lighting. This ruling came just as Major General Thomas Terry announced that it had been "conclusively demonstrated" that current dimout requirements were unsatisfactory. He said that a navy patrol boat had gone twenty-five miles out to sea without seeing any ships until it turned around and discovered it had passed through a convoy, visible against the glow of the landward horizon.[2]

The subject of German submarines was uppermost in many politicians' minds, but no one seemed to have any good answer to the problem. Senator James M. Mead of New York thought that a large fleet of torpedo boats and subchasers would be the best means of combating the U-boat invasion. He cited as evidence the successes of Lieutenant John Bulkley's torpedo boat squadron that sank seven Japanese warships and merchant vessels in Philippine waters before the fall of Corregidor. The editor of the *Galveston Daily News*, however, considered that such boats as Bulkley commanded, although fast and well-armed for their size, were intended for attacks on surface craft. "The PT boats, as our navy calls them, are a development of the present war, and thus far . . . we have comparatively few of them," he wrote. He did not believe that the "large fleet" envisioned by Senator Mead existed. "We must do the best we can with what we have, and the need for action needs no further emphasis than the sinking of 195 ships in the Atlantic and Caribbean and gulf since America's entry into the war."[3]

On May 21, three days after the editorial, *Kapitänleutnant* Hermann Rasch, who had entered the gulf in U-106, sank the tanker *Faja de Oro* off the western end of Cuba. On the twenty-fourth he received an incoming radio message instructing him to refuel in quadrant 70 of the "great square," which was probably east of Florida. Rasch wrote in his log, "As I have been detected off the Cuba coast, I am now proceeding to New Orleans on the route leading from San Antonio to New Orleans, which is marked as the 'echo sounding line' on the map." The German navy must have thought they could somehow send U-boats up the Mississippi River, believing that if merchant ships could travel up and down it, then submarines could as well. Because Commander Erich Würdemann had failed to note in his war diary his near-grounding when he ventured into Southwest Pass, naval headquarters was oblivious of the dangers.

Rasch traveled north, seeing nothing, and dived once for an aircraft. He arrived at the area south of the Mississippi Passes on May 25 and the next day sighted an adversary wildly zigzagging—sometimes three times in one-half hour to one side and then again one hour on the same course. "No system can be found in it," he concluded. The night was lit by a bright moon, and the commander was unable to get close to the ship for fear of being detected, so he was forced to move on, keeping a considerable distance sideways. He ordered battle stations and then canceled it as the adversary zigzagged once more. After the moon disappeared Rasch got into position in front of the "steam cloud" of the vessel and attacked, shortly before dawn. Just as the first torpedo roared out, the ship turned again, and the shot passed under the stern. "The adversary . . . has recognized me, and he turns sharply and sends a Morse message [with name *Carrabulle*]," Rasch reported. The U-boat put on full speed and began firing the machine gun on deck. After an hour and 193 shots, the ship gave up, for the bridge and superstructure were burning furiously. Rasch blasted off the coup de grâce, hit the vessel amidships,

Hermann Rasch, commander of U-106. Photo courtesy of U-Boot-Archiv, Cuxhaven, Germany.

and left it sinking and burning. As daylight was just emerging, the German commander had to leave the scene.

The next night Rasch sighted another ship making frequent zigzags and going to the southeast. "As the moon will not set before sunrise, I have to try to stop him with artillery," he reasoned. "The moon is very high above the horizon, evenly bright." He maneuvered in front of the steamer with his stern facing it and stopped. At a distance of fifteen hundred meters he let loose with the 3.7-cm. gun, at which point he commented, "The steamer isn't panicked—it turns around sharply and now opens fire with its stern gun while sending an SOS for the *Atenas* with position." Rasch turned away and gave up the chase. "An artillery duel, without the benefit of surprise, can only be a success on a dark night," he wrote in his log. The *Atenas,* after making a few repairs, continued her voyage to the Panama Canal, having suffered no casualties.

Rasch remarked that the shipping route he had found seemed to have steady traffic and that his last two attacks showed that on clear, moonlit nights any pursuits would be long-lasting and cost a lot of fuel. Because of possible airplane patrols and ship counterattacks, success in shallower gulf waters seemed doubtful. Rasch's fuel reserves of seventy tons permitted him to use just another fifteen tons if he went on up to New Orleans. From there to the refueling place, taking the shortest possible route for twenty-five hundred nautical miles and without any more attacks, would require fifty tons, leaving a reserve of five. He decided against the New Orleans attempt and began a run at the lowest possible speed to the Yucatán Channel.

As the commander progressed southward, he saw a ship's smoke cloud and approached. As the ship zigzagged, Rasch submerged and sped up for an underwater attack. His first torpedo struck the steamer at the stern, and the crew jumped into the lifeboats and rowed away. Rasch fired a second "eel," and in six minutes the ship was gone. He headed on south, figuring that ship traffic would be frequent coming into the Yucatán Channel and with fewer air patrols.

"New Orleans not reached," he radioed back to headquarters. In his log he wrote, "I should have reported that I was delaying my return journey, as I do not intend to proceed toward home now." An incoming message instructed him that a return trip seemed necessary

Conning tower of U-106, a type IX-B, at Brest, March 6, 1941. Large bottles held distilled water for batteries. Photo courtesy of Bundesarchiv, Koblenz, Germany.

only if he had less than forty tons of fuel left. "Report immediately the reason if you are returning anyway," demanded headquarters.

Rasch replied that he could not carry out the advice about the forty tons. "My fuel calculation . . . is based on the U-boat's experience in 1 1/2 years of long journeys at the front, and was made with great caution." He said that submarines differed considerably in their fuel consumption and that "it should be left to the boats . . . to get along by themselves." Rasch resented headquarters telling him he was overly cautious and sent back a message: "According to the boat's experience, consumption as far as the rendezvous point is at the very best 50 tons. The remaining 15 is for chasing [ships] at the entrance to the Florida Straits."

Back came a reply: "Use possibilities in the gulf." Rasch wrote that he had meant the gulf side of the Florida Straits. He was furious.

By then he was positioned above Cuba's western end and spotted a steamer steering a straight course. He sped up and submerged, but when he came close enough to inspect the vessel he found that it was a Portuguese passenger ship, the *Nyassa,* with its name and flag painted on the side, so he turned off.

Rasch's last attack in the gulf was the sinking of the American freighter, *Hampton Roads,* very close to the western edge of the Yucatán Peninsula. He left having sunk three vessels, but his was not the only U-boat operating in the gulf the last two weeks of May. A second boat, U-753, had entered at the same time and came through the Florida Straits on May 18.[4]

That day a message arrived for *Korvettenkapitän* Alfred von Mannstein, its commander: "Go to Würdemann's operating area [Mississippi Passes]. Further instructions will follow." Von Mannstein began to enter the straits and saw an amphibious plane going north. "Continuous planes of the following types in this area: Lockheed Hudson, a single-wing plane with one engine, a land plane with wings attached medium high, one pontoon aircraft, a biplane, an amphibious aircraft, a sport aircraft and training aircraft," he reported. He wrote that surfacing would be possible only at dusk because of the strong air patrols.

U-753 left Fowey Rock, off the eastern tip of Florida, and started running full speed at periscope depth at 5:00 P.M. Two amphibious planes spotted him and dropped two bombs about two hundred

Kapitänleutnant Alfred von Mannstein, commander of U-753, upon return to La Pallice, France, June 25, 1942, celebrating successes in the Gulf of Mexico. Photo courtesy of Bundesarchiv, Koblenz, Germany.

meters away. He crash-dived, but then a subchaser found him and dropped seven depth charges. No damage occurred. The crew heard three more depth charges in the distance but kept moving. Von Mannstein saw what looked like a group of subchasers, but they did not detect him.

The U-boat had come to the entrance of the Florida Straits, and the commander surmised that a steamer route was about six to eight miles off the coast. He decided to stay there submerged, traveling abeam of the route to and fro, because he thought there was a good possibility of attacking a ship. He saw some smoke clouds and recognized several vessels in convoy with a destroyer, an escort ship, and air cover. The convoy had three columns and was zigzagging very little, going about four knots. Each column had about eight steamers, with protection in front and on each side. He spotted an amphibious aircraft and submerged. The sound room reported asdic (sonar) contact, and the commander decided to attack on the port side of the convoy because he could not detect any zigzagging.

"The destroyer ahead is roaming [probably searching] and the side protection is one subchaser and a fishing boat, which is about 1,800 yards away from the convoy," reported the commander. He said he was free of the subchaser but still had the fishing boat to his stern. He turned to an attack course and planned to fire four shots, noting that "the fattest steamers are unfortunately in the middle column."

Von Mannstein noticed that the port column had zigged and was a thousand meters away. His only possibility was a stern shot or submerging to get to the middle column. "I am going to keep my distance for at least 800 meters, then submerge," he decided.

He ordered both electric engines full speed ahead and went down to twenty meters, where he heard propeller noise on the starboard side. Suddenly the U-boat was pulled upward to seventeen meters. "I felt a light shock," said von Mannstein. "I quickly went down to thirty meters and figured that a steamer had gone out of position." The ship's propellers had sucked the submarine upward, where it struck the ship's bottom, but "it seems that the enemy didn't notice anything," the commander reported. "I took off in a southerly direction."

U-753 surfaced, inspected for damage, and found the bow net deflector broken and the cannon "all bent out of shape and torn at the pivot point." An airplane approached, and they submerged. "In all possible ways I want to keep in touch with this convoy," said von Mannstein. After diving several times for airplanes, he reported that it wouldn't do any good to send messages to other U-boats in the area because they were all out of ammunition. (He could hear their radio communications.)

The convoy steamed out of sight. "I am going after them," the commander decided. "If I go . . . within twenty miles of the coast I will surely be driven under water, because the enemy is staying in the area of the Florida Straits. I want to go south and try again to catch up with them at night southwest of Key West."

U-753 traveled through the straits, constantly driven under by air cover and bombed three more times. Von Mannstein then sent a message describing the convoy, noting that it was on a westerly course at very low speed.

"I cannot afford for anybody [surface vessels] to listen for me because the net deflector is damaged and it makes a rattling noise. I have to get away from here as soon as possible," the captain declared. He observed that airplanes were circling over the place where he last submerged, spelling each other and waiting for surface vessels to come. "The training of the United States air force is getting better," he noted. "Ambition and skill are increasing. Today alone I had twelve crash dives because of airplanes."

When dark came the crew secured the net deflector and lashed down the cannon. Von Mannstein sent a message that the convoy was out of sight, going at eight knots. "I have been chased away by airplanes," he commented. He said that the convoy's course was possibly the Yucatán Channel and that he was going after it. Should he miss it, he planned to search toward the north, assuming that the convoy had headed for the Mississippi delta. A few hours later he heard a radio message from Suhren in U-564, reporting that on May 20 a convoy was seen off the eastern Florida coast. The commander presumed it was the same one he was chasing.

Then he saw the tip of a mast, a single-runner, and von Mannstein sped up to get ahead. As the submarine rushed forward, he saw a ship's smoke cloud and remarked, "Does it have to be just now?" Two at once was too much. He went for the second ship, which was speeding along at thirteen knots, and suddenly the U-boat's gyrocom-

Conning tower of U-753 at Saint Nazaire, France, March 26, 1942. Skull and crossbones emblem with motto reads *Noch und Noch* ("Again and Again"). Photo courtesy of Bundesarchiv, Koblenz, Germany.

pass quit. Ignoring that, von Mannstein fired two torpedoes and missed; he shot two more, and both struck home. "The stern was torn off," he reported, and "it's listing very little." With an accurate coup de grâce, the vessel started to go down. "Unfortunately that cost me two valuable torpedoes," he noted. The U-boat surfaced, and the commander yelled to the crewmen in lifeboats, asking the name of the ship. They said it was the *George Calvert,* headed for Capetown, South Africa, though their destination was actually the Persian Gulf. The survivors reported later that they had seen a white skull and crossbones painted on the conning tower and that one three-inch gun was damaged and lashed to the deck in front of the tower. "The captain," they said, "was of average physique with dark hair and beard, and the entire crew wore shorts. The commander spoke first in German and pretended not to understand English, but he did begin speaking it with hardly any accent."[5]

On May 20 U-753 turned north, and at 8:00 P.M. the commander spotted a vessel with position lights. He started sneaking up to investigate. Without warning, there came an explosion on the ship and a tower of fire reaching one hundred fifty meters. "I presume that was Rasch," von Mannstein surmised. (He was correct—Rasch had attacked the *Faja de Oro*.) A second explosion roared through the night; then the commander saw some boats with lights. "I stay away approximately three miles because I do not want to interfere with the apparent presence of the other U-boat," he explained. In his log he noted the tanker was burning and drifting, and "if it hadn't been torpedoed by a submarine . . . then by a gigantic explosion, and its loss is assured."

After leaving the wreck he sent a radio message that he knew Würdemann in U-506 was out of ammunition and that his own plan was to go up to the Southwest Pass. He asked headquarters if he should try to resupply U-506.

The sub's next encounter occurred with a small steamer near Key West. A torpedo from the stern tube missed, and von Mannstein explained it by saying that the submarine had tipped downward slightly, throwing his shot off. He ordered another one, and this time the "eel's" motor started while it was still in the tube, forcing von Mannstein to get it out as fast as possible. It ran along on the surface for a distance, then careened to the bottom.

A navy ship came into view, a cannon boat of the Erie class. It stopped several times to listen, then went on out of sight. The commander assumed it had been called to the scene of the sinking. Suddenly a light airplane came into sight from the direction of the wreck and flew two hundred meters overhead. "He was asleep," said von Mannstein, who was astounded that the pilot did not observe his submarine just under the surface.

At 10:08 on the night of May 22, the commander saw a sailing ship and planned an artillery attack to let the crew get a bit of training. "We waited for the moon to go under, then tried to approach, but the ship changed course. We are sneaking up on the windward side." With machine guns blasting at it, the ship stopped, and von Mannstein called for a boat. The chief engineer and second watch officer climbed into the raft with a load of explosives and rowed to the ship. As they returned, the fire that they had lit in the cabin started to spread; then several detonations burst out, and the ship started sinking. From the papers they had taken from it, von Mannstein learned that he had sunk a three-masted British schooner, the *E. P. Theriault*, of three hundred fifty tons with a cargo of wood.

Before starting for the Mississippi, the crew took the cannon apart, removed it from the deck, and stowed it away. The log entry stated that the temperature on the bridge was 46 degrees centigrade or 114 degrees Fahrenheit.

Von Mannstein reported that he saw a vessel and that it turned away. "Probably a German submarine. Würdemann?" he guessed. He was right. U-506 had spotted him at the same moment, and Würdemann wrote in his log that he saw "a shadow that was possibly a U-boat—U-753?" They had glimpsed each other as U-506 was leaving the gulf.

U-753 made it to the waters off Southwest Pass and attacked the *Haakon Hauan* on its way to Galveston. The sub did not get to deliver the coup de grâce, however, because a PC boat came up, and the moon was so bright that the submarine could not approach again. After having some engine trouble, von Mannstein decided to sit in front of Southwest Pass and wait for the damaged tanker to show up, but he had no luck.

"I will operate at the outward passage of the Pass from the south and reconnoiter the type of traffic," he decided. He noticed several steamers, the evening group, and said he would surface as soon as possible to catch up with them heading westward (toward Galveston). "I intend to operate west of Ship Shoal, depending on the intensity of the moonlight."

His outgoing message reported that traffic toward the west was in waves, morning and afternoon, departing from Southwest Pass. "In spite of yesterday's new appearance of a submarine, traffic has not stopped. We can assume that the traffic will continue," he declared. The report said that ships going southward had some air protection consisting of flying boats and land planes ("fair to middling"). Sea defenses were PC boats, coastal patrols, and motorboats. "The education grows," he said, and further noted: "They are changing to convoys. . . . The 19th of May in a convoy, while submerging, a zigzagging side column . . . . sucked me up. The attack was a failure and the cannon was damaged."

At Ship Shoal buoy, von Mannstein saw a big fishing fleet with lights a short distance to the north. Then he saw a tanker approaching, headed toward the fleet in fourteen meters of water. "I'm going at him," he reported, but then, "I discontinue the attack because it is getting light fast in the southeast."

U-753 crept north, checking the water depth carefully, because they were getting shallower and shallower. They had just twenty-two meters under the boat, a dangerous situation where they could be seen by aircraft and have no way to dive or maneuver. A big tanker came into view at 2:00 in the afternoon; the commander fired one torpedo and missed. That night von Mannstein tried to attack another tanker, but the moon was too bright, and the ship steered "right through the fishing fleet."

The commander's next report said that there was a large group of fishing boats with lights to the west of Ship Shoal and in between the boats were three dimmed, low-running escorts. "It's a good thing I did not follow the tanker," he commented. This turn of events prompted von Mannstein to draw a map of the Louisiana coast with the freighter and tanker route and the fishing fleet with subchasers hidden in it.

He headed on to the south and planned to station himself near the fishermen when the moon went down and to stay submerged at the twenty-meter depth line. The U-boat had begun to circle around the group of fishermen when the lookout saw a tanker approaching. "Still too bright for attack," the commander noted. The adversary changed course, and clouds passed in front of the moon. Von Mannstein blasted off one torpedo, which hit near the bow and caused a small fire. He shot again and missed; then came the coup de grâce—a huge pillar of flame roared up. He ejected one more "eel," and the sinking vessel hit bottom at the stern, with the end of the ship almost upright in the air. He heard the ship's message giving the name as the Norwegian tanker *Hamlet,* then he left the burning wreck.

The commander's next message to headquarters said that the gulf was rewarding as a main route for tankers. "Water color and layers of water are favorable." He reported that he was out of ammunition and that below Southwest Pass there was "high pressure," presumably referring to air patrols.

The next day a four-engine plane spotted him, dropped a "scare

Crew member of U-753 enjoying a Beck's beer at La Pallice U-boat base, June 25, 1942, after patrol in the Gulf of Mexico. Photo courtesy of Bundesarchiv, Koblenz, Germany.

bomb," circled a few times, then threw out a smoke bomb where U-753 had submerged. "Their tenacity is growing," remarked von Mannstein.

The commander decided that refueling was now inevitable and planned his return trip on the west side of the Yucatán Channel. "I intend to take advantage of every opportunity [on the way]. . . . I have notified Rasch, who is still in the gulf with torpedoes, about rewarding traffic in squares DA 91 and 92 [at Ship Shoal]."

Homeward bound, the crew's spirits rose. They passed some kind of converted ship with a bow protection apparatus guarding the west side of the Florida Straits and were not seen or heard. "The steamer is asleep," exulted von Mannstein. As they happily motored along, the lookout spotted something in the water, and the commander ordered engines stopped. "We fished a brand new truck tire out of the ocean," he said. "I want to take it back to give a boost to the German raw material situation."

The trip through the Florida Straits was a breeze. "There is very little air reconnaissance since it is Sunday and there is a thunderstorm," commented the commander.

In his final report he said that during the sixty-five days of his mission and in spite of tropical conditions, especially in shallow water, and the extra demands made on the crew, "they tackled it with alertness and humor." Health conditions were very good, technical systems had no great failures, and communications were "on the average pretty good." Von Mannstein recommended that messages be sent at night, and that night in the Gulf of Mexico was from about 0400 to 1100 German standard time. He said they had had two weapon failures: one a tube runner, the other their cannon, which unfortunately "couldn't be used, since it was torn off in a collision."

As to the enemy situation, he reported that in May in the western Florida Straits and Old Bahama Channel the switch from single traffic to a convoy system was noticeable, but that in the gulf there were still single vessels. "The strongly trafficked steamer route Mississippi-Galveston is a map explained in enclosure #2." He said the convoy he had seen zigzagged very little and had a formation of three columns with destroyers far ahead and subchasers on the sides. "The sea protection on the whole was weak and not very well trained. It consisted mainly in the northern Florida Straits of PC boats and patrol vessels recruited from customs." He saw no destroyers but heard asdic "without question." Concerning the air protection, he said, "The American air defense in my estimation will probably be quicker than the sea defense to develop into an opponent that we have to take seriously." He described the route from Southwest Pass to the west as patrolled by average air reconnaissance, and on moonlit nights no airplanes were spotted. "In all cases it was possible to remain undetected."[6]

When Hermann Rasch and Alfred von Mannstein finished their patrols in the gulf at the end of May, 1942, the German submarines had scored the biggest successes of the entire war during that month. They sank seventy-one ships of over three hundred fifty thousand tons in the Gulf Sea Frontier and Caribbean waters. The first five sub-marines, U-507, U-506, U-106, U-103, and U-753, did away with twenty-six ships in the Gulf of Mexico. Most of the Gulf Sea Frontier destruction took place near the Mississippi Passes, off the east coast of Florida, and in the Yucatán Channel—with no end in sight.[7]

On May 25, one week after Mayor La Guardia had ordered lights dimmed in New York, Galveston's Mayor Harris wrote a letter to Bob Nesbitt telling him that there had not yet been any requirement to cut down lights on the Gulf Coast. "Of course that may come, but confidentially, there was a board of the Navy Department that went out the other night and watched a tanker go by Galveston Island, keeping the tanker between the lights of the city and the boat, and reported back that there was no illumination of the ship by the lights from shore so that a submarine could stand between it and sink it. This information was given me by the head of the board, Commander Maher, and that may be the reason we have received no orders yet."[8]

7

Riveting

AT TODD SHIPYARDS, across from Galveston on Pelican Island, work went on night and day with repairs of torpedoed ships and arming of merchant vessels. Shipyard officials worried that U-boats might be able to travel into the narrow channel between Bolivar Peninsula and the island. They believed the submarines would have a terrible time turning around, forcing them to exit by the same route and putting the shipyard in danger of attack.

At the beginning of the war, it was a masculine world. All employees at Todd, including secretaries, were men; then the company started hiring anybody and everybody they could find, including women. Shipyard workers were given strict instructions to say nothing about what was going on, not even off-hand comments about daily activities at their jobs. Occasionally the managers threatened to fire employees because they were loose-tongued, and notices were posted everywhere saying, "A slip of the lip could sink a ship."

The government tried to boost America's morale with glowing articles about the "might" of U.S. forces. On May 18, 1942, the navy invited newspaper reporters to visit a school for navy armed guards on Lake Michigan so that they could reveal the progress being made against German U-boats. "Four-inch guns firing today thundered out the navy's defiance of axis submarines lurking in salt water 1,000 miles away," they wrote. The navy had lifted its screen of secrecy regarding the gun crews for merchant ships and told newsmen that each crew had ten men including loaders, spotters, pointers, trainers, and

Todd Shipyards on Pelican Island, Galveston. Merchant ships were outfitted for protection and later brought in for torpedo damage repairs. Photo courtesy of U.S. National Archives.

hot-shell handlers, under the command of a commissioned gunnery officer.

Shortly after dawn, the USS *Wilmette* got underway from the Chicago naval armory and traveled to the firing area seven miles out. A kite was raised with a sleeve target, and the young guardsmen fired at it with .30-caliber Browning machine guns mounted on the stern. "Tracer bullets showed that the lads' aim was good at about 800 yards," the news reported. Next, a one-yard-square yellow flag was set adrift, mounted on a ten-foot pole on a wood float. Seamen brought up the ammunition from the magazines; the skipper called, "Coming on the range"; and the first crew stood by ready to fire. They took bearings on the target, which by now was a speck in the distance, and the ship's whistle sounded, "Open fire." The crew adjusted the gun, and "away thundered the first round." More rounds followed as the officers called, "Down 300 [yards]," "no change," "up 200," "right two," or "left three."

The gunnery officer watched the shell splashes and ordered corrections before the next shot was fired, and the gun captain shouted, "Ready two," or "ready three," as each shell was slammed into the breech by the loaders. As each crew finished its rounds, the *Wilmette* swung around to come back on the range, the guns firing off the starboard beam first, then the port beam. No results of the practice were announced, but the spectators saw "a lot of splashes dangerously close to the fly speck target." At twenty-five hundred to three thousand yards, a hit was credited if it fell no more than fifty yards short, two hundred yards over, or twenty-five yards to either side, on the theory that within this area an enemy sub or ship would be hit directly or damaged by concussion.[1]

The government was trying to demonstrate its efforts to do something in the face of overwhelming German U-boat successes. In Galveston the maritime union planned a memorial service to honor the men who had lost their lives in submarine attacks. Union members decided not to hold a parade but to conduct a ceremony in front of Murdoch's beach pavilion. They carried a wreath with the words "Lest We Forget" in a lifeboat a short distance offshore and placed it on the water. The Veterans of Foreign Wars fired a salute and a trumpeter played taps. Union officials awarded silver torpedoes to the forty merchant seaman survivors of U-boat attacks who were in port that day, many of whom would ship out immediately afterward.[2]

In the same week the paper announced that thirty merchant ships would be launched for National Maritime Day—the biggest mass launching in twenty-five years. The launchings were to take place in nineteen shipyards on all coasts and the Great Lakes, but the schedule was not made public for security reasons. The U.S. merchant ship construction program, largest in world history, was to reach completion of twenty-three hundred vessels by the end of 1943.[3]

On May 20 an American tanker, *Halo,* left the port of Galveston and traveled through the Gulf of Mexico toward New Orleans carrying sixty-three thousand barrels of crude oil. The *Halo,* blacked out and zigzagging rapidly, arrived at a point fifty miles from the Mississippi delta on a calm, clear moonlit night with no other ships around. A torpedo struck with terrific force on the starboard side under the bridge and blew that part of the ship to bits. Ten seconds later a second torpedo hit the same side aft of the bridge and tore the ship apart. The tanker's engines were still running as it plunged to the bottom, all within three minutes.

Twenty-three of the forty-two crewmen who were in the engine room and aft part of the ship abandoned the tanker. They grabbed life preservers and jumped over the side, swimming away as the wreckage roared to the bottom. The fire burned for six hours, and the men huddled together in the water throughout the night and the next day. Then they began to die. On the third day ship wreckage appeared on the surface, and the seven remaining survivors tied boards together with strips of canvas torn from life preservers. Crude oil bubbled up and made a film four inches thick around and on the survivors. During the five days that the men struggled in the water, fifty miles south of the Mississippi Passes, they saw patrol planes every day except two, and the planes never came down to investigate the huge oil slick. Also, a destroyer circled the men three times but passed on by. Finally, on the fifth day, a Mexican cargo ship, *Oaxaca,* arrived and rescued three men on one of the rafts. One was dead, so they buried him at sea; the *Oaxaca* delivered the others to a hospital in Tampico, Mexico. The British tanker SS *Orina* picked up two more men and took them to New Orleans.

The surviving crewmen said that after their ship went down, two submarines surfaced and moved to a spot about a hundred yards away from them and exchanged blinker signals. In the darkness they could make out no details of the subs. These two vessels were U-506, who sank the *Halo,* and U-106, another sub in the gulf at that time.[4]

While the U-boats went on wreaking havoc, the navy ordered merchantmen coming from the Panama Canal to use the Old Bahama Channel and go up the west coast of Florida to get to the northern gulf. Several ship captains disobeyed these instructions and went through the Yucatán Channel instead; they were sunk. So the navy

sent a detachment of B-25 bombers to Havana, and they started patrolling the Yucatán Channel on May 21.

Gulf Sea Frontier historians wrote that the next day "an incident
occurred which was certainly unique in anti-submarine warfare and
the result of rather frantic desperation on the part of a command
whose meager forces had long since been stretched beyond the breaking point." At one o'clock in the afternoon of May 22, the SS *San
Pablo* was shelled by a U-boat just south of the Yucatán Channel.
The unarmed merchant vessel began to try to outrun the submarine.
After the chase had gone on for thirty-five minutes, the Gulf Sea Frontier decided to try an unusual stratagem. It sent a radio message in
plain English saying that aircraft were on the way to assist the ship,
and "as hoped, this message was promptly intercepted by the submarine, which ceased attack and submerged."[5]

As merchant ships in the gulf blew up like a chain of fireworks,
President Roosevelt and congressional leaders put their heads together and decided to discuss once again the idea of a big oil pipeline.
Still reluctant to use vital steel to build it, they mulled over the possibility of digging up unused lines and putting in a pipeline from the
Southwest to Florida or the Ohio River. The oil could then be shipped
on to the East in barges. Naturally, this idea had to be approved by
several government agencies, and nothing was decided.[6]

At Todd Shipyards, work went on full blast. "At the start of the
hostilities, there were only two piers at the yard with two wooden dry
docks, built in World War I," said H. A. Suhler, a former shipyard
worker. "But they were in good shape." He added that they built another pier and brought in a new dry dock that was self-contained.
"They could take this dry dock out to sea, sink it, pump it out—and
it had its own power, pumps, pipe shop, and steel shop."

"We had as many as twenty ships at one time in the yard," recalled
H. A., as he was known. "There were LCIs [landing craft infantry],
LSMs [landing ship machines for troops and vehicles], and destroyers
built somewhere else. They rushed 'em up and sent 'em to us incom-
plete, and we put the ammunition lockers on 'em, finished the quarters, and did other odds and ends." The landing ships had bows that
opened up, and the amphibious tanks would just drive out of the ship
with the men loaded in them.

Todd had a new dry dock that could handle two ships at a time. When the navy found out that destroyers could ram the submarines on the surface, the shipyard started putting "crash bows" on them so that the ship could destroy the submarine but not get hurt in the process. The shipyard rigged up merchant ships with degaussing systems as well, to repel magnetic torpedoes and mines.

"Of course we had a lot of ships in here that had been torpedoed," said Suhler. "We had one that was hit by three Japanese torpedoes: two on one side, then another on the other side, and that straightened the ship back up. We put it in working shape again." Suhler explained that they repaired not only torpedoed ships but some that had run aground to get away from the submarines.

"During the war they brought in a lot of cargo boats, and we converted 'em into troop carriers," H. A. said. "They would take one cargo hold and put tiers of bunks all the way from the top to the bottom, maybe three tiers, and they'd sleep in there just like rats." After the war the ships returned to the shipyard and were converted once more for cargo carrying.

At the Todd Shipyard in Houston a big program was underway for building Liberty ships, but the Galveston yard made only changes or repairs. "We put splinter shielding around the pilot houses so machine guns couldn't penetrate them. The American merchant ships were equipped with a three- or four-inch gun on the stern and machine guns next to the pilot house and on the bow to fight enemy planes or submarines if they were close enough."

H. A. recalled that they had no launching ceremonies during those days—they just converted them, and they sailed off. "Fast as they could, they just went." He said sometimes the men worked three shifts, and the third shift just blasted and painted. The other two did repairs and welding and other odd jobs. The riveting was another important task. "At one time I had eight riveting gangs going, and they drove about a thousand rivets a night. That's real good money."

A riveting gang had a "heater," a man with a ground forge full of coke (a derivative of coal), and he started the fire, heated the coke, then laid the rivets around the fire. When they were hot and all glowed red at once, he reached in with a long steel tong, grabbed a rivet, and threw it up in the air forty or fifty feet. "There was a man standing there with a little bucket," explained Suhler, "round at the top and a triangle to nothing at the bottom, with a handle on it. He caught that rivet in the bucket and passed or threw it down into the hold to the 'driver,' who caught it and put it into the rivet hole, while the 'bucker' on the opposite side flattened it out with a big steel bar and air gun."

The whole crew consisted of a heater, two passers, a driver, and a bucker. "It was hard on a man's kidneys and other organs to drive those rivets, if they didn't know how. That's one thing I never did want to do," said Suhler.

The time it took for the heater to pick the rivet out of the fire, throw it to the passer, who threw it to the driver, who put it in the hole, was five seconds. "You could count five and there went the rivet. It always got to the driver hot," H. A. explained. When the rivets had been driven and cooled, a man went around with a little hammer called a "test hammer," and he would tap all the rivets. If any moved, they had to be taken out and done over.

He said they had women working in the shipyard for the first time in history. "A woman who was a good seamstress could make a pattern for a piece of sheet metal very easily. They also worked as insulators, but not many did welding unless they were exceptionally good at it."

"The shipyard didn't have any protection, but so what?" Suhler remarked. "There were guns at the end of Galveston and on Bolivar, so we had protection." He said they had only a security guard at the gate, but then all the workers and supplies had to come across the water from Galveston by boat.[7]

While the shipyard workers riveted and welded around the clock, news of the survival of nineteen merchant mariners from the torpedoing of their tanker (the *Gulfoil*) appeared in the Galveston paper. The ship, en route from Port Arthur to New York and completely blacked out, was carrying several kinds of petroleum and keeping a straight course. At 10:41 P.M. a torpedo hit the tanker amidships and tore the flying bridge from mainmast to midships house, and the ship began to list about forty degrees. "I was banged about like a pea in a shell," Captain A. Henry Rowe said. A second torpedo hit the engine room fifteen seconds later, before the captain was able to get up on the deck. "The third officer tried to help pull me through the door, but his hands were oily and slippery, and he couldn't hold on to me." As the ship listed, the captain slid out and grabbed the bridge rail, hanging on for dear life until he was sucked under the water when the vessel sank. About four minutes later he was picked up by the men in one of two life rafts.

Third officer John Chalmers had been on watch at the time of the attack and was on the bridge when he saw the torpedo approaching. "It was leaping ahead of a broad white wake at right angles to the ship," he recalled. "There was no chance to give the alarm. The torpedo hit . . . and knocked me off my feet within seconds after I first saw it."

Chalmers said that after the second torpedo exploded, he went down to the bridge deck, found the captain, and asked him if he was all right. The captain replied that he was. The ship was going down fast to starboard, causing the captain to slide across to the rail, and Chalmers fell over the side into a life raft in the water. "Just as I landed on it, the port raft came down and landed on top of me, hitting me in the back. Then I climbed onto the one that had hit me," he said. Along with Chalmers were two others, who started rowing around to look for men. They picked up the captain and several others. "There were men calling for help all over the place. Sometimes we would hear them calling and we would row and row until finally we would lose them in the dark. Occasionally we heard whistles blowing," said one. They rowed for about four hours, as long as they heard any calls for help, and ended up with nine men. Another raft had ten.

Chalmers said the suction of the sinking ship pulled men underwater; some went down about ten feet and were shot back up again, and others never reappeared. All those on the rafts were cut and bruised and had swallowed saltwater with fuel oil, which covered the water around them. During the long day that followed they had plenty of food in the rafts, but their appetites had been killed by the oil.

The next morning they glimpsed a wisp of smoke on the horizon and quickly hoisted a pair of underpants on a boat hook as a distress signal, since their yellow flag was blackened. For a terrible interval, the captain of the rescue ship (the SS *Benjamin Brewster*) seemed in doubt about whether to pick them up, fearing a submarine decoy trap. But he hove to and came to get them; then delivered the weary men to the naval section base in Galveston. The survivors said they saw no patrol boats, aircraft, or ships of any kind until the *Benjamin Brewster* appeared, and all agreed that in spite of their misadventure, they would be going back out to sea as soon as possible. Their rescue tanker would be torpedoed and sunk seven weeks later.[8]

The SS *Carrabulle,* loaded with emulsified liquid asphalt and making her way across the gulf from Good Hope, Louisiana, missed being hit by a torpedo from Rasch in U-106, who fired it before his sub was in the correct position. Rasch then fired a warning shot across *Carrabulle's* bow and sounded his siren. The freighter sent four radio pleas for help as the U-boat chased the ship for an hour, hitting it with a barrage of shells from the deck gun just a ship's length away. The shells tore up the bridge and superstructure, and the captain ordered the crew to abandon ship. One lifeboat with sixteen men was lowered. "As we got away from the ship," one of the survivors recounted, "I would say about 200 feet, the submarine came by and hollered, 'Are you all off the ship?'" The crewman yelled back, "No, there is another boat load to come off." The U-boat roared into high speed and circled the ship, apparently looking for the other lifeboat. At that point U-106 fired a torpedo, hitting the *Carrabulle* amidships, and the explosion coincided with the lowering of the second lifeboat with twenty-four men, including the captain. Twenty-two of them died instantly and two lived, making a total of eighteen survivors, who were picked up by a passing merchant ship, the SS *Thompson Lykes.* The survivors said the submarine was "large, painted light gray, had no streaks or stripes, was about 1,200 tons, had one gun forward and one aft the conning tower and was believed to be German."[9]

After sending four SOS's, they had heard nothing from the United States Navy or Coast Guard. No help was available.

Before the *Carrabulle* and *Gulfoil* met with disaster, a shrimp boat fleet came to the rescue of the *Heredia,* a freighter carrying coffee and bananas to New Orleans, and the *William C. McTarnahan.* Both were sunk by U-506. At the *Heredia* wreck, a patrol plane saw two masts above the water and two makeshift rafts with survivors, including a young girl and boy. The pilot dropped message blocks to the rafts telling them he would bring help. He then flew to a group of six fishing boats nearby and dropped message blocks instructing them to watch where the plane dived in order to locate the survivors. The fishing boats gathered up their nets and followed the plane, which led them to the people in the rafts. A Coast Guard report said: "The intelligent cooperation and prompt action on the part of the masters of the fishing boats was highly commendable and probably resulted in saving the lives of most of those rescued. They had been in the water fifteen hours, and other surface aid could not have reached the spot before nightfall."[10]

When the *William C. McTarnahan* was discovered by a Coast Guard patrol plane, she had a large hole at the waterline and was burning, but not badly. The pilot discovered twenty-seven people in two lifeboats and a raft when he saw their two flares. The plane then flew northwest and directed fifteen fishing boats to the scene of the wreck, and the fishermen promptly rescued all the survivors.[11]

Historian Samuel Eliot Morison remarked: "Unescorted merchant shipping received the full weight of this U-boat blitz, which gave the Gulf Sea Frontier the melancholy distinction of having the most sinkings in May (41 ships, 219,867 gross tons) of any area in any month during this war. . . . And the sad thing is that at least half these sinkings might have been prevented by measures later adopted—coastal convoys for all merchantmen and adequate air coverage."[12]

8

The Dimout

ONE MORNING IN MID-MAY, 1942, Tom Leech was driving down Seawall Boulevard and noticed some county workmen removing debris from the beach. He parked his car, walked down the stairs, and stood watching the men to see what they were doing. One had just picked up an oar coated with oil and shells and was about to throw it into the pile of refuse. "Why don't you wash that off," Leech suggested, "and let's see what ship it came from."

When the workmen dunked it into the shallows and rubbed away some of the oil, the name *William C. McTarnahan* appeared. Leech couldn't believe his eyes; John G. Leech, his son, was captain of this ill-fated tanker and one of the youngest shipmasters to sail from a gulf port. One month ago, the *McTarnahan,* carrying diesel oil, had been blasted and sunk by a German submarine. Leech had survived the ordeal, escaping in a lifeboat. The navy notified Tom Leech the next night that his son was in a hospital in Houma, Louisiana. Leech showed the oar to his son, who was spending the weekend in Galveston, and the captain verified that this was indeed a souvenir of his ordeal.[1]

New U-boat attacks off the coast of Brazil and the torpedoing of a U.S. destroyer, the *Blakeley,* at Saint Lucia prompted a Galveston news editor to comment that the Germans must have secret bases in American waters. "Though it lacks official support, the suspicion that enemy subs are getting fuel and perhaps other supplies on this side is hard to down," he wrote. "President Roosevelt said the other day that the submarine problem is being solved," he went on. The article concluded that the president might be right, but it was hard to see any slackening of the depredations. "Judged by results, present methods of combatting subs which sink ships within sight of our shores can hardly be considered effective. Isn't it time to try something else?" he asked.[2]

Americans did wonder how the U-boats made long trips across the Atlantic, spent six weeks in western waters, and then traveled two thousand miles back to France. No one knew that in April, 1942, the German navy had put into service the enormous *Milchkühe* (milk cows), or U-tankers, that carried 720 tons of diesel fuel, torpedoes, food, tools, and other supplies. The tankers noticeably improved the effectiveness of the U-boats in spite of increasing defensive measures by the United States. Each "milk cow's" supply of fuel oil could replenish twelve of the smaller VII-C boats with four weeks of fuel and five of the larger IX-C boats with eight weeks of fuel, enabling them to carry on operations in the remotest parts of the gulf and Caribbean.

U-459, the first U-tanker built, sailed at the end of March, 1942, carrying diesel oil, food, and other items. "On board our vessel approximately eighty fresh loaves [of bread] can be baked," said *Korvettenkapitän* von Wilamowitz-Möllendorf. "Some 800 of these loaves were baked at night and distributed to various boats and received with great joy. . . . The rye bread that we produced has an excellent taste, is nourishing, and keeps well." He reported that since his rubber dinghy had been lost, he devised an excellent method of transferring supplies to the smaller boats, one that could be used in any weather. First, by using a pennant-pistol, he would shoot a line over, which was attached to the other boat. He would then send mesh-net hammocks or wrapped metal containers packed with perishables via hooks on the ropes. The rendezvous always took place in the mid-Atlantic, beyond the zones of enemy air surveillance, and at first losses were only slight in spite of the slow, cumbersome operation. During transfer of fuel and supplies, both submarines sat exposed on the surface for several hours, vulnerable to air attacks.[3]

These mysterious refurbishings of the U-boats caused many rumors to circulate that German crewmen were rowing to shore at night and walking about town the next day to purchase bread and go to the movies. Stories even had it that some of the Gulf Coast fishermen

Supply U-boat 459 (*left*) refuels U-571 at sea. The "milkcows" operated successfully until late summer, 1943, when all of them were sunk. This photo was taken sometime between March and May, 1942. Photo courtesy of Bundesarchiv, Koblenz, Germany.

were in cahoots with the Germans, giving them fresh fish and information about ship routes. Such tales proliferated from New Jersey to Galveston, and all of them claimed that bread wrappers and theater tickets had been found on captured German U-boat men. None of these adventures actually occurred in the United States. Samuel Eliot Morison, however, commented that the U-boats undoubtedly procured fresh provisions from native schooners in the Caribbean operated by enemy agents, but these were a small factor in their success.[4]

Since nothing seemed to be working against the wily U-boats, a meeting of the Anglo-American Caribbean Commission was held at Trinidad to discuss what could be done. Two of the members, Charles Taussig and Rexford Tugwell, governor of Puerto Rico, thought that a West Indies highway over land and water, with ferries bridging the gaps between islands, "might be the answer to the submarines." They said it should be possible to build fleets of bargelike ferries, "powered perhaps by automobile motors, to dash across those water gaps in the daylight hours and make port . . . long before nightfall, when lurking submarines come to the surface." Once across, the food and supplies could be transshipped to railroad cars or trucks, and the ferry would reload with seafood and sugar for the United States.

Taussig and Tugwell admitted that the plan had some drawbacks: for instance, some of the islands had poor roads and no railroads, and dock facilities were lacking at some potential ferry terminals. The commission members, however, believed that radical measures had to be adopted to deal with the islands' food emergency unless the antisubmarine campaign became more effective.[5]

On June 1 came headlines announcing, "Galveston Dimout Orders Are Given." To protect shipping from the risks of being silhouetted by coastal lights, Major General Richard Donovan, Eighth Corps area commander, issued orders effective June 2 for the dimming of lights along Texas and Louisiana shorelines. The paper said that for the past several nights, Galveston had already been lowering some lighting to protect shipping. The new rules prohibited signs, floodlights, stadium lighting, any exterior illumination except streetlights within five hundred yards of the coast, and all bonfires on the beaches. Streetlights, if visible from the sea, were to be blacked out on the seaward side, shaded from above, and wattage reduced. Individuals were warned to use extreme care with lights and to avoid any suspicion of signaling. Dimout time was to be thirty minutes after sunset to thirty minutes before sunrise, and the navy would continue to control navigation lights and begin patrolling offshore to monitor objectionable illumination. The orders were understood not to apply to Houston and New Orleans.[6]

The next day the editor of the Galveston paper discussed the dimout regulations, saying that the town would suffer "considerable inconvenience" but that there was good reason for it. "We can only hope that the inconvenience will be held to the minimum necessary to accomplish the desired purpose. . . . to keep from silhouetting ships at sea. . . . We feel sure that Galvestonians will cheerfully abide by the dim-out regulations when they are fully understood." He noted that Galveston was the largest community fronting directly on the gulf and that the regulations would apply most drastically in an area within five hundred yards of the shoreline, "which of course take in a considerable slice of this city." He said everyone would miss Treasure Isle's (Galveston's) "glittering diadem of lights" along the seawall and that "time-honored diversions involving driftwood fires upon the beach at night" were gone for the duration. The editor hoped that some way could be found to shield inside lights so that beachfront businesses could continue to operate at night. "It would be a pity to deprive the public of evening recreation on the beachfront if any safe way can be found of avoiding it."[7]

On June 4 Mayor Harris received notification from Washington that construction of the pleasure pier, 85 percent completed, was suspended. Sick at heart, he immediately phoned Major General Donovan in San Antonio and offered to give the pier to the army. "What use the army would make of the pier is not known, due to war conditions. . . . General Donovan will make an investigation of the proposal." Harris said that in the event the army decided not to take it, he hoped that the Reconstruction Finance Corporation could hold off the work suspension order until all the foundation piers were in place and the concrete cap on the deck finished to protect the structure from hurricanes.[8]

A few days earlier news had come in that forty "Axis aliens" had been arrested between Tampico, Mexico, and Laredo, Texas, "some of whom may have been furnishing information to submarine commanders." One German and one Japanese who lived in Matamoros (Mexico) were arrested and taken to a concentration camp. In a series of quick raids the FBI captured a "sportsman who owned a seagoing yacht," a German doctor, and a pharmacist. An agent reported that a "high ranking officer of the Japanese imperial navy who was posing as a humble fisherman" had been arrested in a Mexican resort. All coastal Gulf Sea Frontier cities had been "cleared of axis aliens," and the FBI had Secret Service men in all border towns and throughout Mexico.[9]

Lieutenant Commander E. C. Whitfield of the Coast Guard warned Galvestonians that spreading false rumors about enemy submarines had become serious. "There is no justification for any person passing such rumors in casual conversation," he said. Where there were adequate grounds for suspicion, the facts should be reported to authorities. "There is nothing an enemy propagandist could desire more than to see loyal Americans unjustly accused and to see Americans suspect each other," Whitfield declared. The commander went on to say that repeating unproven accusations was an inexcusable slander and that "everyone can find something better to do to aid in winning the war."[10]

At the same time, the FBI was enlisting locals to help them spy on their neighbors, telling them that their efforts would greatly assist in capturing saboteurs. One genteel Galveston lady sat in a friend's porch swing every afternoon watching the house across the street; then reported to federal agents who was entering and leaving the dwelling.[11]

Announcements of continued U-boat successes in the Atlantic, Gulf of Mexico, and Mediterranean roused Congress to action, and a Senate naval affairs subcommittee decided to make a preliminary investigation of the navy's antisubmarine campaign. Senator Allen J. Ellender of Louisiana, the chairman, said that naval officers might be called for a public hearing. Sixteen ships had been lost in the last five days in the Atlantic, and the total off North and South America had reached 244 since the war started.[12]

"There is no reason to despair of a solution to the submarine problem," wrote the editor of the *Galveston Daily News*. He thought that the recent appointment of Rear Admiral James Kauffman as commander of the Gulf Sea Frontier offered hope of early improvements in the gulf and Caribbean, because Kauffman was a seasoned expert in antisubmarine warfare. Admiral Kauffman said, "We must consider this area as a battlefield until every enemy submarine which enters it is destroyed." Naval authorities commented that the next four or five months would be critical and that antisubmarine activity by planes and ships had driven U-boats southward to the Gulf of Mexico and Caribbean. Furthermore, they reminded everyone that American naval and air forces were still inadequate to cope with the problem and that it was "up to America's shipyards and factories to produce the necessary vessels and planes."

Navy officials explained that the German U-boat combined the characteristics of a destroyer and a submarine because of its speed and guns and that the problem was much more critical than in the last war. "They are using subs with a surface speed of twenty to twenty-two knots, and they carry twelve to sixteen torpedoes," they said. Chairman Ellender said in Washington that "if we are not entirely satisfied that everything possible is being done to halt these sinkings, we are going into the whole matter in public."[13]

Two days later Chairman Carl Vinson of the main naval committee said that "the anti-submarine warfare organization has now passed its growing pains, is well established and is functioning effectively." Vinson reported that the enemy was building more submarines, but they could not build them in the proportion that the United States was increasing the means to combat them. "The naval committee has full confidence that we shall defeat the submarine," he announced.

"In dealing with submarines, we have a tough and clever enemy, and it does not pay to be unduly optimistic," he cautioned. "However . . . the fact remains that in the past few weeks the submarine has largely withdrawn from our Eastern seaboard and is operating farther at sea." He said that the navy was proud of its ship construction progress, but unfortunately, the only types in which it was not well ahead of schedule were those most needed to combat the submersibles. The building of these vessels was getting underway as fast as possible, however.

Vinson referred to criticism based on the success of the English in driving the U-boats from their home waters, saying that "such critics should remember that the British have had three years' experience in coping with the problem and that the British Isles would fit comfortably into the Gulf of Mexico."[14]

Galveston dimmed its waterfront lights on June 1 as Alfred von Mannstein cruised out of the gulf in U-753, having successfully dispatched four merchant ships. For the next ten days there was a slight lull in sinkings; then Erich Rostin in U-158 came on the scene. On June 7 he sank two Panamanian ships—the freighter *Hermis* and the tanker *Sheherazade*—near the Yucatán Channel.

Another of Rostin's victims, the *Cities Service Toledo*, a 1918 tanker loaded with eighty-three thousand barrels of crude oil, had left Corpus Christi headed on a nonzigzag course for Portland, Maine. On the second night out, at about 2:00 A.M., two torpedoes bashed into the ship on one side amidships, and the explosions demolished the starboard lifeboat. "The navy gun crew, except for two men on watch, were asleep in our quarters near the gun," said James

Erich Rostin, commander of U-158. Photo courtesy of U-Boot-Archiv, Cuxhaven, Germany.

Handy, a crew member. "We immediately donned our kapok life jackets and manned our weapon.[15]

"It was extremely hard to see, as it was a moonless pitch-black night, and it took a while for your eyes to get accustomed to the darkness," he continued. Handy said the ship's officers lowered the port forward lifeboat and climbed down to get in it. The merchant crew tried to launch the aft starboard lifeboat, but it capsized in the process. They ran over to the other aft lifeboat and after a lot of struggle got it into the water. "The ship was listing badly to starboard, and they had to push the boat off the side of the ship to get it into the water," Handy said. His gun crew was ready to fire after the first torpedo hit; then they realized that the submarine had surfaced about five hundred yards away. They could not see it but heard the diesel engines and saw a light going from dim to bright. The crew waited to see if the sub would fire a star shell to illuminate the area and then finish off the tanker with a deck gun.

Meanwhile, the rest of the merchant crew was waiting for the gunners, because the lifeboat they had in the water was the last one. The ship continued to list heavily, and "we had elevated our gun almost to the extreme elevation to stay on the sub," Handy said. "We decided not to wait any longer and to go ahead and fire at him, assuming that his light was on the conning tower." Handy said they then shot three rounds but didn't score any hits as the U-boat submerged and fired two more torpedoes into the sinking tanker.

"This last torpedo seemed to be different . . . as it didn't have as much explosive force and threw fire a hundred or more feet in all directions," Handy explained. Immediately, all the crude oil that had been spreading on deck caught fire, and the wooden mast came down in pieces, hitting two of the gun crew. "The fire spread rapidly up the deck, and the gun crew could not get to the lifeboat, so we slid down the side of the ship and swam away.

"I decided to jump from the extreme aft end of the ship, which was about thirty or forty feet from the water," he continued. "I gripped the collar of my life jacket real tight to keep it from breaking my neck and jumped feet first into the oily waves." Handy said it seemed like an eternity before he hit the surface and another eternity before he came back up. "I swam to the lifeboat and pulled myself in, and another gun crewman, Haddad, got in the boat from the other side. We took pieces of the wooden oars and tried to get away from the ship but were unable to do so, as the fire came around the stern of the tanker too fast."

Handy and Haddad jumped out of their lifeboat and started swimming away from the ship and burning oil. Getting through the choppy, goo-covered waves was so difficult they were unable to make much progress away from the fire. "You would swallow a lot of oil and water and get very sick and then throw up and feel pretty good for a while," Handy recalled.

The two had made it about a hundred yards away into the darkness when the water grew rougher. "Haddad and I got separated, and I never saw him again," Handy said. After his shipmate disappeared, Handy could hear the other crewmen yelling to each other. When the sun came up, his eyes started to burn badly from saltwater and from rubbing them to try to remove the oil. "The sun hurt my eyes, too, so bad that I kept them closed most of the time as I floated on my back," he said. On a couple of occasions a large fish tugged at his dungarees, but Handy never saw any sharks. He picked up a Portuguese man o'war, not knowing that its tentacles could severely burn him.

At daylight, a navy PBY (patrol bomber, Y class) flew over; then an air force bomber came in low over the water, circled the burning ship, and left. "I then saw a tanker about three miles away picking up the lifeboat with all the officers in it, and the ship went off to the east. This was the *Belinda*," said Handy.

"About nine o'clock in the morning I was starting to get a little concerned, as my kapok life jacket was becoming more and more waterlogged and wasn't holding me up too well. About ten o'clock another tanker [*Gulfking*] came by about a half mile from me and real near the other guys in the water, and the watch officers heard them yelling." The ship dropped anchor and put out a lifeboat for them while the current carried Handy toward the rescue vessel. He made it to the Jacob's ladder and got his feet into the bottom rung and his arms around it, "but by this time I was too weak to go up the ladder." Then one of the tanker crewmen climbed partway down and helped Handy onto the ship. About an hour later the lifeboat was pulled up on board with the rest of Handy's mates and the body of one of the gun crew. The *Gulfking*, unarmed and loaded with oil, headed east toward Burrwood, Louisiana, and Handy expected to have to abandon ship for the second time. "We didn't have any trouble but did pass two or three torpedoed and burning ships that night and the next day," he recalled.

When they arrived at the Mississippi Passes, a flaming tanker lay between them and shore, preventing the Coast Guard from sending a pilot out to bring the *Gulfking* in, so they lay at anchor the rest of the night. A Coast Guard launch arrived after daylight and transferred the survivors to Burrwood. "A couple of days later I, being the senior member of the gun crew, had to go to Morgan City to help identify bodies brought in from various sunken ships in the gulf," Handy explained. "It was quite a harrowing experience, as some of the bodies had been in the water a week or more." He was able to identify one navy gun crewman and one ship's crewman. Two or three days later the four surviving gunners were sent by train back to the armed guard center in Brooklyn, New York.

"I never suffered any lasting effects of the torpedoing, but for several months it would almost make me sick to smell burning oil, like the exhaust of an automobile," Handy said.[16]

Commander Rostin in U-158, after destroying Handy's ship, the *Cities Service Toledo*, went on to sink the Norwegian tanker *Moira* southeast of Matamoros, Mexico, and the Panamanian tanker *San Blas* in the same vicinity on June 17. His last success was the *Henry Gibbons* on June 23, south of New Orleans.[17]

In Galveston, everybody was wondering why they had to abide by troublesome new dimout regulations. When they read their morning paper, they realized that this was serious business. "It May Cause a Lot of Inconvenience . . . but There's Nobody to Blame but Adolph Hitler; Effectiveness Is Life and Death Matter to Seamen," said the front page. Writer G. C. Griffin explained that the army had started making inspections in launches out in the gulf. After observing the scene, they had concluded that Galveston would have to get along on even less light than when the dimout started. The officials also said there was every reason to believe that the dimouts would be lasting for the duration of the war.

The new measures would be strictly enforced by the police. "Anyone who in peacetime has approached Galveston on the highway at night has noticed that long before he reached the causeway he has seen a glow in the sky," Griffin said. "When the city is . . . lighted at

U-158, with crewmen saluting flag of the Third Reich. Photo courtesy of U-Boot-Archiv, Cuxhaven, Germany.

night, this glow is visible at sea for some distance . . . and when a portion of the horizon at sea is thus illuminated . . . a submarine commander can see a perfect outline of any vessel which is between him and the glow."

The army said it wanted to avoid a total blackout for the entire coast because the problems of crime and traffic accidents would be overwhelming. Thus, officials were requiring that automobiles use only parking lights along Seawall Boulevard and for five blocks from the beach, and no cars at all would be allowed on the sand.

"There are many persons who have cooperated cheerfully with the authorities . . . there are others who have deliberately evaded or defied the dimout regulations," said Griffin. He reiterated that the whole point was not to complain, but "if a person . . . must find someone to blame, let him blame Adolph Hitler." [18]

Two days later came the news that Axis subs had returned to the Gulf of Mexico. "Deadly . . . U-boats have crept back into the gulf . . . free from underwater raiders for two weeks," reported the navy after the sinking of the *San Blas* by U-158. The sinking of this ship and four others elsewhere boosted the sinkings to 270 since Pearl Harbor. The report said that after a U-boat sank a small freighter off the south Cuba coast, a submarine crewman dove into the water and grabbed a life preserver to find out the name of the ship. Off the eastern seaboard, thirteen surviving seamen of a demolished freighter said that the submarine's men apologized for killing some of the freighter's crew and yelled, "Germany and America should not be fighting each other." Before submerging, the commander talked to the survivors about the merits of American and German beer. Americans were fascinated with the U-boats.[19]

In the month of June seven German submarines plied the gulf waters: U-158, U-506, U-504, U-753, U-67, U-129, and U-106. Only four of them had success: U-158, U-67, U-129, and U-106. The twenty-five ships that they torpedoed in May, however, gave Admiral Dönitz immense encouragement for further victories in the gulf.[20]

9

More U-Boat Successes

U-67'S FIFTH WAR CRUISE brought her the most victories of her career. *Kapitänleutnant* Günther Müller-Stockheim sailed from Lorient on May 20, 1942, to the Gulf of Mexico and returned in August flying eight pennants, each signifying a sinking (except for one damaged). Müller-Stockheim managed to sink three merchant ships in June—the *Managua* (Nicaraguan), *Rawleigh Warner* (American), and *Empire Mica* (British)—and damage one, the *Nortind* (Norwegian). In July he decimated four more and was joined by nine additional German submarines, but none of them beat his record. They were U-134, U-154, U-157, U-509, U-171, U-129, U-84, U-166, and U-571.[1]

In fact, there were so many German U-boats in the gulf that month, it's a wonder they didn't torpedo each other. Just after U-67 entered the gulf, the commander took a position south of Mobile. "I will be operating in the shipping lane from Pensacola to Mobile because I do not want to get too close to the coast at night. There is too much light [moonlight]," he noted. Headquarters sent him a message telling him to repeat what he had just said, and he jotted in his log that he would not do it because the signals were too weak.

The hydrophone operator heard a very faint propeller noise, and the commander thought that there must be another submarine stalking around nearby. He had had the same suspicions two times previously, so to avoid trouble he went to full speed and left the scene. "I've had enough of this," he said.

As U-67 approached Mobile, a big land-based plane roared toward

Kapitänleutnant Günther Müller-Stockheim, commander of U-67, on his conning tower. German submarines showed no numbers but displayed their emblems. Photo courtesy of Bundesarchiv, Koblenz, Germany.

them and dropped a bomb, but it was too far away and did no harm. "I am very angry that I have been spotted now," the captain wrote. "Without a doubt, I will stay submerged until dark." He then decided to move over to the east below Port Saint Joe, Florida, because he thought that the ships were not following their usual route but hugging the coast. He spotted an empty life raft and a ring and examined them but found no name on them.

In Müller-Stockheim's next report he said that he had sunk one ship off the north coast of Cuba (the *Managua*) and another off the South Pass, close to the Mississippi delta. Actually, he only damaged the second one, the Norwegian tanker *Nortind*. On June 23 he sank the tanker *Rawleigh Warner* close to the South Pass.

U-67 took up a position on June 27 very close to Port Saint Joe and spotted the light marking Cape San Blas. The commander made out a ship in the distance and took after it as fast as he could. "I am running full speed, but I can barely catch him, because that fellow is very fast," he commented. Then he lost his quarry in a fog bank.

Suddenly he saw a strange sight. "I spot something very long in the moonlight, and it sort of blinks, then disappears again. I don't know what to make of it, so I turn away." The commander said, based on his previous observations, he didn't think it was a porpoise but maybe a periscope. The next thing he spotted was a tugboat pulling a barge. He held his fire because he wished to keep his location a secret.

The next night with a bright moon he saw a shadow crossing his bow. As he crept closer, he could see a little better. "It is very identifiable now as a submarine that looks like a German boat type-IX, but I'm not altogether dead sure," he mused. Therefore, he submerged for a possible attack. Then he heard a "singing" noise, probably that of a propeller. "The other sub apparently has dived, and from what I have seen and learned now, it could absolutely be a German sub, maybe *Korvettenkapitän* Henne, because maybe his radio was inoperative and he could not identify himself," Müller-Stockheim wrote. To avoid a collision, he turned off to port.

The commander said that during the day he stayed submerged on the bottom at a depth of over forty-five meters. "The temperature there is very beneficial [cool]," he noted in his log.

On June 29 just after midnight he torpedoed the British tanker *Empire Mica*, very close to Port Saint Joe. The ship burned fiercely

Crew members of U-67 watching the sinking of the tanker *Empire Mica,* June 29, 1942, just off the south Florida coast at Apalachicola. Photo courtesy of Hans Burck, former U-67 crew member.

after the two shots struck it; then the whole thing broke in two. At that point a fishing boat came on the scene and seemed to be on a collision course with the U-boat. Then another vessel came into view. "Very low silhouette," said Müller-Stockheim, "sort of square with a small bridge. It's not impossible that it's a submarine. Could it be Henne? Is he in this area?"

After hanging around Cape San Blas and seeing nothing but fishing boats, he headed up to Santa Rosa Island just off Pensacola. "I have land in sight," he reported. "There are six searchlights on land, and they have an airplane in one of the lights. I guess maybe it is searchlight training, because afterward one of the airplanes goes into a dive." He could also see fire on the coast. "It almost looks like peacetime," he said.

On July 7 Müller-Stockheim moved over to the Southwest Pass, where he blasted and sank the *Paul H. Harwood*. He overheard a radio station in Pensacola reporting that a submarine had been sighted at 30.14 N, 87.27 W. "This, as [there is] no other boat in this area in position, can only be *Korvettenkapitän* Henne," the commander noted. He was wrong—it was Erich Rostin in U-158.

From his location several hundred miles south of the Mississippi Passes, he noticed several "fast runners with many zigzags." Apparently the shipmasters were now trying to outmaneuver the U-boats as best they could. On July 8 Müller-Stockheim heard violent detonations after seeing a steamer zigzagging off at a distance. "Most probably hit by torpedoes," he surmised. "Assuming a submarine. Here, too, *Korvettenkapitän* Henne would be likely."

Every morning the commander took his boat down to the bottom and remained there during the day. At night he surfaced to make his kills. From a position just south of Mobile, Alabama, he reported to headquarters: "Here the traffic is in groups in both directions, during daytime strong air cover, night with light sea cover [escorts]."

He heard the faint noise of twin screws knocking in the same rhythm and stopped his engines, but the noise continued and faded away on a changing course. "Submarine?" he asked himself.

The next day the commander fired off two torpedoes at a passing tanker, but nothing happened. "I cannot understand this miss," he said, "as the distance was beyond 1,000 meters . . . and the tanker did not change course or speed." He wrote in his log that the ship was riding rather high in front and had a separate device, possibly a depth-charge launcher. "Very disappointed," he remarked, and steered back to the bottom. A short while later he heard loud explosions and again presumed it was U-157 attacking.

The night of July 9, U-67 positioned herself just off the Mississippi Passes. At 10:30 Müller-Stockheim spotted several fishing boats, then saw a tanker anchored "or grounded . . . the latter assumption backed up by the existence of a tugboat." He fired two torpedoes from the stern tubes that hit the *Benjamin Brewster* after thirty-two seconds. "A high, extraordinary, strong and glaring tongue of flame and a second detonation after each of the two hits," he recorded in his log. "Parts of the ship fly through the air and some of them are close to our boat, falling into the water. It seems that ammunition

U-67, one of the most successful U-boats in the Gulf of Mexico. Photo courtesy of U-Boot-Archiv, Cuxhaven, Germany.

was blown up." He could smell an odor of powder, and there was relatively little smoke developing. Then he thought possibly it was a cargo of gasoline. "Departed with double high speed," said the commander.

He stopped at a distance and watched a flying boat circle above the flaming tanker, while further explosions filled the air. A searchlight then came on from the Louisiana coast. He sent a message to headquarters: "Intensive day traffic to the east and west . . . meanwhile, on search westward." Five and a half hours later he noted that the tanker was still burning brightly.

The next morning U-67 wended its way along the coast near Trinity Shoal. His message on July 13 said that there was very busy traffic in daytime going east-west and "visible ships at night at anchor in shallow water."

That night Müller-Stockheim attacked the *R. W. Gallagher* with two torpedoes, causing a "high explosion pillar . . . bridge and front

Crew member of U-67 examining turtle shells after a cruise in the Caribbean. Lorient, France, March, 1942. Photo courtesy of Bundesarchiv, Koblenz, Germany.

mast burn immediately." He said the tanker began blowing its siren as it began to sink, sagging steeply to starboard. He watched as the crew lowered lifeboats, and almost all of them abandoned ship except for the gun crew. "The tanker is heavily armed with four anti-aircraft weapons, machine guns, ack-ack stands, and one cannon." He could see some crewmen on the bow and stern when he fired another "eel" and missed. He shot another and heard the thud of a dud. As the commander reloaded tube 5, the ship sank further.

At this point an escort boat suddenly appeared, so he had to leave the scene immediately. The boat followed, making him think that they had seen him or been directed by rescue boats. Müller-Stockheim accelerated to double full speed, saying, "The diesel vapor is very welcome, because now the escort very likely won't be able to locate us any more." The U-boat slowed down again, trying to get out of the glow of the ship fire. "All over, according to experience, one has to

Reception for U-67, just in from the Gulf of Mexico, August 8, 1942, at Lorient. Eight pennants designate eight sinkings. Commander wears white hat. Photo courtesy of Bundesarchiv, Koblenz, Germany.

count on aircraft," the commander wrote. He heard several more explosions and glimpsed high tongues of flame on the horizon. "It's amazing, but no aircraft are coming."

As U-67 left the scene of the wreck, Müller-Stockheim decided to delay the return trip. "The boat and crew will appreciate the voyage on the surface, because there is mildew all over and short circuits on the boat. I hope to be able to use the remaining eel in combination with artillery in a dim phase of the moon while in the Florida Straits area."

The submarine headed south and left the Gulf of Mexico. About August 1, with no torpedoes and a low oil supply, she neared the Bay of Biscay, where an airplane spotted her and attacked. U-67 dived just as the bombs fell and sustained only slight damage—a few instruments were broken. She made it into Lorient on August 8, 1942, where she received a hero's welcome with bands playing, greetings from Admiral Dönitz, and a crowd of excited citizens with bouquets.[2]

Back in the gulf, U-67 and three of its fellow submarines had damaged or sunk thirteen ships in the month of June.[3]

Korvettenkapitän Wolf Henne of U-157 never made it to his destination off the Mississippi Passes. On June 10 Henne, traveling westward through the Old Bahama Channel, was detected by radio direction finders. Admiral Kauffman, commander of the Gulf Sea Frontier, ordered "all available forces, both air and surface . . . to hunt this submarine to exhaustion and destroy it." Henne, unaware of the situation, attacked and sank an American tanker that night near the north coast of Cuba. Shortly afterward he kept traveling on the surface, believing, like all other Germans, that Allied planes had no radar. Just before dawn a B-18 with radar found U-157, swept low over the heads of the startled crewmen, and tried to drop some bombs. The plane's bomb bays were not quite open on the first pass, however, so the B-18 turned and came back, dropping four depth charges as Henne took his ship down as fast as possible.

Henne escaped this attack, but the worst was yet to come. Three more aircraft arrived to keep an eye out for the submarine, and twelve Coast Guard patrol boats showed up to search. Then the destroyers *Noa* and *Dahlgren* joined them.

The next day, June 11, the pilot of a Pan American Airways plane saw U-157 on the surface, and more aircraft were dispatched, plus another B-18. On the morning of June 12, a B-18 watched the U-boat make a crash dive in the Florida Straits. The cutter *Thetis* found Henne, dropped seven depth charges, and waited. An enormous water bubble broke the surface; then some pieces of broken wood and two pairs of leather pants floated up. There was no doubt: U-157 would never patrol again, and U.S. military officials were jubilant.[4]

"Everybody enjoyed the hunt and it paid dividends in training and morale," wrote Samuel E. Morison, "but the experiment was not repeated for two reasons. The large number of air and surface craft that could be employed on nothing else for several days left shipping unprotected, and it was believed that better results could be obtained . . . by attaching support or killer groups to escort units."[5]

The Gulf Sea Frontier reported that "activity was still intense throughout July. . . . Survivors were picked up almost daily and the sighting of suspicious vessels was a frequent occurrence." The commander estimated that as many as nine submarines were actively engaged in the gulf throughout the month. He was close—there were ten. Army and navy aircraft made repeated sightings, as well as Pan American pilots, merchant vessels, and radio direction finders. "Another source of sightings has not been mentioned," read a footnote in the history of the Gulf Sea Frontier. "Elderly ladies with binoculars were particularly adept at spotting submarines in shoal waters from their front porches."[6]

The report went on to say that enemy subs were operating in four basic areas: the Florida Straits; northwestward of the Dry Tortugas; the Yucatán Channel and southward; and the Mississippi Passes and westward. "The area between Morgan City, Louisiana, and Galveston remained throughout the only unmolested area because of its shoal waters."[7]

The next day Galvestonians kicked off their big victory bond and stamp campaign with a band concert at Menard Park and the hanging in effigy of Adolf Hitler at noon. Thousands of people gathered at Twenty-third and Postoffice streets and watched as Fort Crockett jeeps arrived carrying soldiers, pretty girls, and the stuffed dummy.

L. B. Valadie lifted Hitler by a rope and suspended him over the street corner while the crowd yelled approval. Those who had paid five dollars for bonds and stamps began firing a revolver loaded with blanks at the fuehrer. The first were young boys and girls, who had been saving their money for the occasion; then came a man and his wife who had bought $600 worth of bonds. They took turns firing thirty-six blanks, even though their dollars had purchased 120 shots. Others crowded in to take aim at Hitler. At this point a parade of jeeps and peeps with soldiers from Fort Crockett and Camp Wallace drove up, and a machine-gun unit climbed up to the roof of the E. S. Levy & Company building to "cover" the German despot. A sergeant performed the coup de grâce with a shot from a real revolver, puncturing a balloon inside the effigy's shirt, and the "heart" bled a weak-red fluid as the crowd roared.[8]

In mid-June Congress decided to go ahead with Ickes's pipeline plan because the U-boats were turning crude oil and gasoline shipments into conflagrations in the gulf. "In the long run the result of the war will depend on the result of the race between sinkings and new construction," wrote Admiral Dönitz in his memoirs in April, 1942. "But the hub of both shipbuilding and the production of armament lies in the United States. If, therefore, I go for the hub, and particularly the oil supplies, I am getting at the root of the evil." The admiral had thus far been a man of his word. He knew that the United States urgently needed petroleum products to win the war and that America was confident that no U-boats would come into the Gulf of Mexico or close to eastern shores. After five months of devastation, Congress finally woke up.[9]

Now, at last, came plans to first build a huge pipeline from east Texas oil fields to Salem, Illinois; then join two lines to Philadelphia and New York. As a compromise with Ickes's plan, the twenty-four-inch pipe would be built of seamless steel tubing instead of scarce steel plates and would cost $30 to $40 million. The line would have to be built of new steel, since none of the old pipes was over twenty inches in diameter, and it would carry three hundred thousand barrels of crude oil a day. An additional eight-inch pipeline would be constructed from Port Saint Joe, Florida, across the state to Jacksonville to carry gasoline. On July 19 the National Tube Company shipped to Little Rock, Arkansas, the first trainload of twenty-four-inch seamless steel pipe in forty-foot lengths.[10]

Galvestonians read on July 6 that a Panamanian ship had been torpedoed in the gulf on June 16. This was the San Blas, which had left Galveston enroute to Guatemala alone on a zigzagging course. "Everything was normal," said Chief Officer Ralph Strong of Philadelphia, "when the torpedo struck our port side, tearing away the stern and wrecking the engines. Two torpedoes were aimed at us at about a forty-five-degree angle, but one missed." He said that he was reading in his cabin when he felt the explosion. The captain and several others were killed when the ship rolled over and crushed them as they were trying to lower a lifeboat. Others died because they could not get their life belts on fast enough. The San Blas sank within three to four minutes, and fourteen survivors, including the chief officer, made it into two life rafts, which they lashed together.

They drifted slowly that night as sharks circled their rafts, and one of the men died from his wounds. "We buried him at sea," Strong said. "We recited the Lord's Prayer and gave him a blessing as best we could."

The rafts floated along together, and the men subsisted on a few provisions of milk tablets, chocolate, and graham crackers. Each had two cups of water a day. They put up flags for shelter and canvas sails and took turns rowing, estimating that they should reach land in around six days.

On their third day at sea, two patrol planes flew over but apparently did not see the bobbing rafts. On the thirteenth day a navy PBY found them and landed near them. As the navy crew prepared to pick up the men, they spotted a U-boat. "We had to hurry aboard because we were afraid the submarine might attack the plane," Strong recalled. All the men on the rafts lived through their ordeal, but thirty-three of their fellow crewmen went down with the ship.[11]

"The belief . . . that axis submarines, which continue to take a heavy toll of U.S. and Allied shipping in the gulf and Caribbean, are operating from secret refueling bases in the Caribbean islands and on uninhabited stretches of Central and South American coastlines and that they are receiving information through a well-organized espionage system seems to be borne out by the recent arrest of twenty suspected spies in British Honduras and the Panama Canal Zone," pronounced the editor of the Galveston Daily News. Reacting to reports that army and navy patrols were intensifying their search for these "hideouts," Fort Worth oilman Jack Danciger, consul of Mexico and the Dominican Republic, came up with a suggestion for cleaning out the "Axis sea rats." He said that along the coasts of North and South America, countless sportsmen, who sailed, hunted, and fished there, "are familiar with every foot of these coasts." Danciger believed that under the guidance of the navy or Coast Guard, they could be organized into a patrol "that would soon ferret out these refueling bases and prevent the establishment of others." He further suggested that the navy build thousands of small, armed speedboats for coastal patrol duty. The editor thought that this proposal for a "sub-hunting citizen's army" had considerable merit and should be investigated.[12]

Two weeks later U-171's commander, Günther Pfeffer, left the Atlantic and headed into the Gulf of Mexico after refueling at an unknown position. "I am proceeding to my operational area DA 80

Günther Pfeffer, commander of U-171. Photo courtesy of U-Boot-Archiv, Cuxhaven, Germany.

and 90 [between Galveston and New Orleans] with main focus in front of Galveston," he wrote in his log. On the way there he was bombarded by a flying boat with two or three bombs but sustained no damage. He noticed that the lights were burning brightly at Turk's Island and the Tortugas "under peacetime conditions."

On July 23 Pfeffer entered his assigned area between Galveston and New Orleans. A few days later he sent back a report of his observations: shipping was medium to heavy in groups of small convoys near the coast with corvette-like escorts and steady air coverage, and because of the shallow depth there was no possibility to get into firing position. "I attempted attacks on six steamers but failed due to extensive firing distance," he reported.

Finding the waters off Galveston too shallow to sink any large vessels and having wasted many precious torpedoes, Pfeffer moved over to the Mississippi Passes. On August 13, he spotted a tanker (the *R. M. Parker, Jr.*) and fired two shots. The commander heard two detonations, then fired his artillery four more times with one miss and saw the tanker list heavily. "The bow still sticks a bit out of the water," he noted. The depth was thirty-five meters.[13]

The *R. M. Parker, Jr.* had been traveling alone on a straight course that night with no lights and a silent radio when U-171 struck. Just after midnight the two navy lookouts saw a phosphorescent wake directly astern about twenty-five yards from the ship. They then spotted two points of light moving toward the vessel, but the two torpedoes hit before the alarm could be given. They both exploded on the port side about amidships, causing two tanks to flood and buckling the deck. No distress message could be sent because the mainmast fell in the original explosion, destroying the antennae. The *Parker* was armed, but the men could take no counteroffensive because of the ship's heavy listing and the darkness. After the crew abandoned ship in three lifeboats, the sub surfaced about two hundred fifty yards away and fired five shells into the ship. The first hit the ammunition box at the gun platform, exploding the magazine, and the others hit around the deck and bridge.

"We slid down the lifeline and went into the water, then swam a short distance to the lifeboat," said Edward Haake, one of the navy armed guards. When they had climbed into the boat, one of them thought he saw sharks and whacked the water with his oar.

The men voted to put the second mate in charge, and during the night Haake took off his dog tags and .45-caliber pistol and laid them in the bottom of the boat in case the submarine crew came back and questioned them. "Our instructions were, if asked, we would say we were merchant seamen, and maybe that would prevent us from being prisoners of war," Haake explained. "After daybreak I put on my dog tags and cleaned the pistol." Each mariner had a cup of water and a piece of hardtack for breakfast. "When dawn came we saw the ship's bow out of the water, back to the bridge, listing on its side. A tanker with its compartments empty could float," he said.

Another lifeboat came close to them, and the men decided they should all stay together. Then a PBY patrol plane flew over, and everyone in the rafts stood up, waved their arms frantically, and shouted at the top of their lungs. The plane dropped a message telling them that help was on the way, and a short time later a shrimp boat arrived to rescue them.[14]

Kapitänleutnant Pfeffer scored one more victory, sinking the Mexican tanker *Amatlan* close to the north coast of Mexico on September 4. "Return voyage started," he wrote in his log. "I am heading for Grid Square DE 35 [in the Atlantic east of Florida] for resupplying."

On September 10, when Pfeffer had traveled through the Bay of Biscay and land was in sight, he had to stop to wait for an escort, usually a minesweeper, into the bunkers. He noticed five German planes flying along the coast. Among them was a Ju-52 with minesweeping equipment that flew by him several times, fifty meters away. "Submerging here . . . was out of the question," Pfeffer said. (Too many mines.) He ordered four men to stand watch on the bridge, then later more. "As I had to stay in position, I decided, until being taken up by escort, to cruise up and down in the vicinity, zigzagging at low speed." Shortly afterward, just after the Ju-52 had passed a short distance away, an explosion ripped into the front part of the U-boat. "I assumed it was a mine and ordered both engines stopped," the commander reported. "I thought at first that I would be able to keep the boat on the surface." But his command did not reach the engine room, and he heard the diesels keep on running.

"I ordered 'all men out' [to the deck] . . . and as the boat now showed heaviness in front, called for 'all hands off board.' I heard the engineer in command, who was also on the bridge, shout, 'Life vests up' and repeat the call." Pfeffer saw that the bow torpedo hatch was open, with two men trying to get out of it. He called several times, "Hatch tight!" and emphasized the order by sweeping his hand. They got the hatch closed, but the boat kept getting more and more front-heavy and started to go under.

"I didn't shut the conning tower hatch, as there were still men coming up. When the front edge of the bridge cut under, I jumped." The stern was still out of the water, and Pfeffer could hear the diesels running. "When I came to the surface again, nothing of the boat was to be seen any more." As fast as possible he tried to spread the word to those swimming in the water that they should all stay together to facilitate locating the crew. The first officer proposed that they swim toward the Isle de Croix, and as they were attempting to get there, a German Coast Guard dinghy showed up to save them. Of U-171's crew of fifty-two men, twenty-two died and thirty lived to sail again.[15]

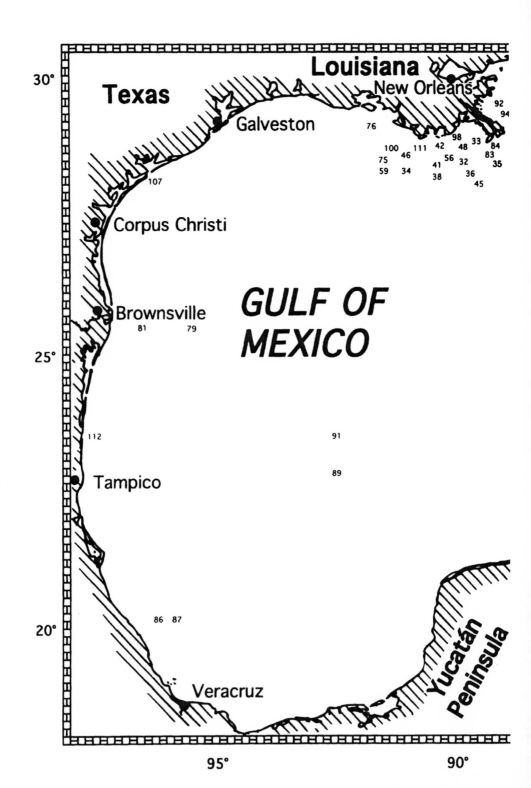

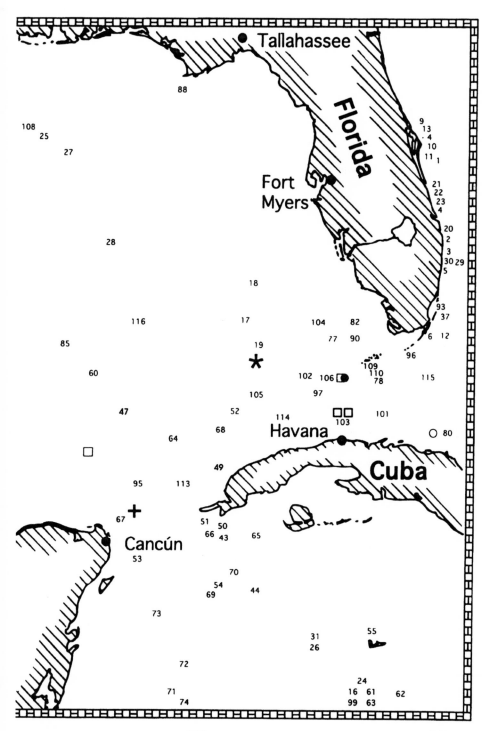

Merchant Vessels Attacked in Gulf Sea Frontier, 1942–43

NO. ON MAP	ALLIANCE	SHIP NAME
1942		
1	a	Pan Massachusetts
2	a	Republic
3	a	Cities Service Empire
4	b	W. D. Anderson
5ᴳ	b	O.A. Knudsen
6	b	Benwood
7ᴳ	b	Daytonian
8ᴳ	b	Athelqueen
9	a	Leslie
10	b	Korsholm
11	b	La Paz
12	b	Sama
13	b	Ocean Venus
14ᴳ	b	Laertes
15	b	Eclipse
16	a	Tuscaloosa City
17	b	Munger T. Ball
18	b	Joseph M. Cudahy
19	b	Norlindo
20	a	Delisle
21	a	Java Arrow
22	b	Amazone
23	a	Halsey
24	a	Green Island
25	a	Alcoa Puritan
26	b	Empire Buffalo
27	b	Ontario
28	b	Torny
29	a	Crijnssen
30	b	Lubrafol
31	b	Calgarolite
32	a	Aurora
33	a	Virginia
34	a	Gulfprince
35	a	Gulfpenn
36	a	David McKelvy
37	b	Potrero del Llano
38	a	Eastern Sun
39	b	Amapala
40ᴳ	a	Nicarao
41	a	Sun
42	a	William C. McTarnahan
43	a	Mercury Sun
44	a	William J. Salman
45	a	Gulfoil
46	a	Heredia
47	a	Ogontz
48	a	Halo
49	b	George Calvert
50	a	Clare
51	a	Elizabeth
52	b	Faja de Oro
53	b	San Pablo
54	a	Samuel Q. Brown
55	b	Hector
56	b	Haakon Hauan
57	a	Carrabulle
58	a	Atenas
59	b	Hamlet
60	b	Mentor
61	a	New Jersey
62	b	Allister
63	b	Bushranger
64	b	Hampton Roads
65	a	Knoxville City
66	b	Nidarnes
67	a	Velma Lykes
68	b	Hermis
69	a	Suwied
70	b	Castilla
71	b	Tela
72	b	Rosenborg
73	a	Merrimack
74	b	Crijnssen
75	b	Sheherazade
76	a	Cities Service Toledo
77	b	Gunvor (mine)
78	b	Managua
79	b	San Blass
80	a	Millinocket
81	b	Moira

82	b	*Bosilijka* (mine)	102	a	*Pennsylvania Sun*
83	b	*Nortind*	103	b	*Gertrude*
84	a	*Rawleigh Warner*	104	b	*Baja California*
85	a	*Henry Gibbons*	105	b	*Port Antonio*
86	b	*Tuxpan*	106	a	*William Cullen Bryant*
87	b	*Las Choapas*	107	b	*Oaxaca*
88	b	*Empire Mica*	108	a	*Robert E. Lee*
89	a	*Cadmus*	109	b	*Santiago de Cuba*
		Edward Luckenbach	110	b	*Manzanillo*
90	b	(mine)	111	a	*R. M. Parker, Jr.*
91	b	*Gundersen*	112	b	*Amatlan*
92	b	*Bayard*	○	c	*Norwalk*
93	b	*Umtata*	*	b	*E. P. Theriault*
94	b	*Paul H. Harwood*	†	b	*Lalita*
95	b	*Tuapse*	□	c	4 freighters
96	a	*J. A. Moffett, Jr.*	●	c	1 tanker
97	b	*Nicholas Cuneo*			
98	a	*Benjamin Brewster*	**1943**		
99	a	*Tachira*	113	b	*Olancho*
100	a	*R. W. Gallagher*	114	b	*Lysefjord*
101	a	*Andrew Jackson*	115	a	*Gulfstate*
			116	a	*Touchet*

Note: a = U.S. registry, b = Allied registry, G = vessel sunk outside Gulf (not shown on map).

10

Fortifications

THE GALVESTON DISTRICT of the Army Corps of Engineers had built
no defensive works on the island since the early 1920s; during 1941,
however, the corps set up a new fortifications section headed by Ed-
win Pearson. His first assignment in mid–1942 appeared on one sheet
of paper with the drawing of a casemate (fortified masonry chamber
for cannons with a slit for firing) around the guns at Fort Crockett's
Battery Hoskins. The old battery had two twelve-inch barbette guns
standing in the open with an earth- and concrete-covered projectile.
Plotting and powder rooms lay between them. The Fortification Division's job was to build a heavy concrete shield for the guns that would
withstand a bombardment of five-thousand-pound shells and to
add special mechanical and electrical equipment to update the big
weapons.[1]

A heavy cloak of secrecy enshrouded the entire undertaking.
"When I had to go down to the head office, it was just like the city
jail," said Adolph Johnson, a former employee. "I had to show an
identification card, and everything in the Fortification Division was
behind barred doors, with a guard holding a shotgun at the entrance.
Everybody was told to keep quiet about things on the outside." Johnson said that for the job they had huge stacks of plans. The work was
quite complicated, because the construction began fifty feet below
ground and rose over the top of the guns. Only a few people had
access to the plans. To get to them, they had to enter a temporary
building, make notes on the necessary information, then later burn
the notes.

San Luis Hotel, Galveston, built atop Battery Hoskins, former gun emplacement at Fort Crockett. Photo from the author's collection.

"It was tough work, but I was young then, and we didn't stop for fifteen to eighteen hours a day. You just kept at it all the time," Johnson recalled. Among themselves, the construction workers agreed that the whole project was a "potential disaster as far as protection for the island or Gulf Coast."[2]

At the same time, the Corps of Engineers was building "military instrument" towers a hundred feet tall, with surface craft detectors to locate enemy vessels and provide directions for the seacoast artillery gunners. These metal towers had a small house on top for the instruments and a ladder going up the side and were located at Fort Crockett, Fort San Jacinto, and Fort Travis on Bolivar Peninsula. Eventually, more were built along the Gulf Coast.[3]

The towers were manned with observers looking out over the gulf

Corps of Engineers workmen pouring concrete at Battery Hoskins, Fort Crockett, 1942. Photo courtesy of U.S. Army Corps of Engineers archives, Galveston, Texas.

waters. "They were expecting the biggest invasion you ever saw to come into Galveston," said Johnson. "With the instruments, they could plot this triangulation—if they saw anything. By taking two of these towers and getting fixes on it, they could figure out the angles, pinpoint on a map exactly where the enemy ship was, and transfer the information to those coast artillery batteries. They were standing there ready to pull the string and blow 'em out of the water."

The two Hoskins guns were set in a saucerlike depression and had concrete roadways from the storage rooms between them. "They had these little carts that carried huge bags of powder and the projectiles. Those shells were pretty good sized—twelve inches in diameter," explained Johnson. He said the guns were manned all the time and

Disappearing seacoast gun, Fort Crockett, June, 1942. Photo courtesy of U.S. National Archives.

when the gunners pushed the carts out to the guns, the construction men had to get out of the way. "They'd load up a gun and just stand there waiting for something to come from one of those towers tellin' 'em what to look for, but there wasn't nothin' out there. Now don't get me wrong, but today, looking back on it, it was kind of like the Keystone Cops," Johnson remarked.

Battery Hoskins had the biggest guns of the area forts, and before the Corps of Engineers started working on them, the guns could turn 360 degrees. "When we got through, the angles were restricted to just out over the gulf in front of the seawall," Johnson said. "The enemy could have just walked right in at the back and taken it with all ease. That took some deep thinking and planning."[4]

On this very subject, a congressman had complained in 1921 that in the past ten years $1,897,000 had been spent on "so-called coastal defense which consists of cannon placed up and down the coast . . . but they cannot hit a military object as well as a bomber can at battle range. . . . These great coast artillery emplacements, made of masonry and steel, which cost millions of dollars, are, in fact, no defense at all. All nations recognize these salient military facts except our own."[5]

But no one bothered to read the *Congressional Record,* and plans went forward in Galveston for Battery Hoskins. First they built wall sections from fifteen to twenty feet thick; then they put roof slabs eight to fourteen feet thick over the guns and magazines. "Man, we poured jillions of yards of concrete up in there. We batched the stuff down on Fifty-third and Fifty-seventh, north of Broadway, and we closed off Fifty-third Street with MP's from Fort Crockett. They blocked the traffic when those concrete trucks were coming," Johnson recounted. The workers started about two or three in the morning and poured all day long. When the concrete mound was finished, they covered the whole thing with sand. "Then over all that, we poured a two-foot-thick burster course of concrete. The theory was, when they came over and dropped those bombs, they would burst on this course and wouldn't penetrate into the powder magazines and things."

Johnson said that just getting the concrete up to the top of the big hill was a terrible chore. "After that we covered it with sand again, about five or six feet thick, and planted all kinds of quick-growing weeds to get some roots in it. Every time it rained, it all washed down to the bottom of the hill, and we'd have to push it all back up again, and that was tough. Boy, we like to never kept that sand up there." Johnson admitted that every once in a while when he thought back on all that he had to sit down and laugh, but in those days it was no laughing matter.[6]

In July, 1942, Galvestonians rallied once again to the war cause with new drives to collect tin cans and waste fats; also, to rummage up yet more rubber goods. A strong appeal went out to housewives to save leftover grease in one-pound cans and turn it in to retail meat dealers, who would pay four cents per pound. They would in turn sell the grease to the nearest soap-making plant.[7]

Two days later Congressman Dave E. Satterfield in Washington told the news that a letter had been found on a captured enemy submarine confirming that cargo U-boats were supplying the subs preying on merchant ships in American waters. Satterfield, who had recently served a tour of duty with the naval reserve as an observer at the American embassy in London, recommended that the United States begin building such supply-carrying submersibles. He said that he had conferred with authorities on the subject, and that unquestionably the construction of an underseas vessel capable of carrying seventy-five hundred tons of cargo was feasible. "Furthermore, such a vessel would be comparatively safe from submarine attacks, by gunfire or torpedoes, as it would proceed submerged at a depth of 100 feet," the congressman explained.

"In addition," he said, "this type of boat, fully loaded and proceeding to a rendezvous, need never surface except under cover of darkness, hence chances of its detection and destruction will be at a . . . minimum." Satterfield ended by saying that when the big naval battle with Japan came up, the United States should not be surprised when the enemy was using "giant submersible aircraft carriers."[8] They actually were.

The navy came out with the statement that new antisubmarine techniques had been "very effective" in the Caribbean. Spokesmen did not say exactly what was being done, but they hinted that the use of convoys was helping. For the past few days there had been no sinkings in the western Caribbean. The improved shipping conditions could be seen in Canal Zone commissaries with new stocks of potatoes, cheese, and fresh vegetables on formerly bare shelves. Island restaurant menus were featuring new items as well.[9]

Because of the submarine scare, Fort Crockett officers decreed that the public could no longer go on most of the beaches, day or night, in the Sabine-Galveston-Freeport area. They warned that armed patrols with orders to shoot would be going on duty and that persons entering the closed areas would be taking a material risk. A few small beaches would stay open, including Stewart Beach and two others on the island.

The reasoning here was undoubtedly fear of saboteurs, and the previous Sunday's funnies referred to the subject in "Jane Arden." Miss

Arden and her boss were boarding an airplane, and she asked where they were going. "To the Gulf Coast—you've read of the submarine sinkings there," he replied.

"Of course—is there a chance to help stop that?"

"There is," he answered. "Because Nazi spies are radioing the submarines whenever one of our ships sails. So we're moving in—every agent we can get is being concentrated there. Those spies must be caught, quick!" [10]

The War Department, concerned about how vulnerable the Louisiana coast was to German U-boats and saboteurs, quietly organized the U.S. Coast Guard Beach Patrol Unit, unofficially known in Louisiana as the "Cajun Coast Guard." Military officials believed that the area needed more than routine offshore patrols and worried that the primitive trappers' huts dotted throughout the coastal marshes would make handy places for enemies to hide. In July, 1942, the Coast Guard, realizing that the only people in the world capable of patrolling such a formidable swamp were the Cajuns and that experienced ones were at a premium, waived physical and age requirements and took all who volunteered for duty. The group formed up with one hundred men, ages eighteen to sixty-five, from the chenière area, the fertile farmland next to the low, sandy ridges that separated the land from treacherous marshes.

The Coast Guard commissioned "Win" Hawkins, a duck-hunting guide, to recruit men and command them. He didn't give orders, just told the Cajuns what needed doing, and they did it. "He knew every trick in the book," one of them recalled. They used Hawkins's hunting lodge as headquarters for their patrols, living at home and riding their own horses, pirogues, and marsh buggies.

The men worked twelve-hour shifts with most of them patrolling, but some operated radios or stood lookout in a fifty-foot-tall camouflaged tower. The Cajuns regularly inspected shrimp boats and other small craft in the area to make sure they had no secret supplies for the German submarines.

Louisiana's coastline was already blacked out, and the men had to rely on memory and instinct to make their way. The darkness caused them no problems. "When it was moonlight, you had that and the stars," said Ralph Sagrera. "When it wasn't, it was really dark, but we knew where we were going—it was like walking around in your house without lights."

Although they never saw any U-boats, the Cajun crew earned the nickname "Swamp Angels" when they started rescuing American airmen from accidents in gulf waters. In December, 1942, a B-26 from Lake Charles had flown out to target practice and crashed one hundred fifty yards from shore. Two of the men drowned at the scene, but the pilot and two others swam in, made it to the marshes, and wandered about for two days almost naked. The mosquitoes attacked them in swarms, forcing them to go underwater for protection with just their noses and mouths out to breathe.

"They were in pretty bad shape when we found them—almost dead," said Elrod Petry of Abbeville. One of the men told the Cajuns, "Just leave me here to die. I can't take another step." They ignored his plea and pulled his half-frozen body, with bloated arms and eyes swollen shut, out of the ooze; loaded him onto a stretcher; and hauled him to safety on a contraption called a marsh buggy, reminiscent of a moon vehicle. This rescue was just one of thirty-five the Cajun men performed as they patrolled the desolate coastline for two years. As Kelly Veazey put it, "We were just doing what we already knew how to do, except we were doing it for our country."[11]

The Coast Guard had become an integral part of the United States Navy and now had the task of operating an information system along American coasts with beach and picket boat patrols and watchtowers. Observation of marine traffic came under naval auspices, and surveillance of local small craft and pleasure boats was assigned to the Coast Guard. All observation and information reports went to the FBI, who now had the duty of obtaining evidence of subversive activity.[12]

On July 25, 1942, orders from Coast Guard headquarters explained the situation: "These beach patrols are not intended as a military protection of our coastline, as this is a function of the Army. The beach patrols are more in the nature of outposts to report activities along the coastline and are not to repel hostile armed units."[13]

To establish a communications system with its local stations, the Coast Guard placed commando jack boxes at intervals of twelve hundred to fifteen hundred feet along the beaches. Patrolmen carried hand-set telephones that could be plugged into the boxes. This entailed laying thousands of miles of submarine cable and installing enormous amounts of equipment that tied into the Bell system. And so the Coast Guard began to act as the "eyes and ears" of the army and navy. They reported suspicious findings to the district naval headquarters, nearby army and navy units, and the local FBI representative. Anything concerning vessels in distress, aircraft crashes or landings, flashing lights, flares, fires, unidentified aircraft or ships, explosions, bombings, splashes, hostile or suspicious vehicles or individuals, underwater or land mines, demolitions, obstacles, chemicals, sabotage, flotsam, wreckage, and unusual objects had to be reported. Recruiting and training began in July, and by December the system was well-organized.[14]

Headquarters of the Gulf Coast area in New Orleans (Eighth Naval District) ordered enlistment of fifty-five hundred men and construction of twenty-five watchtowers. From the Apalachicola River in Florida to Brownsville, Texas, the gulf would be under constant surveillance—the longest coastline assigned to any naval district.[15]

About the same time the beach patrols were set into motion, Congressman Jared Y. Sanders of Louisiana asked that his remarks concerning an article by Henry McLemore in the *Washington Post* on July 18 be placed in the *Congressional Record*. Sanders said the article called attention to the propaganda value of all the newspaper stories describing the submarine commanders' courtesy and thoughtfulness after destroying American ships. "Mr. McLemore's protest against the practice of our press in publishing this type of what is obviously German propaganda is timely," he said.

Sanders reported that he had received a letter from John Schaff in Donaldsonville, Louisiana, pointing out that "many of these news stories which our newspapers print so frequently, might well contain hidden code messages." Schaff said that a package of cigarettes given to a crew member might mean one thing, while other acts and statements might mean something else, enabling the enemy to communicate with each other through the press. "I promptly forwarded Mr. Schaff's letter to Mr. Elmer Davis with the request that he see if something could not be done to stop this practice," said Sanders.[16]

Word came from U.S. navy officials that they were growing moderately optimistic about the outlook for winning the battle against German submarines, which had for the past six months made the western Atlantic a "graveyard for Allied shipping." They claimed the situation was much improved in spite of daily announcements of torpedoed ships because of the newly instituted convoy system along the Atlantic seaboard and in the Caribbean. "In all probability it will be broadened later to include the Gulf of Mexico and the sea lanes to South American ports," officials said.

There was no denying that U-boat attacks had been costly: since Pearl Harbor three hundred vessels had gone down, and American shipyards had been unable to keep up with the losses. But steadily increasing ship production was bringing a ray of hope.

Navy officials announced that use of convoys along the East Coast had chased the submarines southward. "Have you read of any sinkings within fifty miles of the Atlantic coast lately?" asked Navy Secretary Frank Knox. Convoys in the Caribbean and Gulf of Mexico were expected to be equally effective in ridding the sea lanes of the underwater raiders.

When German U-boats first began attacks near U.S. shores, the American public and some military officials minimized the importance of the submarines, believing they would not be able to continue their hostilities and that they had been sent over for "nuisance purposes." When their attacks went on and on, however, the need for convoys became increasingly evident. Convoys had already proven effective by the British long before America entered the war, but American navy officials refused to follow their example until the U-boats had done massive damage.

The United States began to increase blimp patrols off the Atlantic coast, build Y-guns for launching depth charges from ships, and speed up production of sound-detecting equipment. The navy instituted a submarine combat school with twelve hundred men to train for manning the new patrol and escort boats, and the British sent over some of their submarine chasers to help the cause.[17]

Industrial giant Henry J. Kaiser, who was building Liberty cargo ships faster than anyone in history, said in a launching ceremony speech that America wasn't building and probably couldn't ever build enough ships to beat the submarines. He said he was convinced that the problems of getting men and supplies to the global war fronts could best be solved by building a great fleet of cargo-carrying planes.

Aircraft sound detectors, Fort Crockett, World War II. Photo courtesy of *Galveston Daily News*.

Kaiser referred to the Martin seventy-ton flying boat, which could carry fourteen tons of equipment and troops. He claimed that within ten months, nine of the larger shipyards could be turning out five thousand Martin cargo planes a year.[18]

The U-boat scare was reaching epidemic proportions. The whole country was obsessed with it. "Jane Arden," in the Sunday comic section, showed our heroine and a secret agent leaping away from a crashed car. "Up with your hands," ordered the agent as he pointed a gun at someone. The next scene revealed a moving van knocked sideways by the agent's car and several police standing near a palm tree. "This is it, Chief! Here's their short wave radio!" said the agent.

"Put the bracelets on those Nazis," replied the policeman.[19]

When Navy Secretary Knox announced that convoys would begin in the Gulf of Mexico when sufficient naval craft were available, his voice was noticed. The editor of the *Galveston Daily News* wrote that in World War II as well as World War I, no good substitute had been found for the convoy system. "The effectiveness of arming [merchant ships] is limited by the fact that attacks usually occur at night.

Even in daytime a torpedoed ship sometimes goes down before anyone aboard gets sight of the attacker." The editor said that convoying
really was a must. Within a few days of the editorial, Günther Pfeffer
in U-171 observed that shipping vessels in the Gulf of Mexico had
formed into small groups hugging the coastline.[20]

Readers of the paper noticed an item of interest: the report from a
Galveston merchant mariner whose ship had been torpedoed in the
Caribbean. Raymond Smithson said that when his ship went down,
he and Cornelius O'Connor jumped overboard and were separated
from the rest of the crew. They found some bits of wreckage in the
sea and created a makeshift raft, where they floated and waited for
help. The raft was just big enough for one person, so they took turns
swimming while one rested. The men said that three naval patrol
planes approached but made no attempt to land in the choppy seas.

"Well, there we were, swimming around our raft . . . when all of a
sudden a damn-big black thing loomed up in front of us," said
O'Connor. "It was a big sub, about 200 feet long with a goat's head
painted on its conning tower." He said that two men appeared on
deck and that he yelled for help. The Germans threw them a line
and pulled the two men up onto the boat, then led them over to the
conning tower.

O'Connor stated that he saw four men out on the deck: a fat man,
a short man wearing glasses, and the two seamen who pulled him
aboard. He said he asked the Germans to take them over to a raft
they had seen after the ship sank, but at that moment a plane flew
over and dropped a flare, interrupting their conversation.

"The German officer shoved us down the conning tower hatch, and
the crewmen stumbled after us. That submarine crash-dived in one
hell of a big hurry," he said.

"We were a side-show attraction. Faces stared at us from all angles,
up and down the companionways. They were curious." O'Connor
said that in a few minutes they were blindfolded and led through a
door forward to the torpedo room. An officer asked O'Connor how
the American people felt about the war. When the captive told him
the Americans firmly believed they would win, the officer scoffed and
said the German people were stronger than the American people
thought. Smithson said the crewmen gave them some rum and tried
to convince them Germany was going to win the war.

After about two hours the sub commander ordered his boat to surface, and the two prisoners were led to the deck, where a small wooden raft "about the size of a bed" was given to them. The Germans gave them directions to shore and told them good-bye.[21]

11

Kühlmann and the

Robert E. Lee

JOHN NAUMCZIK, handsome young army recruit from Illinois, arrived at Fort Crockett in the spring of 1942 to be a searchlight operator with the Twentieth Coast Artillery. In the earliest days of radar, the signal corps used aircraft position finders both to locate enemy planes and train spotlights on them and to control gunfire. The army placed a series of lights mounted on thirty-foot towers along the Texas coast from Corpus Christi to Sabine Pass, and at the beginning of the war the Florida National Guard manned the ones at Fort Crockett. The guardsmen trained the new army recruits, who then reported for extensive mechanical training in Louisiana. Back in Galveston, Naumczik recalled that they had alerts every morning from 4:00 to 7:00, which meant they had to climb up the towers and stay there in the open for three hours to be ready in case of emergency. "That must have been a critical time of day when they expected attacks," he said. If they received a report from one of the observation towers of a suspicious vessel out in the gulf, their job was to train one spotlight on the ship for two minutes. Then another light would come in and illuminate it, then another, so the enemy could not locate the source of the beams.[1]

The Army Corps of Engineers initiated a frantic building pace readying the island for enemy invasion. In addition to the casemating of Battery Hoskins and the erection of steel observation towers, the corps constructed two new gun batteries: one at Fort San Jacinto on the east end (Battery 235), and the other across the water at Fort Travis on Bolivar (Battery 236). At the old Battery Mercer at San

Searchlight and antiaircraft gun training in the Coast Artillery, Fort Crockett, World War II. Photo courtesy of *Galveston Daily News*.

Jacinto, they installed air conditioning and gas proofing and turned it into the Harbor Entrance Control Post to direct Galveston's defenses.[2]

On July 24, the town civil defense leaders staged a "war incident" to keep their workers alert and ready for action. One of the wardens phoned in a supposed bombing at Twenty-sixth Street, reporting several casualties and seven people "trapped under wreckage." He told them there were unexploded and incendiary bombs and poison gas there, with fumes traveling northwesterly. Shortly afterward, auxiliary police arrived, blocked off traffic, and put up signs marking broken water and gas mains. They roped off and marked an "unexploded bomb," and fire engines came screaming up to put out any raging fires.

Wrecking and decontamination squads picked up victims either un-

Workmen building barracks and putting up tents at Fort San Jacinto, Galveston, February, 1943. Photo courtesy of U.S. Army Corps of Engineers archives, Galveston, Texas.

der imaginary wreckage or "gassed" and laid them on the southwest lawn of the post office building. Then the white-helmeted air raid wardens with first-aid kits ran up to the "victims," lying on the grass with tags describing their injuries. The wardens quickly checked out the bodies and applied splints and bandages to the proper parts. Next, the stretcher bearers arrived, carried the injured across the driveway to another section of the lawn, and placed them on cots, where doctors and nurses examined them. The Red Cross motor corps came on the scene and removed all the casualties; then the all-clear signal sounded. The show was over, and the throng of people watching from the sidewalks went home. Everybody said it was a great success.[3]

As Galveston continued to gird up for battle, the shocking news came out on August 1 that forty-nine-year-old Mayor Brantly Harris had died of a heart attack the morning before. For the past several months his health had been steadily deteriorating, but the mayor refused to change any of his old habits and his heart finally gave out. Because he struggled so hard to get the city prepared for enemy bombing, one might have said that he was the town's first war casualty. His position was filled immediately by mayor pro tem Henry W. Flagg, Sr.

There was no time to mourn. War preparations had to go forward. Already the townspeople had grown used to seeing the khaki-clad police auxiliary on street corners along the seawall, tooting their whistles at motorists to enforce dimout regulations. "There is nothing spectacular about the service they are performing," said the paper, "but back of it is the earnest desire of these men—many with bulging waistlines, disappearing hair, aching arches and other tell-tale signs of middle-age—to do what they can to win the war." They were playing an important role in the protection of merchant shipping and would be able to do other wartime duties.[4]

Jane Arden's U-boat spy adventures continued in the comic strips: her FBI agent friend had failed to uncover a Nazi agent inside a moving van sending messages to U-boats in the gulf. On July 27, the agent and Jane visited a radio station and told the owner-director that someone was signaling German submarines from his station.

"But that's impossible," the owner said.

"This is war—nothing is impossible," Jane told him.

The agent joined in: "You're a loyal American—but how about all your advertisers?"

Jane: "What's to prevent someone from slipping a code message into a commercial announcement?"

"Well, here's a copy of everything we're using today—I'll help you all I can!" replied the owner.[5]

Elmer Davis, head of the news censorship department, never gave the Germans credit for military skill or intelligence; his writers were duty-bound to put the enemy in the worst possible light and to avoid taking any blame for America's lack of preparedness. It was easier to divert attention from internal problems with stories of saboteurs secretly informing the Axis from U.S. shores. Most of what the enemy needed to know, they could read in the newspapers.

At a New Orleans navy base, a phone call came for young Galvestonian Ballinger Mills. It was his pregnant wife, Cissie, telling him to come home immediately. "Why?" he asked.

"There's a Commander Cunningham here from the Naval Intelligence Office and an FBI agent. They want to see you as soon as possible," she replied. The commander arranged for Ballinger to take a train to Galveston that night, and the next morning the two men promptly appeared at the Mills home on Avenue O.

"We want to rent your upstairs northwest bedroom. We'll pay whatever you say."

"But the room isn't for rent," said Cissie.

"No matter, we're taking it over. And it will be anywhere from three weeks to three months. Just tell us how much."

"One dollar, then." So the arrangement was made, and Ballinger went back to his base.

Cissie called Ballinger a couple of days later, saying, "There's all sorts of stuff going on here. After you left, they moved the furniture out of the room, everything except two chairs, and they brought in all kinds of equipment, and they told me that *nobody* could come into that room. They have two men, one navy, the other an FBI agent, on duty twenty-four hours a day." Ballinger asked her what on earth the men were doing. "I don't know," she told him.

Five weeks later the men thanked Cissie kindly for the use of the bedroom and left. Shortly afterward Commander Cunningham, who was stationed at New Orleans, called the couple to explain their activities. He made them promise not to repeat a word he told them for the duration of the war. "You know that there are sinkings by German submarines of the convoys that go out on Tuesdays and Fridays from Galveston. Well, there have been clandestine radio signals from someplace on the island to the submarines. We localized it in about a twelve-block area, so we rented three different rooms and finally discovered where the signals were coming from." The commander explained that they had found an amazing antenna the height of a house at 2924 Avenue O, where the German brewmaster for Southern Select Brewery lived. "The antenna was telescoped down during the daytime so you couldn't see it and raised at night. We went in there, and they had all the equipment," said Cunningham. Ballinger asked them what they were going to do with the German agents. "They've been placed in a concentration camp in Oklahoma," replied Cunningham.[6]

In the Caribbean, convoys were just beginning to be successful. The navy hoped that the day would soon come when enough warships would be available to form killer groups for hunting and destroying enemy submarines. Convoying required heavily armed escort vessels to protect merchant ships with defensive action only; the escort ships could not go off to chase U-boats and leave the convoy vulnerable to attack. Whenever confrontations took place, the men in the escorts had no way of knowing whether they had damaged or destroyed the German submarines. Oil slicks proved nothing, for sometimes the U-boats lost small amounts of diesel oil from their exterior storage tanks.

From May through September, 1942, the German submarines relentlessly attacked ships in the Caribbean and Gulf of Mexico, sinking an average of one and one-half vessels per day and destroying over a million gross tons. Because of such losses, the Office of Price Administration in Washington proclaimed that Texas and Louisiana were suffering from a severe shortage of sugar. Despite that announcement, the Kempners, a local distinguished, pioneering family whose fortunes were made from cotton, sugar, and other enterprises, had just closed down their bulging sugar warehouses.[7]

Just before convoys were organized in the Caribbean, U-166, under the command of *Kapitänleutnant* Hans-Günther Kühlmann, made a trial run. He then took aboard torpedoes, ammunition, fuel, and provisions and sailed from Lorient on June 17. His mission: to lay mines and conduct warfare in the Gulf of Mexico. Headquarters ordered him to report his fuel situation after he passed fifty degrees west, because his U-boat, a type IX-C, was considerably larger than the others sent to the gulf and required more diesel oil.

On June 20 Kühlmann reported that he had been caught by aircraft searchlights and had a few bombs dropped near him, but had sustained no damage. When he passed the fifty-degree mark on June 30 heading westward toward southern Florida, he reported that he had two hundred tons of fuel left. On July 10 he spotted a convoy of two steamers with two destroyers and fired six torpedoes, but they all

Hans-Günther Kühlmann, commander of U-166. Photo courtesy of U-Boot-Archiv, Cuxhaven, Germany.

missed. Four days later he reported having sunk one sailing vessel of three thousand tons.

On July 11 Kühlmann blasted and sank the sailing boat *Carmen* (eighty-four tons) with gunfire south of Haiti and next dispatched the American freighter *Oneida* two days later near the east end of Cuba. On July 16 Kühlmann used his artillery to sink the trawler *Gertrude*, a sixteen-tonner. On July 27, after laying nine mines near the mouth of the Mississippi River, he radioed his superiors that he had fulfilled his mission (minelaying) in grid square DA 93, accomplished on July 24 and 25. No more messages were ever heard from Hans-Günther Kühlmann. German headquarters requested him to report his situation on August 3. "In spite of several challenges, we have received no answer," they reported. "We can't find any reason for the disappearance." They posted one star by U-166 from August 3 to September 2, and on January 28, 1943, they posted two stars, assuming her total loss.[8]

On July 30, U-166 encountered the 1924 cargo-passenger carrier *Robert E. Lee.* The old ship, built for the coastal trade, had deckhouses with wooden sides and heavily painted canvas tops. The promenade deck had square windows instead of ports across the front. She had left Port-of-Spain, Trinidad, on July 20, headed for Tampa in a convoy with navy escort. Her passengers, American construction workers, their families, and others who were survivors of Caribbean sinkings, were crammed into the small cabins, four of them in two-person rooms. Conditions were terrible, with intense heat and very little water for washing and drinking.

After a couple of days at sea, a group of passengers approached the chief mate to ask for a tradeout. "We would sand scrub the promenade deck, which was very dirty, if we could have coffee in the crew's mess . . . plus a bucket and a couple of cakes of soap. . . . The deal was made and we scrubbed down the deck and got our coffee every day in return, plus the bucket and soap," said one of them.

The convoy made it to Key West, where it dispersed, and word went around that the *Lee* was going to Tampa for fuel and water, then on to New Orleans. The travelers, anxious to escape from their miserable situation, asked the captain if he would let them debark at Tampa, and he agreed.

The old ship, now with a patrol corvette (PC) escort, PC 566, anchored at the Edgemont Key Light and signaled for a pilot to take her in. The answer came back that there was none, and at that point the shipmaster decided to go on to New Orleans. The escort broke radio silence to advise the commander of the Gulf Sea Frontier that the *Robert E. Lee* could not get a pilot at Tampa and was continuing to New Orleans. The commander replied that the escort should stay

Passenger-freighter *Robert E. Lee,* sunk by Kühlmann in U-166 south of New Orleans on July 30, 1942. Photo courtesy of Steamship Historical Society Collection, University of Baltimore Library.

with the ship to New Orleans and advise the port director of their arrival. At 7:16 that morning, the frontier commander instructed the Pensacola Naval Air Station to send air cover for the ship and her escort, but the planes were unable to find them.

That afternoon, July 30, with clear weather, calm seas, and excellent visibility, the escort was a half mile in front of the *Lee* as they approached the Southwest Pass. PC 566 radioed New Orleans to inform them what time they would be getting to the pass and to ask for a pilot. As they were sending the message, a group of passengers and a few of the crew on the *Lee* noticed something streaking along in the water parallel to the ship and close to the surface. They were having a lively discussion about whether it could be a shark or a porpoise when the object made an abrupt ninety-degree turn and smashed into the ship just aft of the engine room.

"When the torpedo struck, I happened to be just finishing getting dressed after taking a bucket bath," said Captain Barton Holmes, "and in fact, I was in the act of strapping on my watch. . . . I remember saying, 'Here we go again.'"

The explosion completely destroyed the number three hold, blasted up through the "B" and "C" decks, put the engines out of commission, damaged the steering gear, and demolished the radio. Most of the ship's windows were open at the time of the attack, and as the doomed ship listed, water rushed in and hastened the sinking of the vessel. The deckhouses had so many coats of paint on their canvas covers that they just fell in when the torpedo hit.

The ship started going down so quickly that many passengers and crew members frantically donned life jackets and jumped overboard. The crew did manage to lower six lifeboats and sixteen life rafts, and these were quickly filled. "We were badly overloaded and the boat's freeboard was only a couple of inches; however, the sea was smooth as glass," said Captain Holmes. "The water was filled with people, rafts and boats. The *Lee* was now standing on its stern and going down fast."

Minutes after the ship disappeared, the escort crew saw a periscope and dropped six depth charges, resulting in a small oil slick where the periscope had last been seen. As the survivors scrambled for safety, PC 566 sent a distress signal.

"The escort was underway at full speed dropping depth charges close by," said the *Lee*'s captain. "After all the racket stopped, we paddled around looking for anyone alive in the water. Those we reached were dead, either from the concussion of the depth charges or having their necks broken by jumping into the water with a cork life jacket on. Then the sharks came and took over."[9]

One of the *Lee*'s crew members, G. D. Vernial, said that after the torpedo hit, chaos and confusion reigned. He jumped overboard with a sprained ankle and bleeding head and made it into a lifeboat. "The vast area . . . off the Mississippi River was littered with debris and floating bodies. Oil and blood stained the sides of our boat." Vernial helped pick up bodies from the water and carried the wounded on board the corvette. "With my hospital experience, I applied first aid to the most critical ones. I dressed those dying from blood loss and wounds," he recalled. The ship's doctor had no time to even speak as he untiringly treated those in dire distress.

Survivors of the ordeal filled the naval hospital in New Orleans, where some of them died. "To my great surprise, none of the men that I took care of died at all," Vernial said. "I felt very proud—it was the crowning glory of my career."[10]

On August 1, two days after the *Robert E. Lee* went down, a memorandum went to the commander of the Gulf Sea Frontier from R. S. Edwards, deputy chief of staff of the United States Fleet, headquarters of the commander in chief. The memo said, "In connection with the sinking of the SS *Robert E. Lee,* it appears that (a) ComGulfSeaFron should have told PC 566 to contact the Port Director, New Orleans 'after arrival' instead of 'on arrival.'"[11]

Two days after the *Robert E. Lee* went to a watery grave, Henry White, pilot, and George Boggs, Jr., radioman, were patrolling in a Coast Guard plane off the swampy Louisiana coast, twenty miles south of Isles Dernieres. At 1:37 P.M., White saw a submarine sitting on the surface. "His conning tower and part of his deck were exposed," said Boggs. White immediately sent an SSS message telling its position and began circling to make an attack from the stern. At that point Hans-Günther Kühlmann in U-166 noticed the plane and started a crash dive.

"Henry had to change his plan," recalled Boggs. "He shouted that he would have to hit it broadside, then he armed the charge and had me check to be sure it was armed." Boggs looked out the window to inspect the 325-pound depth charge to ascertain that the lock was unfastened and that the arming wire was firmly attached.

"We started our dive from 1,500 feet. As we headed down, Henry had trouble getting the aircraft to dive steep enough; it kept wanting to pull out," said the radioman.

"Bo, you'll have to release the charge—I'm busy with the throttles. Now when I say NOW I mean NOW!" yelled White.

"We continued our approach, and at about 250 feet Henry shouted, 'NOW!'" Boggs continued. With that, he released the charge, then opened his window to watch the bomb fall. The U-boat was by now completely submerged, and it looked as though the depth charge had landed about twenty feet away from it. A big geyser of water roared up as it hit.

"By this time the wing obscured any further observations," Boggs went on. "We then pulled out of the dive and started circling the position. We saw only an oil slick . . . from light to medium."

Henry White sent a radio message back to Houma, Louisiana, and Biloxi, Mississippi, reporting that he had sighted a surfaced submarine, made an attack, and possibly done some damage. The two men circled the area for two hours and were relieved by another Coast Guard patrol plane. Back at Houma, the FBI interrogated the two and advised them not to divulge any of their adventures because of security reasons. "We figured we either destroyed or badly damaged the U-boat. . . . We never knew until the fall of the German Empire that we had destroyed U-166," said George Boggs.[12]

On July 24 and 25, U-166 was cruising on the surface setting mines afloat and had gone undetected. Kühlmann reported on July 27 that her minelaying operations were completed. On July 30 she overheard PC 566 sending a radio message to the New Orleans harbormaster and knew exactly where to find the *Robert E. Lee*. Two days later U-166 met her doom. The mystery will never be solved as to why Kühlmann's submarine was on the surface so near shore that day— was he laying more mines or getting some fresh air? As it turned out later, U-166 was the only German U-boat sunk in the Gulf of Mexico proper, although U-157 was very close to it. News of the possible sinking of U-166 did not reach the American public because the U.S. navy was not sure they had sunk it, and they did not want the Germans to know what they were doing.

While Kühlmann had been busy putting out mines (none of which caused any damage), nine other German submarines roved gulf waters and sank twenty ships in July. Gulf Sea Frontier headquarters at Key West was going crazy with continual reports of enemy submarines, and it was difficult to tell if the information was real or imagined. The reports said that Pan American pilots operating southward from Miami consistently mentioned seeing U-boats on their overwater flights. The Seventh Naval District and Gulf Sea Frontier intelligence offices offered the pilots a special course in enemy submarine recognition to improve their accuracy. Many pilots voluntarily took the course and became excellent assistants to the frontiers by reporting locations of U-boats.[13]

The United States Navy was at a severe disadvantage from February to December, 1942, in that neither they nor the British could decipher radio messages sent by the German navy. On the other hand, the U-boats knew exactly what the Allied ships were saying when they called for help and gave their locations in longitude and latitude. Ship captains, when their vessels were sinking, made every effort to throw their codebooks overboard, weighted with concrete chunks or locked in iron boxes; they had no way of knowing that all their trouble was a waste of time. The Americans could pick up the German submarine messages with radio direction finders and determine the boat's location, but that was all.

The Germans had an elaborate Enigma cipher machine on every U-boat. It looked something like a typewriter in a metal box: the operator pressed keys with German letters, and eight rotors converted the letters into coded language. The operator wrote down the message and sent it off to headquarters, or vice versa.

Before February 1, 1942, the British had been able to decode the German messages and even gave vital information about U-boat locations to the United States Navy, which chose to ignore the whole thing. When the Germans altered their code in February, the British deciphering experts did not break it until ten months later, after Admiral Dönitz's submarine commanders had decimated shipping along America's eastern and southern coasts and the Caribbean. After December, 1942, the Allies picked up U-boat messages and used them to their advantage while the Germans wondered why their naval problems were growing worse.[14]

Just after Kühlmann's ship went down off the Louisiana coast, the navy started the first real convoy system in the Gulf of Mexico. Good results of convoying had already been seen on the East Coast and in the Caribbean, and now the time had come to get organized in the gulf. To protect tankers that frequently traveled between southern ports, the navy designated the route between Galveston and the Mississippi Passes as the first convoy lane. This route took the ships through shallow coastal Louisiana waters past the Ship Shoal buoy, past the Southwest Pass buoy, and into the river delta. There was no other way to go: shallow waters offered more protection, even though German submarines had done some of their worst damage where the convoy route hugged the Louisiana coast.[15]

From the time the Gulf Sea Frontier had been established in February, 1942, "shipping in this area was largely chaotic and often operated at the discretion of the Master of each vessel," wrote naval historians. They said many ships came into frontier ports without the command knowing anything about their arrivals or departures. "The problem of exercising full control over merchant vessels was of course international in scope (and diplomatically ticklish at best)," the historians explained.

At first shipmasters, confident that no enemy would venture into the Gulf of Mexico, went any direction they wanted and told the navy nothing about their intended routes. But they gradually began to realize that their sole protection lay in reporting their movements to naval authorities. The first appearance of the U-boats in the Florida Straits speeded up their cooperation. In fact, navy historians said that all shipmasters who disobeyed military instructions and went on unauthorized courses had their vessels torpedoed.[16]

To operate the convoy system, the navy set up the Shipping and Routing Control Division with three offices: the main one in Key West, Florida; one at Pilottown, Louisiana, at the Southwest Pass; and the third one in Galveston. There the port directors helped coordinate groups of ships operating within Gulf Sea Frontier waters and those going into adjacent frontiers. The route between Galveston and Pilottown had the designation GM-MG, and the first group of vessels made the trip on July 30.

The system entailed amassing merchant vessels in the convoy anchorages until enough ships were gathered that were heading in a similar direction. Twenty or thirty ships might sit at anchor for a week or ten days awaiting the formation of a group, thus causing a tremendous loss in shipping time.

To solve the delay problem, the interlocking convoy system came into being in late August. Oceanwide in scope, the new plan, using advance scheduling, ended the lengthy waiting periods and allowed continuous movement for shipping. The interlocking routes went between Key West and New York (KN-NK), Key West and Galveston (KH-HK), Key West and Pilottown (KP-PK), and Key West and Guantanamo, Cuba (KG-GK).

HK convoys formed in Galveston Bay and consisted of ships from Houston, Texas City, and Galveston bound for New York, Trinidad, and North Africa, as well as Key West. They would meet two other convoys south of Key West on a designated day and time, and then regroup to continue their way to other ports.

Staying in formation was not an easy thing. The ships, with no lights at night, had to go the same speed and stay a specified distance apart without radio communications. They accomplished this with flags or quick light signals and by dragging a line with a noisemaking buoy off the stern as a space marker for the ship behind. "The halyard was about a thousand yards long and had a little gadget on the end that made a swirling noise in the water. You could put it right alongside your bridge, and if all the ships were doing eight knots, they'd go along just like they were," explained Captain Glenn Tronstad. At night each ship had a small light on its stern that could be seen by the ship behind as well, but the swirling buoy could be used even in fog.[17]

"Every time we got ready to make a trip, we'd have what they called a captain's conference—usually the radio operator and the captain, who would go up to the commodore at the Federal Building in Galveston," said Tronstad. "Anybody that was in this convoy would get instructions, and we wouldn't know just exactly what route the convoy would take, because the orders were sealed until we got out to sea."

Tronstad said they traveled with destroyer escorts, and the head ship was the station keeper, going eight knots. Some vessels could go faster, but they all had to go the speed of the slowest one. "Some of the old-time ships had the reciprocating engines and some had old diesels, and their speed was about ten knots. So if they didn't press them too much, say about eight or nine knots, they could keep pretty good station," he recalled. "But if they did have problems, they'd bellow off some smoke and be listed as 'stragglers.' That's where the U-boats came in—they looked for stragglers, all alone."

"We also zigzagged, using flashing lights or whistle signals," he continued. "And when you're navigating, you have to use exact time, so the lead ship would get a time tick from his nongenerating radio and send up a ball at noon, and we'd all look at it. Soon as it was right high noon, that time ball would come down and everybody would say, 'Mark,' and set their clocks according to that."

Tronstad said he was fortunate in that as a ship's crewman he saw only one submarine, down off the coast of Mexico. The gunner was getting ready to fire at the supposed antagonist when the captain said, "Wait. I don't believe that's an enemy. I think it's a friendly sub." This was just a feeling he had, according to Tronstad. And true enough, it turned out to be an American submarine. The sub captain said that he knew he shouldn't have been traveling on the surface but he had an injured man aboard and was rushing at top speed to get him to a hospital.[18]

In August, when convoys were moving across the Gulf of Mexico, the Caribbean, and the Atlantic coast, the lopsided battle picture began to tilt the other way. "The U-boats were forced to fight for their prey," navy historians wrote. "Most shipping was under convoy and enjoyed the protection of both surface and air escort, and the arrival of radar-equipped planes permitted night coverage as well." America seemed to be getting the upper hand, and the Germans now had to search hard to find any more "sitting ducks."[19]

12

The Big Inch Goes In

AS SOON AS THE WAR PRODUCTION BOARD authorized steel for the new oil pipeline from Texas to the East Coast, Secretary of the Interior Harold Ickes asked Jesse Jones, secretary of commerce and chairman of the Reconstruction Finance Corporation, to arrange for the financing and construction of the project. Jones agreed to do it with the condition that the oil industry form a nonprofit corporation to supervise construction and operate the line. Eleven eastern oil companies immediately organized what was called the War Emergency Pipelines, Incorporated, in June, 1942. Charter provisions stipulated no dividends or profits would accrue to any stockholders because of the government contracts. The corporation signed a construction agreement to build the "Big Inch" for the government, starting with the section from Texas to Salem, Illinois, to be extended to Philadelphia and New York. The final line, 1,475 miles long and twenty-four inches in diameter, would move three hundred thousand barrels a day to the eastern seaboard and cost $95 million. A second, twenty-inch, line would be built from Texas to Seymour, Indiana, then to the New York area. This would become the "Little Big Inch."

As convoys were getting organized in the gulf, the first seamless steel pipe went into the ground near Little Rock, Arkansas, on August 3 to begin the largest petroleum conduit in the world. Five months later workers had completed the first section from Longview, Texas, to Little Rock, and oil began to flow just before midnight on December 31, 1942, a few minutes before the deadline of January 1, 1943.

The work went on at a breakneck pace—over the Allegheny Mountains, under thirty large rivers and streams, below two hundred creeks, and under hundreds of roads and railroad crossings. Each day the crews finished an average of 3.6 miles, and the entire grueling job took a record-breaking 350 days. Construction equipment and manpower were scarce, and available equipment was hastily adjusted to handle the giant overweight tubing. On July 19, 1943, the workers made their final weld on the big line at Phoenixville, Pennsylvania, and a ceremony was held for the occasion with Secretary Ickes and other government notables attending.

The tremendous pipeline, made of 3/8-inch-thick steel pipe, had been tested to pressures of 750 to 800 pounds per square inch with no failures. Some of the branch-line pipes had been found to have defects and were rejected, and the testing continued until everything was satisfactory. The oil companies built twenty-eight pumping stations fifty miles apart, each with three centrifugal pumps to keep the oil flowing. Fifty-one steel storage tanks holding 3,836,000 barrels were erected at Longview; Norris City, Illinois; Phoenixville, Pennsylvania; and Linden, New Jersey. By the end of June, 1943, the Big Inch had already transported about 21 million barrels of crude. But in retrospect one might say the frantic project had come a bit late, considering that the U-boats had already done their worst damage in the Gulf of Mexico.[1]

By early fall of 1942, the Galveston paper was bombarding its readers with war reminders and urgings to save things. Rubber was badly needed, and a cartoon showed that 400 feet of garden hose would make one bomber tire, 1,850 rubber bands would make one cartridge-inflated life belt, and that 1,252 pairs of rubber gloves would make a set of deicers for a long-range bomber. Paul Nicholls, head of the city scrap drive, said that the quota per month would be 675 tons and that designated depots would be set up for deposits. "Galvestonians must yield every bit of scrap metal not essential to everyday life," he told them. The army at Fort Crockett would pick up all the junk, haul it off, and sell it. Nicholls reported that grease collection was slowly increasing.[2]

In England, where war had created drastic shortages of everything, King George announced that in order to conserve resources, the royal family would henceforth take baths in only five inches of water. The king, playing a major role in efforts to save fuel, ordered every bathtub in the royal household painted with a black or red line at the five-inch level and posted notices reminding users of the necessity for fuel economy.

Likewise, the monarch directed that only one light bulb would be allowed in bathrooms and all palace bedrooms and that extra bulbs would be taken out. At Buckingham Palace and Windsor Castle, no central heating was being used, and the king had forbidden any fires in the fireplaces. Only on orders from a physician could a fire be lit in a bedroom. The number of functioning boilers had been limited so that four days a week there was no hot water in some areas of Windsor Castle, and the occupants of those rooms would have to haul it from the kitchen.[3]

To get people's minds off growing scarcities, propaganda against Hitler and his Nazi military pervaded the news. Galveston's E. S. Levy & Company inserted a small advertisement with a picture of a Hitler doll bending over with pins stuck in his derrière. Labeled "Hotzi Notzi" and "Stick Him," the doll was priced at only fifty cents. "A copy of the little image President Roosevelt has on his desk at the White House. Use him for your own pleasure," the ad urged.[4]

Problems with too much light on the island persisted in spite of dimout regulations. Major Ralph Barry told local air raid wardens throughout the entire city to see to it that no outside lighting appeared in their districts except for streetlights and a few other exceptions. One warden asked Chief Warden F. F. Kay if it was allowable for a person to use his garage or back yard light to drive his car into the garage. "No," Kay replied.

Chief Kay also informed the wardens that army higher-ups had told him Galveston's dimout was "very unsatisfactory, and that unless regulations were more strictly enforced, the army might order a complete blackout every night."[5]

The news editor exhorted people to take more care. "Hide that light," he wrote, saying that the merchant ships at sea would be safer if Galveston reduced outside illumination to the absolute minimum. Nothing but streetlights was supposed to be shining, and those at a fraction of their normal wattage. "These regulations are designed to eliminate the loom which might silhouette ships near shore and make them easy targets for enemy submarines. There is no doubt whatsoever as to the necessity for these precautions. Several ships have been sunk in the gulf within a few miles of shore."[6]

The police chief told the auxiliary police that they must see that cars entering the five-block strip along the seawall had only parking lights on and that the drivers were on their way home. No one could travel through the area unless it was the only way to get to their house, and the speed limit there was ten miles an hour.[7]

The Coast Guard needed volunteers to help patrol Galveston and Bolivar beaches. They announced their program, saying, "Got a horse? If so, you may be the man for the new beach patrol." The job entailed protecting the shore from submarine-borne spy "invasions" as well as routine duties such as looking out for ships in distress and suspicious items on the beaches. Men with horses could volunteer themselves in company with their mounts, or they could just lend their animals with harnesses and saddles. The Coast Guard especially wanted experienced riders and sportsmen who had served in the cavalry or mounted police or were otherwise well-trained.[8]

Galveston had very few horses, but Bolivar Peninsula had some reliable steeds and expert riders as well. The Coast Guard took over the old Sea View Hotel at High Island, twenty-seven miles down the peninsula, and set up a stable of area horses. Two local families, the Lynns and the Whites, donated their beach or ranch houses to use. "They had another camp at Breeze Inn, down the beach toward Sabine Pass," recalled George Hamilton, one of the volunteers. The inn was an old beer joint leased from a rancher named Broussard, and the men slept on cots set up on the dance floor the first night.[9]

"We rode our own horses; then later they sent some cavalry horses in . . . we had to ride those old things," said Hamilton. He said the cavalry nags hadn't been ridden for "Lord knows how long," and they had old army McClelland saddles, which were "little bitty, with nothing on them and a crack down the middle where you sit."

Hamilton and his mates rode in pairs from White's ranch at High Island down the beach until they met the riders from Breeze Inn, about fifteen miles, then rode back. They did this every night and stayed at White's, getting off for weekends. "I don't know what the deal was. We didn't run into any Germans or anything," he remarked.

One day, as Hamilton and his buddy were riding along, they spotted a large, strange object sitting on the sand. "We didn't know what it was, and we were kind of scared of it. And we only had our shot-guns," he recalled. They rode back to the main post at the Sea View Hotel and reported it, whereupon a crew in jeeps drove down to the site to investigate. It turned out to be an old ship's boiler.[10]

Coastguardsmen at the Sea View Hotel played Ping-Pong or boxed in a big upstairs recreation room. Some of them, after finishing a long patrol, occasionally stopped at "This Is It," the "Green Light," or "Windy's Place" for refreshments. The old man who ran "Windy's" would let them in the back door if they were in uniform, sell them a beer, and tell them to lock up when they left because he was going home. "Windy's" was their favorite place.

Many a new recruit struggled to master horseback riding when he arrived at High Island, never having been even close to a four-footed charger. "Some of them would get up on one side and fall off the other side," said Glenn Cudd, one of the recruits.[11]

Late in August, the Coast Guard geared up its "Dogs for Defense" program with the training of eighteen hundred canines for beach pa-trol. These were mostly German shepherds, Doberman pinschers, and Airedales, and they went out only at night.Generally, one man walked with his dog on a leash for about one mile of beach. The dogs, ever alert, could sense the presence of strangers and were formidable ad-versaries. One man patrolling near Plymouth, Massachusetts, almost walked off a cliff but was stopped when his canine companion re-fused to take another step.[12]

To improve communications, the Coast Guard planned to install a Navy-type TRC (Tactical Radio Control) radio transmitter at Galves-ton station WNU to allow remote control of the station's transmitters. Because they were having trouble sending distress and enemy-sighting signals by Teletype, the Coast Guard calculated that a point-to-point radio circuit between WNU and Washington would be advanta-geous.[13]

Apparently the rookie beach patrollers missed an item in the begin-ning, because two young women, while walking along the shore eight miles from town, discovered a bullet-riddled life preserver. A picture in the paper showed the two of them holding it up between them. It seemed they had upstaged the Coast Guard by discovering the first "suspicious" object.[14]

On August 3 a Senate subcommittee listened to the testimony of seventy-five-year-old August Simon Lake, one of the world's leading figures in submarine development and whose invention of the undersea torpedo boat in 1889 had been put to use by the United States Navy. He told the attentive senators that he had perfected a "secret silencing device" that could pave the way for a fleet of submersible freighters and that these vessels could elude planes, ships, and other undersea craft with ease. Lake stated that it was entirely practical to have a "silent submarine" and that he thought the enemy was now using underwater freighters. The committee, already considering the possibilities of cargo planes, paid attention as the elderly man described the sub carriers that could transport seventy-five hundred tons of oil, tanks, guns, munitions, and men to fighting zones. Lake said that shipyards could use the same materials and equipment used to produce Liberty ships and still have some steel left.

When questioned further, the inventor told the senators that he envisioned the possibility of building the huge submarines of concrete. The use of such a material, however, would require "considerable experimentation, and I would prefer steel," he said. He estimated the cost at $2,125,000 each and the time for construction at five or six months.

Lake read a letter he had received from Navy Secretary Knox saying he thought the silencer idea was "feasible" and that the submarines would be comparatively safe from torpedoes and shell fire if submerged a hundred feet. With his new invention, a sub could come within fifty yards of a surface ship. "I guarantee nobody on the ship could see or hear it," he claimed.

Furthermore, the inventor thought it was a fallacy to attempt to stop the enemy submarine depredations by warships or airplanes. "But unfortunately there is no way in which the submarine menace can be abolished," he remarked. Reports were now saying that subs were sinking U.S. ships twice as fast as they could be built, but he thought that if the truth were known, the ratio was more like four times. "It seems to me, therefore, that it would be far wiser for us to build ships which cannot be seen or heard and consequently not be sunk," he concluded.[15]

Lake had spent several years before the war in Germany, England, Russia, and Austria as an advisory engineer designing and building torpedo boats. He felt sure that the Germans were using cargo-carrying submersibles to supply their submarines operating off America's shores. The old man was right—they were.[16]

Patriotism in the United States was reaching a fever pitch. Factories, shipyards, aircraft construction plants, and other industries hammered and tonged, belching out clouds of steam and showers of sparks. Workers prided themselves in keeping long hours, while government propaganda urged them to ever-greater productivity. We were losing the war. In San Francisco the Western Pipe and Steel Company fired 150 shipyard workers for "shirking their jobs." Company officials explained their actions by saying they were fully behind the navy's "work or fight" policy and that they had given the men's names to the draft board for removal from deferred classification. The navy had asked that all shirkers be eliminated from yards where naval vessels were under construction.

"We don't want slackers in our shipyards or defense plants," said the secretary of the local AFL. "They prevent the great majority of honest, industrious workers from doing their work."[17]

In Galveston the hue and cry went up for collection of scrap metal. From his San Antonio headquarters, Major General Richard Donovan explained that old cannons or other relics with historical value would be left alone. Many of the guns in parks and courthouse yards had much sentimental value and would not be touched. Thousands of cannons and other weapons from World War I, however, were serving no useful purpose and would help the war effort. (In 1942 these weapons were merely twenty-five or so years old and not considered antiques.) General Donovan and his assistant planned to remove several of these war remnants from the state capital grounds and from Camp Mabry in Austin, with the full cooperation of Governor Stevenson. "These huge cannon will net many thousands of pounds of the vitally needed scrap, and will be moved away by the army within the next two or three weeks," Donovan announced.

The general clarified the army's position in scrap collecting by saying that its aim was to furnish transportation for removing scrap from central collecting points and to expedite the work of collecting thousands of tons of metal from military reservations. He said that citizens who wanted to could sell scrap metal to dealers, whose prices were under government controls. "The government needs it immediately and is seeking the cooperation of the entire nation," he urged.[18]

The American public was growing angry, believing that the war effort was coming along too slowly because of Washington's inefficiency. The president was thought to be blameless, except for his reluctance to fire anyone, but much criticism was arising toward the various war agencies. *Fortune* magazine wrote Mr. Roosevelt an open letter advising him to hold a thorough court-martial of his war administration.[19]

German submarine activity in the gulf continued with the episode of U-508. "An uncommonly saucy U-boat," wrote Samuel Eliot Morison, "gave the Gulf Sea Frontier a final kick in the teeth on 12 August. It attacked a small Key West-Havana convoy escorted by two PCs seven miles south of Sand Key Light." U-508, commanded by *Kapitänleutnant* Georg Staats, torpedoed and sank two Cuban freighters, the *Santiago de Cuba* and the *Manzanillo.* Just afterward, students in the Key West Sound School could see the smoke from their windows. The *Dahlgren,* a destroyer, and several training ships, just going out for their daily exercises, quickly formed a "killer" group. The thirteen vessels plus several airplanes searched the area for three days and two nights, but they never found Georg Staats. The submariner continued his patrol, attacking two more ships in convoys before he left the Gulf of Mexico.[20]

The U-boats, now facing convoys everywhere, gave them no slack. Military optimists who thought that the new group system would suddenly repel submarine attacks saw no immediate results. In July, August, and September of 1942 the German submersibles sank seventy-five ships, most of them under escort in the Caribbean.[21]

Navy historians, looking back after the war, remarked that "it was unquestionably in August that the German undersea raiders were definitely defeated in the Gulf Sea Frontier." This was true, but the raiders had just moved southward. "Anti-submarine measures were a major influence on the number [of U-boats] operating, because as soon as they became effective in a given area, Admiral Dönitz pulled his boats out," wrote Morison.[22]

When September rolled around, the Galveston Coast Guard let out the news that they were soon going to take over the majestic Galvez Hotel, one of many hostelries the government had requisitioned for military use. In this case they picked the oldest and grandest one in town. Built on Seawall Boulevard in 1911, the Spanish-style resort with its tall palm trees had an elegant penthouse on top, surrounded by four turrets. In the penthouse lived Sam Maceo, gambling kingpin, who could look out the windows and see his Balinese Room on a long pier in the gulf. When Maceo heard the news, he moved out and arranged to start building a large house in the west part of town.[23]

Hotel manager Winthrop P. Younger said that vacationers would still be able to find accommodations in the Buccaneer, Jean Laffite, and other places. A few days later, signs went up on all hotel entrances telling the public that no one would be admitted. All luncheons and meetings were canceled, but no date had been set for the Coast Guard to move in, because permanent guests had to find other living quarters.[24]

Keeping stride with events of the gulf U-boat war, comics heroine Jane Arden continued her search for saboteurs. She had discovered that a man named Fred Krish, playing the role of hillbilly "Uncle Eben" at a coastal radio station, was sending out coded messages to the U-boats. The question was, Where did he get his information? To find out, Jane went to the station to watch a live broadcast, posing as a fan.

"I'm *very* interested in your program!" she said to "Uncle Eben."

"Wal set y'se'f right down hyar, but don't flash your smile on the boys. That away, er I won't git a speck o' music out'n em," he replied.

The program started while Jane sat and watched.

A few days later Jane and her FBI agent friend paid a visit to the port director and verified that he designated the route by which ships left every day.

"I decide in the morning—the order is dictated to my secretary—the orders are typed and delivered to the ship captains by special messenger," the director explained.

Jane asked him if there was a chance of a leak, and he said he didn't think so because a squad of marines was carrying the messages.

Port Director: "And yet that message is radioed to the Nazi U-boats each day—but how?"

"That just leaves you, your secretary, or one of the ship captains," said Jane.

Further investigations revealed that a sheet of carbon paper was missing from the ship messages. They decided to set a trap, so Jane hid in a locker to see who was taking the carbon papers. That night the janitor arrived with his push broom and started rifling through the pile of trash papers to be burned.

"I've already read every scrap of paper by then—ah—here we are, the carbon paper they used in typing the sailing orders," he muttered. "Seven ships—twenty-one o'clock—route three—bah! Now we'll sink 'em all."

The janitor-spy heard Jane's watch ticking and discovered her in the locker, whereupon she claimed that she was a spy also and prevailed upon him to leave the building with her. As we would expect, the FBI was ready to pounce and did indeed capture the culprit. In actuality, no U-boats received messages from hidden radios in the United States, but many people thought they did. It was the era of suspicion.[25]

Jane's spy adventures in the gulf concluded at the end of August, just as news began to come out that the U-boat menace was slackening. Secretary Knox told reporters that things seemed to be getting better every day, because attacks along U.S. shores had steadily diminished, but the problem was by no means solved. He thought that the use of private boat patrols, blimps, and army air surveillance had been very effective, together with convoying on the Atlantic seaboard and the Caribbean. "The minute you make it tough for the German U-boats along our coasts and off the British Isles," he said, "they hunt new areas—the high seas far from land."

Net results showed that only half as many vessels were sunk in the western Atlantic and Caribbean in August as in July—thirty-four ships compared to sixty-eight.

Secretary Knox announced that American shipyards were producing new vessels at ever-increasing rates: sixty-eight cargo carriers and tankers were completed in August. For the first time, America began to feel a guarded optimism.[26]

13

Pounce on Every Ounce

AT FORT CROCKETT ONE DAY, Private John Naumczik was standing guard duty at the base of a military instrument tower on the grounds of the fort. He saw Colonel Schwepp, base commander, drive up with another officer and their wives. Naumczik, standing in front of the concrete-walled plotting room beneath the tower, watched as they emerged from the car and strolled over to where he stood. When they came closer he said, "Halt!"

"Do you know who I am?" asked Colonel Schwepp.

"I believe so, sir."

The colonel put his hand on the plotting-room door handle, and with that John raised his rifle and said, "Your pass, sir."

The colonel extracted his pass and held it out. But John, new in the military game, forgot protocol. "Put it on the ground, sir," he said.

Now the colonel had turned red and his teeth were clenched. He did as he was told. Naumczik picked up the pass, looked at it, and gave it back to him. The party then proceeded to enter the highly secret plotting room for a tour.

The next morning at daylight John had just finished guard duty and was ready to go collapse in his tent when Captain Laird walked up. "My God, John, what happened? What did you do to Colonel Schwepp?"

The private told him he had just refused to let him go into the plotting room without showing a pass.

"You shouldn't have made him put it on the ground," chided Laird.

"That just added insult to injury in front of the major and their wives. I'm going to have to hide you."

The captain ordered John to get into a waiting jeep, then drove him out to a remote spot on the west beach. There he let him out at a tent and gave him a water-cooled machine gun. "What am I supposed to do here?" John asked, feeling immensely weary.

"Well, if you see an assault coming in, you cut loose with that machine gun, but first you call for help," replied Laird.

"How do I get out of here?" John asked.

"They'll come get you. But be on the lookout for Schwepp—he couldn't find you."

Naumczik's orders were to sit in the tent and watch through his binoculars for approaching enemies. It was beastly hot, and John could scarcely keep his eyes open. After a short while he saw a jeep coming down the beach. It was Colonel Schwepp and two other officers. The colonel jumped out, and John saluted him.

"Where's your canteen?" barked Schwepp.

"In the tent, sir."

"Where's your bayonet?"

"I don't have a bayonet, sir. I just came back from furlough and they didn't have any."

"Next time I see you, you'd better have a bayonet."

The colonel drove off, still tight-lipped. Several days went by, and one morning, while John was standing in formation with his fellow searchlight operators, Colonel Schwepp walked up to him. "Get a haircut," he ordered.

John's hair had just been cut, but he said nothing. The colonel did not let the private forget his transgression for quite a while.[1]

Over at Gray's Iron Works, a shipbuilding facility on Pelican Island, plans went forward for speakers and rallies to keep workers in a fighting spirit. The Maritime Commission had been visiting shipyards in Houston, Beaumont, and Mobile, giving employees firsthand accounts of war experiences and urging them to concentrate on their jobs. The commission's aim was to convince workers of their extreme importance in ship production. The first speaker was Demitri Goulandris, a merchant sailor who had been torpedoed twice; the second was James MacPhee of the Canadian army, who had fought at Dunkirk and was injured by a bomb fragment. During World War

I, members of the armed forces had participated in a national program in which they delivered patriotic speeches at plants and shipyards. As a result, morale improved and production increased. The
same program was being instituted for the second great war.[2]

Galvestonians, fired up with scrap collecting, began to donate personal items for the war effort. David Rogers gave his collection of
antique weapons, including a Revolutionary War flintlock pistol, a
dueling pistol, a bullfighter's sword, an 1893 Spanish Mauser rifle, a
German and a Japanese navy swords, two Franco-Prussian bayonets,
three Civil War bayonets, and three Civil War cavalry swords. A few
days later, Peter Erhard of the First National Bank announced that
the bank would scrap its original safe, installed in 1865. Salvage
workers had yet to figure out how to remove the ponderous metal
box from its vault, but they were sure they would find some way. A
week later, the paper showed a photograph of four burly army workmen trying to lift the five-ton safe. As they hauled it out of the bank,
its immense weight broke the concrete sidewalk in several places before they could load it onto their truck.[3]

Paul Nicholls, head of the scrap drive, said he and his committee
wouldn't be satisfied until "every ounce of scrap metal on the island
was unearthed." The committee had already found 20,000 pounds of
old, unused metal in downtown office buildings, and the Girl Scouts
had rounded up 1,268 pounds of junk. At Menard Park on Seawall
Boulevard, two World War I cannons were dismantled, picked up by
army trucks, and thrown onto the growing piles. Next, the city made
plans to pull up abandoned streetcar rails to be sold to the government. Mayor Harris had signed a contract in June with the War Production Board for removal of the rails at a price of $36,000. A.
Bornefield, city commissioner of streets, explained that some repair
work would be necessary to eliminate large holes but that there was
a problem getting shell and asphalt to fill them. "We will do the best
we can under the circumstances," he promised.[4]

On September 26 a short flag-raising ceremony took place in front
of the Galvez Hotel, recently converted into Coast Guard barracks.
As the American flag went up, a bugler played "To the Colors." Lieutenant W. G. Ethridge, commanding officer, spoke to the assembled
men, telling them how important their service would be; then dis-
missed them to go about their duties. He passed on the news that the

former hotel manager, James Gray, had enlisted in the Coast Guard and was now assigned for duty there. The hotel bedrooms had been stripped of all furniture, and the lobby had a only few chairs and sofas left. Ethridge could not say how many men would be stationed there because of secrecy, but he did say that the Coastguardsmen would be sleeping, eating, and provided with entertainment in the Galvez.[5]

Within a few weeks, the hotel was transformed. The bridal suite now housed a half-dozen men, a bugler announced mess in the dining room, a ship's bell rang every hour and half-hour in the main lobby, and the ladies' restroom was now the officers' wardroom (dining salon).[6]

That same day, Henry Flagg, the new mayor, issued a proclamation for "Binocular Drive Week." The mayor announced that the United States Navy had issued an urgent appeal for the use of privately owned binoculars during the war. Citizens were asked to phone in a full description of their lenses to be donated, because Zeiss or Bausch & Lomb were preferred in the larger sizes. The navy would pay one dollar for use of the binoculars and requested that people be careful in boxing them up to avoid damage. Citizens were also advised to enclose a card with their name and address. Navy officials said no guarantee could be made for safe return of the binoculars, because they might be lost at sea.[7]

One day later Mrs. Will Rogers presented the first pair for the navy to Gertrude Girardeau of the American Red Cross, who gave them to Gus Amundson, campaign chairman. The navy then announced that twenty other people had offered glasses, but they were not the type wanted. Only Zeiss and Bausch & Lomb of 7x50, 6x30, 7x35, 8x40, or 8x50 would be accepted.[8]

Dr. William Marr said he was going to send in a pair of 10x50 Zeiss night glasses, one of the most powerful ones made. He had originally purchased them from a Captain John Phelan, who had loaned them to the navy during World War I. The navy returned the binoculars to him in 1918.

A navy lieutenant in Dallas wrote a letter to national newspapers saying, "I don't need to emphasize how important it is that officers standing watch far out at sea, with enemy craft lurking nearby, have the best glasses that we can obtain. . . . These things and more are dependent upon how quickly the lookout can spot an Axis submarine periscope or the wake of a torpedo."[9]

The scrap drives were gaining momentum. Schoolchildren, air raid wardens, volunteer industrial workers, and housewives pitched in. At the Queen Theater, a "Scrap Matinee" took place, and local citizens piled five tons of junk in front. The pile, so tall it almost touched the marquee, contained old guns, beds, nuts and bolts, lawn mowers, meat grinders, and a motion picture projection machine donated by the Queen. "Our engineers worked all Friday night to clean out our warehouse," said John Browning, Interstate Theater manager. "Our contribution to the pile added considerably to the tonnage."

Workers at the Galveston wharves took the afternoon off to comb the waterfront for bits of scrap metal, and employees of Gray's Iron Works made a similar effort around their buildings. Scrap drive chairman Paul Nicholls said that scrap piles were now appearing on vacant lots and that they were "getting higher and higher." In Denver, a local citizen proudly put his automobile bumper in the junk heap and replaced it with a wooden one, saying, "Gone to Hirohito."[10]

The Texas Highway Department did a good deed by putting into operation two "nail pickers." The machine had an eight-foot magnet suspended four inches from the ground that would pick up nails, nuts, bolts, and other pieces of metal as it moved behind a truck going five miles an hour. Besides collecting valuable scrap metal, the "nail-pickers" would save motorists' tires and tubes.[11]

Colonel Homer Garrison, head of the Texas Department of Public Safety, swore in nine thousand Galveston schoolchildren as Texas Rangers and charged them to "go on the march immediately and ransack thoroughly every section of the city for scrap metal." Meanwhile, air raid wardens worked toward a plan to have each block in town collect its own scrap. Housewives were expected to find everything they could and put it out for the children to pick up. WPA (Works Progress Administration) workers were ripping up the old streetcar tracks, and plans were made to extract a seven-mile-long stretch of abandoned oil pipeline. The city commissioners voted to donate the metal streetlight poles along Seawall Boulevard and replace them with concrete ones.[12]

The city waterworks prepared to get rid of its obsolete machinery at its Alta Loma pumping plant. Such items as diesel engines and old boilers would be contributed. The editor of the *Galveston Daily News* urged the Fire Department to give up an old steam pumper containing "several thousand pounds of steel and brass which Uncle Sam would be glad to get." He believed that if this relic of horse-and-buggy days had no potential value for fire fighting, then converting it into armament would be a "fitting finale to an honorable career." He called the old pumper a "museum piece" and said he frankly would hate to see it go, but many individuals were donating their relics, and "certainly this is no time for putting sentiment ahead of the war effort." [13]

The editorial recommending the scrapping of the old steam pumper fire engine was noticed by George Gymer, city police and fire commissioner, who declared that it would be donated. "To the old-time fireman, the suggestion . . . that the old horse-drawn engine be turned over to Uncle Sam for junk smelled of sacrilege," he said. "However, I agree . . . that since we are engaged in an all-out struggle . . . the old fire engine with its large amount of brass, copper, iron and steel can justifiably be sacrificed." He went on to explain that Mayor Flagg and the other commissioners had to vote on the proposal to make it final. Furthermore, he said if the decision were made to scrap the old engine, it would be used in the annual fire prevention parade the following week so everyone could see it for the last time.

Gymer told reporters that the horse-drawn pumper was the oldest of its kind in Texas and probably in the South. Bought by the city in 1891, The American Lafrance Fire Steamer cost $9,000 and was built in Seneca Falls, New York. The contraption was coal-fueled, and one fireman sat in the front driving the horses, with another in the rear shoveling coal. Following close behind came a horse-drawn cart carrying more fire fighters with hoses and ladders. The grand red pumper measured about thirteen feet long and had four big iron wheels. In the middle sat the large black steam engine and a hefty water hose. Since its retirement, generations of firemen had been keeping it in mint condition at the back of the central fire station, making sure all its parts stayed cleaned, polished, and gleaming. [14]

Three days later, while George Gymer was on vacation, Mayor Flagg called Lawrence Dorsey, acting fire commissioner, and Frank Best, chief of the fire department, and asked them to make a survey to see if the old fire pumper could be put back into use. The mayor had been besieged with phone calls and letters from people who had read in the paper that a valuable historical item was going to be scrapped. They urged him to either reinstate it or at least save it. Some thought the pumper might be helpful in emergencies or to assist in fire fighting at the west end of town, although it had not seen service since 1915. Chief Best looked the pumper over and said that the engine was iron, not copper, and that it could be fixed and possibly used on a boat. He suggested the city keep the pumper until scrap needs became more drastic. But Commissioner Tompkins responded that there was no question about the government's need for scrap and that he was in favor of keeping the pumper only if it could be reconditioned and put back into use. Tompkins was opposed to keeping it as a relic or for sentimental reasons. The committee said they would get an estimate of the cost of repairs and also find out exactly what metals the pumper was made of.[15]

The next day the paper observed that a "scrap" had developed over the old steam pumper. Gymer, although on vacation, gave out the information that an official at Gray's Iron Works had discouraged him from making repairs. But John McDonough, the president of McDonough Iron Works, inspected the machine with his boilermaker and reported that it was in good shape and could be repaired at nominal cost. "Although I am in full sympathy with the present scrap drive, it is my opinion that the small amount of scrap that could be salvaged from . . . this engine would be greatly offset by its standby value in case of an emergency," he wrote.

To cap things off, several people who had seen the old engine in a recent parade said that the pumper was not the one everybody was thinking about. They claimed that it was one of several obsolete pumpers owned by the Fire Department and that the one in question had been in use at Gray's Iron Works for some time. For some mysterious reason, no more news of the historic fire engine was reported, so the altercation probably went on for some time. But in the end the preservationists prevailed, and the wonderful antique stayed safe in the local fire station. Fifty years later, it found a home in the Galveston Railroad Museum.[16]

Following right along with patriotic fervor, Dan Kempner, owner of the Prudential Building (formerly Fellman Dry Goods Company), donated "Shimmying Sadie," the first elevator in Texas, to the scrap drive. The old elevator, installed in 1905 by the Otis Elevator Company, had been removed when the building was remodeled, and the parts—cages, motors, and cables—had long been obsolete. A local company agent verified that the elevator had been labeled "Otis Elevator Company of Texas No. 1." The agent then remarked that he believed if the elevator were able to talk, "it would agree that it could be put to no better use at this time than the patriotic purpose of adding to Galveston's very successful scrap drive."[17]

The Dan Kempners, ever civic-minded (Mrs. Kempner headed the American Women's Volunteer Service), had been used to a life of luxury for many years. Every other year they loaded up their daughter, Mary Jean; the maid; the chauffeur; many trunks and suitcases; and the family car, a sleek silver-gray Renault, and shipped themselves off to Europe. Mrs. Kempner's niece, Lyda, and her husband, Arthur, coveted the elegant car so much that they asked permission to drive around in it now and then. Every time they did, the two discussed how they could ever afford to buy it, if the chance arose. Suddenly, with no warning at all, Dan Kempner donated the Renault to the scrap drive. Lyda and Art were flabbergasted. They asked him why on earth he had done such a deed and told him they had wanted to buy it. "It was the patriotic thing to do, that's all," he replied.[18]

I. H. Kempner, Dan's brother, drove every Friday to his Sugar Land refinery and farms, where he collected five-pound bags of sugar, packages of butter, and crates of live chickens for each Kempner household. He made sure to pick up the exact amount of sugar allowed by the rationing rules and no more, regardless of their large numbers of family and servants. When he arrived in the alley behind his house at Fifteenth and Broadway, a group of Kempner family chauffeurs met him in their limousines to take home the food allotment.

All four Kempner households participated in the scrap drives to a remarkable degree: they saved grease, rubber bands, string, and old metal objects. "Every Saturday my cousins and I would pull our little red wagon around to each house and pick up large cans of grease, sacks of tinfoil, rubber bands, and whatever else they had collected and deliver it to the fire station," said Lyda Thomas, granddaughter of I. H.[19]

I. H. Kempner wrote to his daughter Cecile in 1942: "I have come to the conclusion that rationing and severe tax restrictions . . . are

necessary to awaken our people to the fact that sacrifices are necessary on the part of every one of us and cannot be passed to the other
fellow. . . . The truth is *we are losing the war.*" His belief that each
person must help in every possible way was so strong that he wrote
to each of his five children telling them they were honor-bound to
strictly follow the rationing rules, and he gave each of them a book
entitled *How to Cook with Honey.* He told them *they* especially
should set a good example. Lyda Quinn, I. H.'s daughter, recalled
that her grandmother Kempner loved sugar but that he still wouldn't
let her or anyone else in the family have more than their share.[20]

A nationwide drive went into gear to procure every ounce of scrap
in the United States. A three-week campaign recruited children and
their parents to make a "clean sweep," and already a weight lifter had
given up his weights. Someone else pulled up several iron benches,
urns, railings, and statues from a cemetery.[21]

In July, the War Production Board proposed that the old battleship
Oregon be scrapped. The famous ship had completed a stormy race
from the West Coast around South America to Santiago, Cuba, in
1898 to attack the Spanish fleet and in 1925 was retired and put on
exhibit in Portland. James V. Forrestal, undersecretary of the navy,
opposed the scrapping of the *Oregon* because he said the vessel was
"one of the historic symbols of this nation." Oregon residents and
officials added their protests, and the idea was dropped.

But as the months went by and the need for metal became desperate, navy officials regretfully announced in October that they intended to cut up the 10,288-ton battleship and use it for the war
effort. President Roosevelt agreed, and the old ship went to its doom.
The president did stipulate, though, that the 5,865-ton cruiser *Olympia,* the nation's last naval relic of the Spanish-American war, be
saved. Commodore George Dewey, on board the *Olympia* at the
battle of Manila, had given the command to Captain G. V. Gridley:
"You may fire when you are ready, Gridley." Dewey's flagship, *Olympia,* and her five sister ships made it through the battle and sank all
seven Spanish vessels.[22]

Ships were going down so frequently in western oceans that one
enterprising soul proclaimed he was going to salvage hundreds of
them after the war. Harry Reiseberg, former chief of the Bureau of
Navigation Tonnage and Licensing, said that he had already used div-

ing bells and iron robots to recover treasures from the ocean floor. An experienced salvage expedition director, Reiseberg said he was seeking a patent for a dry dock 520 feet long and 210 feet wide. It would have thirty hoisting machines that would lower sixteen tongs 300 feet long with 7,500 feet of cable and could lift the ship hulls. "The device will cost less than one freighter," he said. "And I expect to recover an armada of ships."[23]

After a lull in sinkings in the Gulf of Mexico, action accelerated again in the Atlantic. A convoy, under escort by four small Norwegian corvettes and the British destroyer *Viscount,* was visited by a U-boat "wolf pack," which attacked in groups of seven or so in daytime and at night. The battle went on for forty-eight hours. The *Viscount* went after the submarines nine times, and the corvettes made several daring attempts to ram the U-boats as the battle became wilder and wilder. At night the skies were lit by the eerie crisscrossing of flares, star shells, and tracer bullets as the subs and ships blasted each other. Despite all this, the commander of the destroyer commended the Norwegians for their "uncanny skill" in locating the U-boats. On each corvette, an officer stationed high on the mast and every man on deck served as lookouts. When *Viscount* commander Waterhouse heard one of them shout, "Tallyho!" he quickly checked the bearings and found a submarine. At one point the corvette HMS *Potentille* rushed up to a diving U-boat and dropped a circle of depth charges. Twelve minutes later, she sighted another only three hundred yards away and let loose with her guns, scoring several hits. She sped up to ram the U-boat but missed by just a few feet, then dropped another pattern of depth charges.

Another submarine attempted to crash-dive when the *Viscount* approached and shelled it. Her bow tipped up out of the water at a fifty-degree angle, and the boat slid down stern first, appearing to be out of control. The *Viscount* dropped several depth charges and considered the U-boat destroyed. This battle typified the troubles of convoys in late 1942, but at least ships in groups were surviving much better than they had when traveling alone.[24]

14

December 7 Again

"IT IS MY OPINION that we will have the submarine situation in the gulf pretty well under control in sixty days," said Congressman Albert Thomas of Texas after a conference with Lieutenant General B. B. Somervell. "New ships are being built . . . and it stands to reason that the Texas port facilities should be utilized fully in the war program." He said there was an enormous area of storage space in Houston, for instance, that could be used for storing army supplies. Houston port officials sent pleas to the general to use their warehouses and docks.[1]

John McKnight, a reporter for the Associated Press, took a thirty-two-hundred-mile flying tour of American bases in the Caribbean to get an overview of the U-boat war there. "It's getting tougher for the Nazi submarines," he observed. "The threat . . . hasn't been eliminated, and air force and navy officers say they've 'scotched the sea serpents, not killed them.'" McKnight said that a higher percentage of attacks on the U-boats were effective and that the submersibles were having to stay down longer in the daytime and attack at night, when conditions were more difficult. Officers at the bases gave several reasons why fewer ships were being sunk in the Caribbean: new and deadlier explosives were being used, bomber crews were better trained, Brazil was now fighting with a small navy and air force, and it was possible that Hitler had transferred some of the U-boats out of the Caribbean.[2]

Three days later came the news that seven cargo ships had been sunk off the northern coast of South America. This was the highest number of submarine victims in that area over a seven-day period in more than two months and seemed to signal a new U-boat offensive in Caribbean waters.

At the same time Mexico had finished building a bridge a half-mile long over the Suchiate River on the Guatemala-Mexico border, and the first freight trains loaded with rubber, sugar, coffee, bananas, and raw materials chugged northward from Central America. Before the bridge was complete, shipments had to be unloaded from freight cars, carted to the bank of the river (there was no wharf), and poled across in tiny boats. The new route was being heralded as "torpedo-proof," although the bridge itself was something of a hodgepodge job. Builders threw it together in about three months at the rate of thirty-seven feet a day, and crews used prefabricated sections kept for replacement on damaged bridges, for the most part. The beams were of different sizes and lengths, and when they didn't fit, the workers improvised— shortening a piece here and lengthening a piece there—by bolting them together.[3]

Congress went into action to increase defenses against U-boats by announcing the construction of a $10 million lighter-than-air base in Hitchcock, a few miles from Galveston. The new base would be one of a series along the Gulf and Atlantic coasts for antisubmarine patrol, using navy blimps and bombers. Officials of the Galveston Chamber of Commerce thought that the site would be permanent and a great protection during the war emergency.[4]

At the same time, aircraft observers received orders to report any "suspicious or unusual incident which indicates enemy action." The army was asking that ground observers throughout Texas file "red flash" messages as well as reports on aircraft. These would indicate the presence of parachutes; the landing of airborne troops; the dropping of bombs; aircraft accidents; the landing of planes at places other than airfields; the dropping of articles from planes; unexplainable flashes, flares, explosions, or gunfire; the presence of a submarine or enemy warship; the shelling of the coast by a submarine or warship; torpedoing, burning, or other attacks on a ship; the presence of lifeboats or life rafts; the landing of troops and equipment such as tanks and artillery; or any other unusual incidents indicating enemy action.[5]

Higher-ups in the U.S. military feared actual invasions, seeing that the German submarines had come so close to shore and had sunk so many ships in the gulf and Caribbean. "I am surprised we didn't have orders to fire on some of the coastal cities," said Peter Petersen, who served on U-518 in the gulf. "That would have really stirred things up." The U-boats, however, never had orders to fire at anything except Allied ships.[6]

Shipbuilding surged ahead, and a submarine chaser, the first of a series of naval craft to be built at a Galveston shipyard, was presented to the public on November 11, 1942. Suzanne Cohen christened the new SC-1057, built at Gulf Marine Ways—then the chaser got stuck halfway down the launching ramp. After several hours of pulling and tugging, the subchaser entered the water.

"There is no way of telling how many more enemy submarines may be sunk, how many American lives may be saved, and how much nearer the war may be brought to an end," remarked former Texas governor James V. Allred. "Eleven months ago we were humiliated when we found that a treacherous enemy had found our forces not alert. Today we are thrilled beyond expression to know how our forces, by their alertness . . . and efforts have succeeded in landing all along the Mediterranean and Atlantic coast of Africa." Allred told the crowd that the building of this subchaser represented the effort that must be used by every working American, producing or building, to help win the war.[7]

Two weeks later the 220-foot tanker *Seven Sisters,* the largest ship ever launched in Galveston, was christened at Gray's Iron Works on Pelican Island. Mrs. Jack Walmsley whacked a champagne bottle on the sparkling new vessel just before it slid into the water. Two more Liberty ships had just been completed and sent out of the Houston shipbuilding yards, and it looked as though Gulf Coast ship construction was going full steam ahead.[8]

Galveston businessmen who could not qualify for the draft joined the Coast Guard Auxiliary and worked in twelve-hour shifts patrolling the island waters in their fishing boats and yachts. They kept a vigilant eye out for submarines, attacks on shipping, and navigational hazards.[9]

In November, Sergeant John Naumczik was sent away from his base at Fort Crockett to Fort Monroe, Virginia, to study a new type of radar. "At first I was supposed to study the 268 radar, which went with the searchlights. Then all of a sudden they told me I was going to be on a different one, and I didn't know what they were talking about—it was seacoast radar," he said. The new radar would be used to coordinate the guns at Galveston, and when John returned to Fort Crockett, a radar station had been set up. "It looked like a water tower, with a tin shack at the bottom, where the operators stayed, controlling the antenna. This was the SCR 296, seacoast radar."

Naumczik explained that the station was highly secret, and no one except Colonel Schwepp was allowed to go inside. Guards with dogs were stationed in front, and none of the troops knew what the tower was except the few men who worked in it. Most of the men thought it was just a water tower. Not long after the first radar tower was installed at Fort Crockett, a second one was erected in the area of Fort San Jacinto.

"We had crews that worked the radar, and it was tiring and hard on the eyes, looking at those scopes. It was like a small television screen, and two of us would watch it continually," John recalled.

The radar crew stayed in contact with the harbor entrance command and told them of any targets that came up on their screens. "We could pick up anything, even an oil barrel. It was calibrated for one hundred thousand yards, actually fifty-six miles. The harbor command report must have gone to an air base, because if we picked up an object other than a convoy ship, a bomber would soon appear," John went on.

One day they saw a big signal bounce up and reported it to the harbor command. John ran outside, climbed up the tower, and hadn't gone twenty feet when he spotted a big destroyer escort entering Galveston Bay. "We thought, 'how did he get in here?' He had come out of the Houston Ship Channel and turned his radar on—it almost blew our minds."

One day "B" Battery wanted to practice-fire at a towed target, using the big ten-inch guns and with the help of radar. That day the water was rough, and the radar operator had a difficult time telling through the scope whether the towing Coast Guard cutter and the target were far enough apart. Naumczik instructed the captain of the "B" Battery not to fire, and the captain retorted, "Yes, we are going to fire."

"You can't let them do it—it's too rough out there. We can't separate the targets."

"I'll have your neck, Sergeant!" said the captain.

When the captain informed the navy operations commander of the problem, the commander said, "And I'll have yours if you fire." [10]

Radar had so improved the military detection program and the accuracy of the big guns that a hue-and-cry went up for more men to join the Coast Artillery. A full-page ad enjoined young patriots to step forth and sign up, saying, "How would you like to shoot the wing off a Junkers bomber—or watch a Zero come tumbling down in flames under your fire?" And: "Coast Artillery men operate giant searchlights to hunt the night raiders. They use automatic weapons so startling and effective that they've made Hitler shake in his boots." Duties included manning antiaircraft searchlights on the "Moonlight Cavalry," operating the "big ears" (aircraft sound detectors), and firing gigantic coast defense guns. [11]

November came and went. On December first, Galvestonians rushed around filling jugs, five-gallon cans, quart jars, and car tanks with all the gasoline they could find. "We're filling up everything but our pockets," someone said to a filling station operator. Gas rationing was due to start the next day, and everyone wanted to have a reserve, despite the dangers of storing the flammable fluid. Cars lined up for blocks until midnight trying to obtain as much of the fuel as they could carry home. [12]

At the same time, the Galveston Civilian Defense Committee announced that the city would have its first daytime air raid alert on Monday, December 7, cooperating with a statewide practice ordered by the army. "Soldiers on the home front should learn just as fast as soldiers on the fighting front that ignorance means death," the army said. "Galvestonians must be ready to go into action when the sirens sound."

Rules were as follows:

1. Cars were to pull over to the curb when the sirens went off and remain until the all-clear was sounded, but in the event of an actual air raid, car occupants should run to the nearest building.
2. All buses had to stop and riders were to stay in their seats. Trains would continue to travel, but arriving passengers would stay in the depot.

Trainees with listening device ("ears") for an antiaircraft battery at Fort Crockett, June, 1942. Photo courtesy of U.S. National Archives.

3. Pedestrians were to go into the nearest building.
4. People in buildings should go into hallways and stay away from windows and doors.
5. Funeral processions in progress could go ahead, but none could begin during the alert.
6. Civilian defense workers would be supervising, wearing helmets and armbands.
7. Major Hopson would have army planes fly over the city to add to the realism of the test.
8. One trial "incident" had to be conducted.[13]

A few days after this announcement, the navy issued its first full report on events at Pearl Harbor the previous year. Officials said the Japanese bombing had sunk or damaged all eight American battleships in the Hawaiian area, ten other ships, and a floating dry dock. The job of raising and repairing the ships had been rushed, they said, and several had rejoined the fleet, although the *Arizona* was counted as a total loss. Those back in service were the battleships *Pennsylvania, Maryland,* and *Tennessee;* the cruisers *Helena, Honolulu,* and *Raleigh;* the seaplane tender *Curtiss;* and the repair ship *Vestal.* The ones sunk or damaged so severely they would serve "no military purpose for some time" were the battleships *Arizona, Oklahoma, California, Nevada,* and *West Virginia;* the destroyers *Shaw, Cassin,* and *Downes;* the minelayer *Oglala;* the target ship *Utah;* and a floating dry dock.

The eight battleships had represented almost half the navy's strength when the war started, and losses of eighty navy and ninety-seven army planes had been counted. Officers and enlisted men in the navy and Marine Corps who were killed numbered 2,117, with 960 missing and 871 wounded who survived. Among army officers and enlisted men, 226 perished and 396 were wounded, most of whom had recovered. The navy estimated that all this devastation had been inflicted by 105 Japanese planes at 7:55 A.M., just as the watches were changing and while many of the personnel were at Sunday services.[14]

Freshly reminded of the horrors of Pearl Harbor, local citizens organized to be ready for an air raid practice, "so that any possible real air raid will not catch the city unprepared," announced local civil defense directors. Galvestonians read the rules in the newspaper and stayed alert for the sirens to sound between 7:00 A.M. and 7:00 P.M. on December 7.

The first sirens began to wail at 5:30 that afternoon, and pandemonium broke out. Crowds of workers rushed onto buses, other pedestrians ran to sheltered places to get out of the cold, and cars whizzed off in all directions. Air raid wardens, civilian defense workers, and fire fighters went immediately to their posts as army bombers buzzed low overhead. The wardens, stationed at nearly every street corner, tooted their whistles continuously to stop cars. Some people came out onto the streets just to see what was going on. Although the first siren was just a standby signal, everyone took it to be the real thing.

At 5:47 the sirens screamed a second time to indicate the actual air raid, but this time it was thought to be the all-clear signal. During all this bedlam, an imaginary "incendiary bomb" went off at Twenty-second and Avenue E. Rescue and demolition squads together with medical teams immediately rushed in to rescue persons "trapped in buildings" and give medical aid. Demolition units then destroyed the "bomb" before it could set anything afire. The practice incident went off in goodly fashion, but coordinators admitted that the signals had been a mess. At 6:15 a third siren rang out indicating the all-clear, but many had already left the scene and gone home.

D. G. Kobs, in charge of communications, said that some parts were needed to coordinate the signals and that these were on the way. The new system would have a central control office with an officer on duty. "All in all, despite the flaws, it was a good test," said W. J. Aicklen, head of the Civilian Defense Commission. "It must be remembered that this was our first test. That more such tests are needed is evident." [15]

Citizens were happy to hear that lighted Christmas trees could be placed in home windows, provided they were not decorated with an excess of lights (no bright ones) and were placed several feet back of the window. "Only the usual number of colored lights can be put on," instructed the air raid wardens, "plus no outdoor lights at all." If anyone violated the rules, their name would be turned in to higher military and civilian authorities. There had been problems with more and more lights appearing in the downtown area because of merchants' Christmas displays. It was hard to keep everything dark at Christmastime. [16]

In early January, 1943, after the news of the British destroyers' success in sinking two U-boats, Admiral Stark remarked that enemy submarines were the number one naval problem. "Our present shipping losses by U-boat attacks are something to be mighty uncomfortable about," he said at a Washington conference. In London, A. V. Alexander, First Lord of the Admiralty, said, "We are in the difficult, serious stage of the war at sea and the U-boat must be beaten before victory is assured." [17]

At the end of January, the air raid warning committee gave notice that all air raid sirens had been synchronized and would be operated from one central control button. A volunteer operator would be on duty twenty-four hours a day to receive a signal from Washington. When he pushed the local button, sirens would wail simultaneously at six locations around town and would be turned off at the same moment. With this new plan it was hoped that no more confusion would result from air raid practices. [18]

On Tuesday, February 9, a two-man Japanese submarine "captured" at Pearl Harbor came to Galveston under the auspices of the Treasury Department to raise money for the war effort. The eighty-one-foot sub had washed ashore during the invasion at Oahu because of an error and was found by the U.S. military. After a few vital parts were removed for study, the little submersible was shipped to the states, placed on a huge trailer truck, and hauled around the country to be viewed by the public. Anyone who bought war bonds or stamps could look into the interior and see two "Japanese" in uniform at their battle stations, ready to launch two torpedoes. Because the only entrance was a sixteen-inch hatch in the conning tower, thirty viewing ports had been cut on both sides of the hull and covered with Plexiglass. Ladders on each end of the trailer allowed viewers to climb up for a close inspection.

The morning of the celebration, schools were closed. The truck bearing the submarine crossed the causeway at 9:30 and was met by two army marching bands, antiaircraft weapons on trailers, the police chief, and units from Fort Crockett and Camp Wallace. As the parade marched into town, it grew larger and larger with the addition of Boy Scouts and Girl Scouts; army, navy, and Coast Guard; two high school ROTC bands; Texas defense guards; Red Cross workers; AWVS; and the Coast Guard Auxiliary. Once the speeches were over, thousands of curious citizens bought war bonds or stamps in booths near the submarine and climbed aboard the trailer to take a look. All in all, the show made a big hit with everyone.[19]

In early March, construction at the Hitchcock blimp base got underway with the announcement that it would house several blimps, intended to be a formidable threat against U-boats in the gulf. Little did anyone realize that the major offensive by German submarines was almost finished in those southern waters.

The gulf had been free of U-boats from September 4, 1942—when U-171 sank the Mexican tanker *Amatlan*—until February of the following year. Admiral Dönitz had sent them to the Caribbean and Atlantic. "As a result of the strong air and sea patrols and the introduction of the convoy system, the situation which we had long anticipated . . . had now materialized," he wrote in his memoirs. "There seemed to be no justification for keeping boats there any longer, so I withdrew them." True enough, the admiral did pull them out of the gulf, but he redeployed them there in 1943—a fact he failed to mention in his writings. U-boat veteran Peter Petersen said he thought Dönitz sent them back to the gulf to keep the American forces spread out and stirred up.[20]

From February to December, 1942, the British lost their ability to decode secret German navy signals because the Germans had changed their cipher machine. American army and navy bases could locate the U-boats, however, using radio direction finders that tracked the location from which submarines sent signals to their headquarters, although their signals were sent sparingly. Even when the navy had exact latitudes and longitudes for U-boats, its planes and ships were spread so thin that little could be done about attacking.

Historians of the Gulf Sea Frontier noted that the year 1943 "introduced a new type of undersea tactical warfare by the enemy in these waters." The new approach took the form of "long periods of quiet followed by cautious and rapid attacks when the German U-boat commanders were of the opinion they had lulled our forces into complacency." The historians remarked that the first two months of 1943, like the last few of 1942, saw "little positive enemy activity." Actually, no U-boats were operating in the gulf. The only incident of note was the collision of a British warship, HMS *Hunter*, and an American tanker, the *Pan Carolina,* in the fog near the Mississippi Passes. Little damage was done and one man drowned.[21]

Finally, in February, after a seven-month lull, *Kapitänleutnant* Heinrich Schäfer in U-183 quietly entered the chilly gulf waters. His only success was the 2,394-ton Honduran banana ship *Olancho,* sunk on March 11 between Yucatán and Cuba. "The *Olancho* was violating her routing instructions," navy historians wrote. "All independent shipping at that time was so routed as to enjoy coastal patrol to the maximum extent and was specifically instructed to cross the Yucatán Channel during daylight hours only." The banana carrier met her fate by not being escorted and by traveling alone at night.[22]

The Gulf Sea Frontier command anticipated possible renewed attacks off the Mississippi Passes and set up a special series of airboat patrols. The patrols originated from the *Christiana,* a seaplane tender berthed just off Timbalier Island along the Louisiana coast. This 145-foot craft had been built in 1892 and served in World War I as a lighthouse service tender; then was reclassified in 1942 and moved from base to base in the Caribbean, wherever submarine activity was the worst.[23]

At this point U-155 entered the "Golf von Mexico." *Kapitänleutnant* Adolf Piening wrote in his war diary as he cruised along near the west side of southern Florida: "Up to now I have not been noticed. I intend, if there is no [ship] traffic in the present area, to leave during the full moon to go to the center of the gulf and operate at the junction of the steamer routes from New Orleans to Yucatán and from Galveston to Tampico and Florida." He noted that it was impossible to operate in the Florida Straits because of the brightness of the moon. At night he stayed below the surface and came up every morning to check out the situation.

On March 17, a message from headquarters came in asking Piening for a short report on traffic. The commander replied, "No traffic," and sent the message a second time, but it was not received. That night he wrote that he had been forced to send another short signal, and "therefore my presence in the gulf is known." At this time, the American military could not only locate the U-boats by their radio messages but could decode them as well, although the Germans were unaware of it.

Two days later Piening was in the middle of the gulf, south of Mobile. After four days of submerging and surfacing and seeing nothing, he spotted a passenger freighter brightly lit with blue and white lights. "It is hard to see," he said. "Probably Argentine." He let it pass.

The next day he saw a smokestack and made an underwater approach. "At the stern they carry a big banner, but the colors are not recognizable. It is probably Swedish." He chased the ship, then let it go. Shortly afterward, his instruments signaled that he had been hit by a radar beam from a ship.

The following day Piening decided that judging by his observations so far, the gulf traffic was traveling in the shallow coastal waters, because he had seen very little sea or air defense. "I intend to go again to my original position off Florida at the quarter moon and afterwards through the Florida Straits," he wrote.

An outgoing radio message on April 9 informed headquarters that he had sunk a tanker and a freighter off the western end of Cuba and that in the daytime there was strong air cover. He also reported that several times he saw blimps. "All navigational lights as in peacetime, and searchlights along the coast," he observed. The commander told them he had fourteen torpedoes left and eighty tons of fuel.

Piening summarized his observations, concluding that operating in the Gulf of Mexico seemed less than promising, because presumably there was only minor ship traffic. "Oil pipelines to the East Coast are likely to have been finished, meanwhile, as well as utmost use of railroad lines for supply to East Coast," he reported. So the captain knew all about the "Big Inch," the gasoline shortages, and the increased use of railroads for petroleum shipments.

"I saw newly built vessels in the shallow waterways along the coast, but shallow water operations are difficult, because the 100-meter line is always far from the coast," he continued. "At crossroads, the mine laying operations were successful." (The pages from Piening's war diary regarding his two sinkings and minelaying were missing.)

The commander said he stayed at periscope depth during the daytime, except to come up occasionally for a better look. In the middle of the gulf he reported that there was no defense. Piening said his operations between Key West and Havana had been successful, although in the daytime there was air protection but no sea escorts. He thought that ship traffic had been curtailed because of his two sinkings, however. "In the northern part of the Florida Straits, the traffic is probably near the coast," he wrote. "At nighttime I could not go closer than ten nautical miles because of sound detection and search-lights."[24]

The United States Navy knew that an enemy submarine was operating somewhere within the Gulf Sea Frontier during April, and a radio direction finder had fixed its position at twenty-six degrees north, eighty-six degrees west on March 30. U-155 sank the unescorted Norwegian cargo ship *Lysefjord* on April 1, and survivors reported that she went down in one minute. The area had been under patrol that night by a blimp and an army plane, but neither saw the sinking.

Scarcely twenty-four hours later, an American tanker, the *Gulf-state,* was hit by a torpedo, and she sank in one and a half minutes. The ship was carrying gasoline, and the fuel burned on the water so fiercely that observers in the Florida Keys saw the huge glow.

"Every possible effort was made by this Command to locate the submarine responsible for the attacks, and search of an expanding area continued through April 6," historians wrote. "No contact was ever made."[25]

15

U-Boat Disasters

"CELEBRATE HIS BIRTHDAY. It's April 20 [1943]. Let's give him a rousing party—with gunpowder made from the used cooking fats American women have saved," declared an ad in the *Galveston Daily News*. A profile bust of Hitler glowered darkly above the words, surrounded by little swastikas. "Every drop is desperately wanted. Save at least a tablespoon a day. Rush each canful to your meat dealer."

While townspeople made an effort to save grease, the Coast Guard settled in at the Galvez Hotel. "We had seven steel double-deck bunks in each room," said John Kinietz, a recruit. "That made fourteen men sharing one bathroom, and sometimes two rooms shared one. You should have seen us trying to shave in the morning." The second floor was off-limits to the men, because the entire floor was occupied by WAACs and WAVES. "There were about fifteen hundred people crammed into that hotel," Kinietz said, "and it was like a prison." The heat was terrible, and no one was allowed to look out the windows, day or night. Curtains had to remain shut at all times, and a guard watched from the grounds to see if anyone peeked out. If so, they were reported.

John's duties entailed patrolling by foot along the seawall from Stewart Beach to Sixty-first Street, where at night it was very dark. He carried only a billy club for protection and kept a lookout for unauthorized people and submarines. At other times he did patrol duty on the Intracoastal Canal, where the Coast Guard stopped ships coming into Galveston harbor to put seals on their radios so they could not be used on shore. The radios were released when the ships returned to sea—all for security reasons. The guardsmen also checked fuel levels on shrimp boats leaving and entering Pier 19 to make sure they were not carrying diesel oil to enemy subs. "The Coast Guard knew how much they would use for shrimping," said John.[1]

On April 17 Radio Galveston intercepted a message that a British merchant vessel, the *City Castle,* was being attacked and torpedoed in the Gulf Sea Frontier. Investigations revealed that the ship was nowhere near the gulf or Florida, and the navy then discovered that Radio Galveston had been the victim of three or four hoaxes within the past few weeks. Another hoax occurred on April 27. The commander of the Gulf Sea Frontier ordered the Eighth Naval District to conduct a complete investigation in the Galveston area to determine if an illegal radio station might be operating there.[2]

At the end of April, 1943, the frontier commander speculated that one or two U-boats would continue to appear in the Gulf Sea Frontier from time to time. This would force shipping into convoys, thereby causing delays in moving cargoes. The navy assumed that the U-boats would be very difficult to locate and attack, because their tactics had become noticeably wary to avoid detection. In their last three ship sinkings the U-boats were never seen, suggesting that the commanders knew that air coverage was better than ever. Because none was sighted, it was presumed they were staying submerged from dawn until dark and that they were equipped with radar-detecting devices. "These tactics . . . materially reduced the efficiency of their operations; nevertheless, the mere known presence of one or two enemy units in the waters under this Command tended to reduce the total amount of shipping in the area and to force shipping into convoys," the navy said. "It had the secondary effect of increasing our employment of planes and escort vessels." Everything the officials surmised was true.[3]

On April 27, the U.S. Coast Guard cutter *Icarus* sank a German submarine off the Atlantic Coast and captured thirty-three of her crewmen, the first time U-boat prisoners had been taken. About that time the army proudly announced that it had Lightning fighter planes that could cross the ocean "under their own power." A group of two-engine Lockheed P-38 Lightnings attempted the first crossing: one was lost at sea, six others made emergency bad-weather landings and were damaged, and one made it the last three hundred miles on a single engine. One of the world's fastest fighters, the Lightning could now span oceans by means of two 165-gallon gasoline tanks fastened under its wings. New vistas were opening up for greater American victories.[4]

The British, at the end of December, 1942, cracked the German naval code again, and they must have felt a kind of grim enjoyment at hearing the advice and information passing between German headquarters and the submarines. On May 27 the interceptors picked up a message sent from Adolf Piening in U-155. This message told German headquarters that operations in the Florida Straits showed great promise of success between Key West and Havana and that in daytime there was air-escorted traffic but no sea escorts. "Operation in the middle of the Gulf of Mexico offers little hope of success since there is no traffic. It is supposed that there is traffic in the shallow waters along the north and east coast," Piening reported.[5]

Another message, sent to a U-boat, said, "The first night always offers the greatest chance of success." Another: "On moonlit nights, when in contact with a convoy, attempt as quickly as possible to get into shooting position." And: "In the presence of escort vessels employing radar, always try to escape on the surface, as the enemy will in most cases soon discontinue the chase."[6]

On May 29, Admiral Dönitz issued specific orders: "Stay on the surface and fight back in all doubtful cases. Use every means to train your crews for this and make them visualize the dangers of being bombed at slight depths." This new ruling had a drastic effect on some of the commanders and their crews. The admiral continued: "When cruising or standing in disposition, do everything to exclude surprise attacks. Either run on electric engines, in order to hear aircraft ahead of time, or in favorable weather conditions, submerge."[7]

Permanent Order number thirteen came out saying that the danger of being surprised by aircraft using radar, especially at night, was great. "Submarines outbound or inbound in the Bay of Biscay must proceed submerged."[8]

Dönitz advised that the tactics used in coastal areas of America, the Caribbean, and the mid- to south Atlantic, as well as in the open sea, "are to be according to the situation and the decision of the commanding officer." He cautioned U-boat crews to approach lifeboats or rafts for purposes of identification only or when the harmless character of the rafts had been definitely established by close observation. "After shooting down airplanes, do not approach the wreck," he warned.[9]

In a message to Boehme in U-450, headquarters told him to stay together in the water in case he had to abandon ship beforehand. "Tie yourselves together with rags or heaving lines. Take pistols and ammunition along, and fire stars hourly."[10]

U-177 was informed on June 15, 1943, that on June 5 a daughter had been born to Koch, fireman first class. "Mother and child doing well. Congratulations. Flotilla."[11]

German submarine commanders carried with them and knew by heart their U-boat commander's handbook, an invaluable guide for operations and emergencies. One of the primary admonitions for attacks was the motto: "He who sees first wins!" Each message transmitted to headquarters had to give the sub's location, which enabled the high command to keep track of its boats but also allowed the Allies to find them. Another major rule required that commanders carry out attacks with "indomitable resolution and steadfastness, until final success, resulting in the annihilation of the enemy, has been achieved."[12]

If all was lost and capture looked imminent, the captain was to blow up his boat. First he had to place blasting charges around to create several big leaks, then more charges to destroy highly secret equipment (wireless transmitter, sound locator and target detecting devices, periscopes, fire control system, etc.). "If there are not enough blasting cartridges . . . available . . . the equipment must be smashed, so that it becomes useless."

Next, the commander was to destroy secret documents by acid treatment, tying all other documents in a bundle—especially the wireless code data—and weighting the bundles with iron objects for throwing overboard after surfacing. Then he was to prepare a brief message to report to headquarters "the destruction by yourself of the submarine, if it should still be possible to surface."

After the submarine had surfaced for the last time, the commander was to open the diesel head and foot valves and empty all compressed air tanks. "If it becomes necessary to blow up the boat in close proximity to the pursuing enemy . . . the commander should at this mo-

Initial housing of blimps in hangar, largest wood structure in the world, at Hitchcock Naval Air Station, November 30, 1943. Photo courtesy of U.S. National Archives.

ment still be concerned chiefly with the possibilities of hurting and destroying the enemy, and should use his last weapons to try to fight him," the book advised. Then the adversary should be kept in check with all available guns until the destruction of the submarine was complete.[13]

On May 18 a blimp squadron, ZedRon-22, went into commission at Houma, Louisiana, and four days later the Naval Air Station at Hitchcock was commissioned, under the command of Charles W. Roland, USN. The enormous wooden hangar, 960 feet long, 328 feet wide, and seventeen stories high, had room for six blimps and was one of the largest wood buildings in the world.[14]

Twenty miles from Galveston, the new thirty-five-hundred-acre

Naval Air Station gave area residents confidence that they would henceforth be protected by the mighty airships patrolling the gulf. A big commissioning ceremony was supposed to be held in front of the administration building, but a sudden downpour forced the crowd into a nearby storage house for the speeches, because the main hangar was as yet unfinished. One week later the first lighter-than-air, K-62, landed at the new base, and on June 12 Blimp Squadron Twenty-three came in to begin antisubmarine operations. These football-shaped silver balloons, 251 feet long and 62 feet high, cruised at forty-seven miles an hour and had a maximum speed of seventy-five, with twelve-man crews and a range of two thousand miles.[15]

One month later, at midnight on July 18, blimp K-74, from another southern base, was cruising along on routine night patrol. While in the Florida Straits at an altitude of five hundred feet, the airship picked up a blip on its radar. The crewmen took their battle stations and changed course to the direction of the bearing. Then, half a mile to port, they saw a submarine silhouetted in the moonlight, very close to the coast of Cuba and going about fifteen knots. They observed no sign of life aboard as they circled twice, so they decided to attack. When they had come within two hundred yards the U-boat opened fire with .50-caliber guns, and the blimp returned fire with her forward gun.

The command to release bombs was given, but the bombardier, a new and inexperienced crew member, operated the release incorrectly, and the airship sailed over the submarine with the bombs still in their racks. At this point both the blimp and the U-boat began circling, firing continuously at each other. As the blimp passed over the target a second time the bombs again failed to release, the sub kept firing, and the blimp went out of control, rising sharply. The submarine continued to shoot for a few minutes as the airship lost altitude and settled in the water some distance away. Then the U-boat disappeared.

The next day rescue boats picked up nine members of the blimp crew, but the bombardier was missing. He had become separated from the rest of the group and apparently was attacked by a shark—there were several swimming around the survivors.[16]

An intensive boat and aircraft search went on. About twenty-four hours later a PV-1 sighted the wake of a submarine, then saw U-134 traveling on the surface near the spot where the blimp went down.

The plane dropped a series of six 350-pound depth charges, but the first one fell short. The second hit the base of the conning tower and was followed shortly after by a huge geyser of water as it exploded. The last four could not be seen, because the tail of the plane obscured the pilot's vision when he started climbing to regain altitude after the attack. When the plane returned to the area the submarine had disappeared, and the military presumed that it was badly damaged and probably sunk.[17]

The navy called the loss of the blimp "unfortunate, especially in view of the most regrettable failure to drop bombs, whereby the submarine escaped almost certain destruction, nevertheless is partly compensated for by the conclusions drawn from the incident and . . . recommendations . . . with a view toward avoiding the recurrence of a similar happening." No mention was made of the fact that blimps were not supposed to attack U-boats, but the crew had seen no one on the deck and took a chance. They might have succeeded if their bomb doors had opened. The navy decided, however, that the value of the blimps in antisubmarine warfare still appeared to remain unquestioned. Peter Petersen, U-boat control room operator, said his crew members always dreaded the sight of blimps because they knew the airships could radio their location to air and navy forces.[18]

A second submarine, patrolling the gulf from May through July, 1943, was *Kapitänleutnant* Herbert Uhlig's U-527. The submarine made the customary preparations for her second patrol with a trial run, and everything seemed satisfactory. She took on oil, torpedoes, and provisions and prepared to depart from the Keroman bunker. Crew members felt something ominous in the farewell ceremony when the flotilla commander, *Korvettenkapitän* Kuhnke, finished his address with "Aufwiedersehen, Kamaraden," instead of the customary "Heil Hitler." They stood in awkward silence and did not respond until Kuhnke repeated his words. In the early afternoon of May 10, U-527 left Lorient on the flood tide and was accompanied by a minesweeper until dark.

Two days later, at forty-seven degrees north, nine degrees west, the submarine came upon a large ship that had been storm damaged and was being towed back to England. Her corvette escort depth-charged the U-boat about fifteen times, but Uhlig's vessel escaped unscathed.

U-527 continued on a westerly course and passed south of Ber-

Kapitänleutnant Herbert Uhlig, age twenty-seven, commander of U-527.
Photo courtesy of U-Boot-Archiv, Cuxhaven, Germany.

muda to her first operational area. Here she fired two torpedoes in an unsuccessful attack on a fast ship traveling alone. She then went around to the north end of the Bahamas and headed for Florida. While traveling toward the Florida Straits, Uhlig sighted the Great Isaac lighthouse at night and later the glow of Miami, approximately forty miles away. The trip down the coast and through the straits brought no unusual events and was made mostly at night. Every day they saw at least one blimp in the early morning or late evening, and the men nicknamed them *harmlose Tiere* (harmless creatures). U-527 submerged each time one floated into view, however.

About a week after leaving Bermuda the sub arrived in the Gulf of Mexico, where her patrol area was approximately midway between Tampa, Florida, and Havana, Cuba. *Kapitänleutnant* Uhlig had given a gulf chart to the navigator only a few days before, and at that point the crew knew where it was going.

The men, somewhat bemused by the variety of air- and surface craft in the gulf, decided that their patrol was ill-advised, dangerous, and unprofitable for a U-boat. One of the first vessels they saw and couldn't identify escaped on a zigzag path after they fired four torpedoes at her. This was U-527's last attack, and around July 2 or 3 she began her trip home, leaving on the same course as when she entered.[19]

Much later, in June, 1946, Herbert Uhlig wrote a letter to the families of his comrades who were killed as they were returning. He told them that after three years as a prisoner of war in the United States, he had made it back to Germany to inform the dependents of his fallen comrades about the events that had occurred when U-527 was sunk.

"On the way home I had to head for a point some hundred nautical miles south of the Azores for refueling," he began. "Three days ahead of rendezvous point with the 'supplier,' I was attacked by an aircraft which dropped two bombs." One of the bombs did not explode, and the other hit the fast-diving boat close to the conning tower, which caused a bunker to leak. Oil started to drift out onto the water.

Three nearby destroyers saw the oil and roared into pursuit after the U-boat, dropping depth charges. The barrage started at one o'clock in the afternoon and went on until dusk, when Uhlig supposed that the destroyers (he didn't know how many) had departed.

He rose to periscope depth, looked around, and saw the three destroyers in scattered positions. "And then I quickly dove down again. At the same time the destroyers came toward me, and they bombarded me the whole night until quarter of eight in the morning," the commander recalled. After a lull of two hours, Uhlig again went to periscope depth, saw nothing, started the engines, and ordered the crew to straighten things up and get back into normal positions. "Then we saw that everything on board was in a pretty bad mess," he said. "During the trip to the rendezvous point, some of the heavy damages were repaired; meanwhile, the other sub had been sunk, so that I resupplied from another boat, and we started the trip to Lorient together."

On July 23, the helmsman sighted an aircraft approaching a short distance away. "As it would have been too late for submerging, and we were traveling together, I decided to stay surfaced and repel the adversary by the .2-centimeter guns. By doing this, I acted according to an order that in case two submarines are together, aircraft have to be fought above the surface," he explained. When he first spotted the plane, Uhlig, with very little time to spare, ordered the yellow flag hoisted on the side of his boat to warn U-648, the other sub, of the approaching aircraft. He then radioed Commander Stahl to ask whether he had seen the signal. "I am sorry to report that my partner, the other submarine, did something inconceivable to me, and crash dived," he related. "So I was left alone now having to face the enemy. Of course the aircraft attacked my surfaced boat."

Uhlig made ready for his defense and gave the command "Open fire" at the second he thought most favorable. The stern gun blasted off one shell, then quit; and the rear machine gunner was too far right to do any good. "As a result, the aircraft carrier–based bomber was able to drop six bombs without hindrance, well aimed in lowest flight level," he wrote. One of the bombs hit on the port side on the edge of the conning tower and caused a tremendous explosion.

After a few seconds the crew members told Uhlig they could not keep U-527 afloat, and he ordered all his men overboard. Although he was suffering from several injuries, he helped them climb out of the conning tower hatch. Suddenly, "I was caught by the sinking of my boat so that I was pulled under the surface by the suction. Only at a depth of approximately ten meters did I happen to succeed in

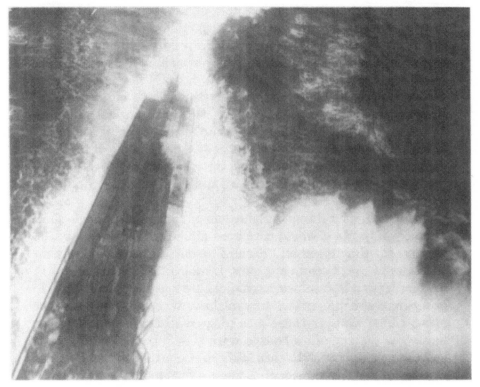

Navy carrier plane attacking U-527 near the Azores, July 23, 1943. The submarine had just completed a patrol in the Gulf of Mexico. Photo courtesy of U.S. National Archives.

getting out of the pull, inflate my life vest and struggle to the surface, where I gathered the survivors and urged them to keep together," the commander recalled. Uhlig said that after a while the first watch officer died, and thirteen men remained. Forty had disappeared.

"The time between the bomb explosions until the sinking of the boat I estimated . . . as approximately forty seconds. I presumed that the fewest of my comrades died by being drowned, and I supposed that the greatest part of them lost their lives immediately by deadly injuries caused by the detonations," he wrote.

Uhlig told the relatives that he was still suffering from the grief and pain of the forty deaths, but two facts consoled him: he could not have acted differently, and he would do the same thing again. "All comrades . . . gave their lives fully believing in the victory of the German forces and did not have to live to see the bitter breakdown. These thoughts not only meant finding solace for myself but also helped make it easier for me to write this letter . . . Assuring you of my deepest compassion, Herbert Uhlig."

The commander gave further details of the sinking when interviewed by his son Ralph fifty years later, saying that the airplane had thrown out a smoke buoy at the attack site to facilitate rescue operations. The destroyer *Clemson* then came up and sent out a rubber dinghy so that the U-boat crew could climb into it, and a motorboat pulled the dinghy back to the ship. The men had been in the water for about three hours, but the water temperature was warm enough for them to survive, being somewhat near the Azores.

"We were taken on board, and each of us received a sea rescue bag. In it were a toothbrush, a towel and soap—everything that one needs at first after being rescued," said the commander. The ship's captain gave Uhlig a package of cigarettes, which he divided among his crew members and himself. "Then they left us alone for a while, because some of us were injured. I had a couple of breaks and open wounds."

In the next few days they were transferred from the *Clemson* to the *Bogue* (the attack plane's carrier) and traveled toward Casablanca. On board the *Bogue* Uhlig and another officer were placed in a large room and his crew in other quarters. A navy lieutenant looked after their needs, supplying them with fresh bed linens, towels, and good food. He also took them for half-hour walks on deck every day and allowed them to visit the ship's chaplain. "The lieutenant spoke a little German, but we spoke better English than he spoke German. All in all, we were allowed to live with dignity," Uhlig recalled.

On the *Bogue* Uhlig met the officer who was the pilot of the plane that had sunk him. "He came to our room, and he shook our hands, and he said in so many words he was sorry, but that one of us, he or we, had to be sunk," said the commander.

When they arrived at Casablanca, they were transported to a field hospital, where doctors examined them and treated their wounds. "We were x-rayed, and they found that I had a skull fracture," Uhlig wrote. "At that place we were treated very well and allowed to go in and out. We were in kind of a holding situation until we had a freighter that could take us from Casablanca to Staten Island. On the trip across we were again treated well and had one steward that took care of us."

They landed at New York, and Uhlig and one other officer then traveled to Crossville, Tennessee, a camp for officers. A train took them from there to Papago Park, Arizona, where they lived in an officers' camp, with other crew members quartered nearby in separate barracks.

Uhlig and one of his fellow officers devised a plan to escape at the beginning of 1945 (their duty was to get out). "We were ready with all the preparations, like cash and civil clothing, and we thought we could stay outside the camp, and so on," he recalled. They had devised a finely detailed plan, figuring they would try to get to San Francisco or Los Angeles and catch a neutral ship that would take them to Germany or a neutral country. "But just before we could carry out our plan, a group at a neighboring camp broke out. I think about thirty prisoners tried to escape," Uhlig said.

Three U-boat commanders, including *Kapitän* zur See Wattenberg of U-162, were among a group of prisoners who were especially strong in their socialistic and naziistic beliefs and had been housed in separate barracks. After much planning, they decided to build a two-hundred-foot tunnel to freedom, starting beneath an outdoor coal box and coming out at a canal that ran by the camp. The digging took many months, and it was later suspected that they used their coal-stove shovels to cut through the rocky ground. The three commanders disappeared into the tunnel on a trial run, emerged south of the camp, and walked 130 miles to the Mexican border. Forty miles into Mexico, prison authorities found them and brought them back to Papago Park, not realizing that the prisoners had used a secret passage. The German commanders then had all the information necessary to put into effect the mass breakout.[20]

The day of the escape, another bunch of prisoners stirred up a demonstration. While the guards were quelling the riot with teargas and clubs, the U-boat men made their getaway. The three commanders, joined by twenty-two others, fled the prison yard. They lugged one-hundred-pound packs filled with clothing, cereals, canned goods, medical supplies, maps, and cigarettes.[21]

"When the guards discovered that the men were missing, they sent out a massive search party with dogs and airplanes and everything it took to catch them," said Uhlig. "This naturally ruined our escape strategy." They never even tried to get out of Papago Park, duty or not.

"We all believed in the final German victory—that is what held us up," said Uhlig. "I even wanted to go home so I could get into action again."

In 1946 Uhlig and the others were sent by train from Papago Park to the East Coast, where they joined many prisoners of war from all over the country in an encampment near New York. There they were visited by a Dr. Törpisch, who conducted intensive denazification interviews with them. Uhlig and friends were then put on board a Liberty ship and sent back to Hamburg. "We arrived at the train station in Altona, and in our compartment we opened a little vent and looked out," he recalled. "The first thing we saw was a very poor worker laboring on the train tracks. He told us how everything looked, and he said, 'In Germany everything is completely ruined, and there's nothing else we can do and nothing else we can accomplish.'"

"It was a very nerve-racking time, a time of terrible hunger," said the commander. Uhlig received letters and care packages from two people: the officer who had taken care of him on the *Bogue* and a farmer for whom he had worked while in the Arizona prison camp. The former U-boat captain, educated solely for navy duty, worked in a refinery for a while, as an interpreter for the British, and as a trainer of German fishermen. Later he had a chance to study dentistry at Kiel University and obtained his degree as a doctor of dental surgery. Never once did he regret his part in the U-boat service or any actions he took at sea. He had done his best.[22]

Close to the time that Uhlig sailed into the Gulf of Mexico in U-527, Galveston was planning another blackout for air raid training. The first week in May, everyone was ready. On a clear, balmy night twenty-five hundred helmeted civilian defense workers stood by to go into action at their posts. Throughout the early evening an air of expectancy hovered over Galveston, as people awaited the practice air raid. Heads of various civilian defense units were gathered in the central control room, where a battery of telephone operators sat, ready to receive reports of violators. When the names came in, the operators would broadcast them over the radio in hopes that the perpetrators would correct their mistakes. The object was to get the island as black as possible so that if enemy planes were ever to appear on a bombing raid, the primary targets would be invisible. After all, if fighters could now cross the Atlantic, the fearful raids were more than possible.

About 8:45 the blue signal went on in the control room, and the first warning siren began to howl. This indicated that householders and store owners were to dim their lights quickly and that "enemy" planes had been detected. Marine industries along the waterfront lowered all illumination, and only the bright lights at the Todd-Galveston Dry Docks threw up a blinding glare on Pelican Island.

At 9:00 the red signal flashed and the second siren sounded, indicating that an attack was imminent. At that point, pedestrians ran to shelters, all cars and buses pulled over to the curb, homeowners turned off their lights, and Todd Dry Docks went into complete blackness, though for only five minutes. The roar of "enemy" bombers flying over the island added a feeling of authenticity and peril.

Police cars cruised through the darkened streets with headlights hooded, casting eerie shadows as they moved. Auxiliary police and regular patrolmen walked about the town looking for unauthorized lights. When they discovered a problem, the wardens called the property owner or knocked on the door to get fast compliance.

At 9:20 another siren wailed, indicating that enemy planes had left the area but that they might return. Instead of another dimout, which the signal called for, all lights flicked on immediately. When the all-clear signal sounded at 9:30, the city was already lit up and back in motion.

At the critical blackout time, W. J. Aicklen, defense coordinator, and his party were standing atop grain elevator B of Galveston Wharves to look over the city. They noticed only one failure, a bright light in the downtown area that reflected on the American National Insurance Building, but aside from this one slip-up, "blackness was very nearly perfect." Aicklen called the air raid test "a great success."[23]

"Galveston did very well in Thursday night's test blackout—much better than in the first test held in January, 1942," wrote the news editor. He commented that it was still hard for some people to realize that the enemy could strike them in their own homes and that experiences like the blackout might help folks envision the horrible consequences of not being ready. "A few stores in the downtown district failed to extinguish their lights, and the resulting glow might have had serious consequences if the planes . . . had been manned by enemies instead of friends," the editor pointed out. He said that even a few lights would be enough to guide the bombers to their targets. "Nothing short of perfection would suffice . . . if the city were called upon to sustain an enemy attack." [24]

16

The 1943 Storm

"THE UNITED NATIONS are meeting with mounting success in their war on the submarine menace," declared the British Air Ministry. In the last ten days of April "giant" aircraft on dawn patrols in the Atlantic had sunk five U-boats, as evidenced by oil, wreckage, and survivors drifting in the waves. "The battles provided new evidence, both of the power of air attack on submarines and of the strength of the U-boats defensive flak," the ministry said. "In all five cases the U-boats attempted to give battle on the surface with their guns."[1]

Admiral Dönitz's strategy wasn't working. The German submarines were being caught off-guard by more and more aircraft zooming down out of the sun or clouds. Because of the constant noise of the waves and wind and their low position in the water, the U-boats had a difficult time seeing or hearing planes approach. Once the enemy came into view, there was usually insufficient time to dive to a safe depth. The admiral's plan for them to stay on the surface and shoot back made the U-boats sitting ducks for aircraft.

The destruction of Herbert Uhlig's U-527 was a perfect example; in addition, the aircraft carrier *Bogue* was one of many carriers achieving great successes over the U-boats. The "baby flattop" was one of the first included in the pioneer antisubmarine hunter-killer groups, and during her career from February, 1943, to April, 1945, the *Bogue* or her escorts and planes sank thirteen enemy submarines.[2]

On June 2 the First Lord of the Admiralty, A. V. Alexander, informed the House of Commons that the destruction of German undersea raiders had accelerated to the point where losses apparently exceeded the number of submersibles being built and that the number of U-boats operating in the Atlantic seemed to be diminishing. Alexander reported that the sinkings in the last twelve months exceeded the number of subs sunk in all the previous months of the war.[3]

On the night of June 9, during a plane-spotting test, a diligent watcher in Madisonville, Texas, sent an emergency message to Houston that a strange plane was in the Houston-Galveston territory. Camp Wallace officers received the signal that "hostile aircraft were virtually right over us."

Officials in Galveston's warning-reception center, after receiving the erroneous message, called Fort Crockett, who advised them to request a confirmation of the report from the warning center in Houston. Before they had time to get an answer, Fort Crockett received another confirmation. With that, the blue warning alert siren went awry and gave out a short "bleep," which was not heard in most of the city. Those who did hear it had no idea what was going on. Then the red alert siren wailed loudly, and most of the air raid wardens donned their helmets and ran to their posts, ordering lights out. Other wardens, not knowing what to do, phoned the chief air raid warden, S. S. Kay.

At first Kay told some of the wardens the signal meant nothing; then, when he learned the alert was genuine, he found that the wardens had gone to their positions anyway. "They reacted automatically to the red alert, which is, after all, what we want," he said.

John Curtin and William Schneider, wardens of zones 1 and 8, admitted they were confused as to what was happening when they heard the second siren. They were glad to see that their sector wardens were on the job and that motorists had pulled over to the side of the road with their lights out.

According to a report from the causeway bridge operator, Camp Wallace, Texas City, and Freeport were completely blacked out. No lights showed at Fort Crockett, and the men there were stationed by the big guns.

In some areas of town no siren was heard and there was no blackout. People living near Thirty-seventh and Seawall Boulevard said that they heard nothing and kept their lights on, and motorists continued to drive around.

The civilian defense coordinator, W. J. Aicklen, said he had been on the job and that all the sirens had blown everywhere. He reported that all defense personnel were at their positions and that the auxiliary police, rescue squads, and doctors had rushed to their posts. Aicklen pointed out that no all-clear had sounded, because the flickering of streetlights was supposed to give that signal. This did occur at 10:32 P.M. He concluded that Galvestonians had cooperated "splendidly" but that there had been some criticism. Somebody phoned up the *Galveston Daily News* and said, "I just want to know what kind of a burlesque blackout that was," and hung up.[4]

Galvestonians received the good news early in July that the new local army air base would begin operations two months ahead of schedule with the arrival of twenty-five B-17 bombers. Major Henry Coles, commanding officer, said that groups of twenty to fifty flying fortresses would be arriving and departing daily from the new base. "The number of planes coming here will vary from day to day," he explained. He said he had talked to some of the flyers in the first group and that they were "all young and alert Americans . . . enthusiastic about their training." Most of them would be flying over enemy territory very soon.

Winston Churchill and the United States government announced that losses of Allied and neutral merchant ships from U-boat attacks in June were "the lowest since America entered the war" and that trans-Atlantic convoys were "practically unmolested." U-boat attacks were now in widely scattered areas. The officials further stated that sinkings of Axis submarines were "substantial and satisfactory" and that every opportunity was being taken to attack U-boats departing from and returning to their bunkers in France.[5]

The navy said that its "baby flattops" were playing a major role in the U-boat battles. One of these stubby, ugly little carriers, accompanying a slow-going convoy across the Atlantic, beat off two German wolf packs. Planes from the carriers sank two U-boats, and forty-one prisoners were picked up by destroyers. Eight other submarines failed to damage a single merchant ship. A few days after this news came out, a plane from the small carrier *Bogue* sank Herbert Uhlig's U-527.[6]

The "Big Inch" pipeline, linking Longview, Texas, and Linden, New Jersey, was now complete. At dedication ceremonies in Phoenixville, Pennsylvania, Interior Secretary Harold Ickes spoke from a flag-draped platform after workmen finished the final weld on the last section. "The nation's problem," he said, "is to assure that our fighting men and machines go into battle confident that behind them there is no break in the line of petroleum supply, no limit to the volume of oil they need for the bloody job of blasting every enemy into unconditional defeat."[7]

On July 25 the temperature on Galveston Island soared to ninety-five degrees, the highest temperature recorded since July 8, 1939. The following day was slightly cooler at ninety-three, and big crowds gathered at Stewart Beach to seek relief from the sultry heat and threatening thunderstorms.[8]

At 1:15 A.M. on July 27, the U.S. Weather Bureau issued a bulletin saying that a tropical disturbance had appeared about seventy miles south-southeast of Port Arthur, Texas, moving west-northwest at ten to twelve miles per hour. It was expected to move inland near Galveston about daybreak. The storm would be accompanied by strong, shifting winds reaching fifty to sixty miles per hour with heavy squalls near the center.

Many such storms had buffeted the Gulf Coast, and each one was as unpredictable as the last. There was nothing to do but get ready, and Galvestonians began their routine preparations: buying canned goods, boarding up storefronts and windows, closing storm blinds, and storing canned food and bottled water. U-boat commander Herbert Uhlig had just cruised out of the gulf three weeks before, little realizing that he had barely missed a hurricane.[9]

The radio warned citizens to secure their vessels and floating property. The county courthouse announced that it would be open for people who lived in low-lying areas, and many property owners from the west end of the island came in to spend the night. Fort Crockett and the navy section base were securing their posts, and men at the air base were tying down their planes. The pilots said they would fly the aircraft out if the storm should become too dangerous.

Weather bureau officials announced that for security reasons they would not issue wind, tide, or barometric readings but that so far the storm did not seem a very serious threat. At 7:30 P.M. on the twenty-sixth, the disturbance lay about one hundred twenty miles south of Burrwood, Louisiana, moving slowly to the northwest.[10]

Then, at mid-morning on July 27, the storm roared down on Galveston. "Severe hurricane . . . near Houston, Texas . . . with winds near 100 miles per hour . . . and gales 50 to 60 miles per hour away from center," reported the U.S. Weather Bureau. "Gales and heavy rains will extend about 200 miles over area west through north to northeast of Houston by daybreak."[11]

Sergeant John Naumczik, Illinois native, and a friend from Ohio looked out their barracks window at Fort Crockett the morning of the storm and said to each other, "It doesn't look too bad—let's go on over to the commissary." As soon as they opened the door they saw a one-by-four plank embedded in a palm tree. That should have given them a clue, but they were confident. "The minute we went out the door, the wind didn't hit us, but the minute we got onto the sidewalk, we *took* it. The wind must have been blowing about sixty or seventy miles an hour, and it knocked us off our feet." The two soldiers crawled and scrambled over to the PX, where they found shelter. They had to spend the night there because they could not get back to their barracks.[12]

The paper described the storm as "widespread and extensive," and some elderly residents described it as "the worst storm since 1915." Many downtown businesses sustained severe damage to buildings, merchandise, and signs; many houses were demolished or had roofs blown off; windows were broken everywhere; large trees were uprooted; and streets were filled with tree limbs and piles of lumber from wrecked homes. Telephone service had practically disappeared, no telegraph service was available, and water pressure was so low that almost nothing came out of the taps. Downtown the water was two to three feet deep, and electric power was out throughout most of the island. The city warned people to boil their water and be careful of spoiled food caused by lack of refrigeration.

The weather bureau's wind gauge blew away at 1:30 in the afternoon when the storm was at its height, but veteran seamen guessed that the wind approached ninety miles per hour at times. Over six inches of rain fell in the twelve-hour period between 7:30 in the morning and 7:30 that night, and at first no serious injuries were reported. That was July 27.

At the new army air base all personnel were evacuated, but a few soldiers who stayed behind in the barracks suffered slight injuries from flying debris. Three and a half feet of water covered the airfield, and no one knew whether the new runways had survived. The bombers had been flown out the night before. The wind velocity recorded at the base was seventy-eight miles per hour at 4:00 in the afternoon with gusts reaching eighty-five. Reports from the Hitchcock Naval Air Station said they had made it through without any damage, and Commander Roland reported that because of their superior drainage system they had had no flooding at all.

Throngs of refugees from the west end of the island crowded into the county courthouse with their pallets and bundles of belongings. They spread them out on benches in the hallways and courtrooms and settled in for the night. Several hundred people were stranded in the Santa Fe Building, and the numbers grew as refugees began to pour in. The building's restaurant was jammed, and the waiters served food until everything was gone. Many people spent their time looking out of the upper-story windows at the effects of the ferocious wind and blinding rain on surrounding buildings. Others played cards or sang favorite songs. That afternoon the wind pushed a railroad gondola car out of the yards at the west end of the city and smashed it into the Santa Fe Building. The car hit a huge reinforced brick pillar supporting the rear of the building, reducing the column to rubble. The pier halted the car's headlong flight, however, preventing it from hurtling into the depot waiting room where many people could have been crushed.[13]

Older residents of Galveston reported that the scene around the Santa Fe depot was almost as bad as it had been in the 1915 storm. All kinds of trucks and cars were stranded in the streets as high water rose to the tops of the fenders and poured inside. The wind ripped doors open and broke windows, and two witnesses reported that the wind tore the fenders off one car and the hood off another.

Particles of gravel from the roofs of surrounding buildings were hurled several hundred feet against the windows of the Santa Fe Building so that people inside thought that sleet or hail was mixed with the rain. Almost all the windows in hotels and office buildings had been blown in, and the William Schadt Building, a three-story brick structure, collapsed into a pile of rubble. Telephone wires were strewn about where poles were down.

On July 29, the local paper announced that twelve people were dead and that property damage was over $10 million. At the height of the storm, July 26, the tugboat *Titan* had left Corpus Christi that Monday morning. Heading for Port Neches and towing a barge, it ran into the center of the hurricane. Crewmen of the tugboat and barge spent forty-eight hours wallowing around in rough seas before most of them made it to shore. The barge men were sunburned and blistered from the salt spray and had had nothing to drink for two days. "We saw two ships on the horizon," recalled eighteen-year-old fireman Robert Boothly. One of his fellow crewmen, named Rooks, put a life raft over the side and said, "I'm going to make a break for those ships. I think I can make it."

Rooks plunged into the billowing waves, went under, and his friends never saw him again. The rest of them leaped from the barge into the water and managed to get aboard the raft. When the fourteen-man crew of the sinking *Titan* jumped overboard to get into their small rubber raft, one of them saw two others thrashing wildly in the sea. He swam over and tried to save them, with the result that all three drowned. The rest of the men floated to shore at High Island, about thirty miles away from Galveston on Bolivar Peninsula.[14]

The *Galveston,* a dredge belonging to the Army Corps of Engineers, was working out near the end of the north jetty on Bolivar Peninsula when the hurricane came in. The turbulent seas jerked the vessel from its anchorage and swept it onto the jetty rocks. The crew stayed aboard until 2:30 the next morning, when the *Galveston* started to go to pieces. When the hull split open, the crew launched a lifeboat, and the older men and those who could not swim managed to row to the jetty. They threw a line to some of the men who had climbed onto the rocks, and those remaining on the dredge pulled themselves with the rope to the jetty.

The Coast Guard, who had heard their SOS, sent out a thirty-six-foot launch. When it approached the wreck site, huge waves threw it out of control and killed the motor. The boat began to crash against the rocks, and some of the crew members were thrown into the water. Others jumped onto the rocks. All of them reached safety, and fifteen minutes later a Coast Guard pilot boat, *Texas,* arrived and picked them up.

The *Texas* had fought its way through the Bolivar Roads channel but was unable to come near the jetty from the south side because of high waves. The commander reported that the waves between the two jetties were "precipitous," causing him to detour out into the gulf and come around to leeward of the jetty. They rescued twenty-four men.[15]

During the breakup of the dredge, some of the crewmen had been thrown into the water wearing life jackets, and they swam and floated to shore. Justice of the Peace Andrew Johnson, who lived ten miles from the wreck area, went out into the storm to check on his sheep and cattle. There he saw a group of dredge survivors staggering and crawling up out of the surf onto the beach. "They were all exhausted and in a state of shock," said Johnson's daughter Barbara. Some of the men were unable to walk, and the judge put them on his horse and delivered them to his house. Other dredge crewmen were not so fortunate, and their bodies washed ashore along with the living ones.

The Johnson farmhouse had turned into a place of refuge on the day of the storm. Pauline Johnson said that some Coast Artillery soldiers stationed in the military instrument towers along the beaches had been picked up by an army truck. The truck tried to make it back to Fort Travis but couldn't because of vicious winds and high water. The soldiers reached the Johnsons' house and parked at the base of the front steps. "The tin on our roof started flying off, and the back of the army truck had a canvas top. The tin was slicing the top of the truck," recalled Pauline. "The soldiers got out and crawled, holding onto whatever they could, into the house."

No ferries were running, and there was no help to be had anywhere. Bolivar residents were stranded. Inside the Johnson house the crowd included the four Johnson children, a couple named Meyers with their son, twenty soldiers, eight men from the sunken dredge boat, Judge Andrew Johnson and his wife, and their farmhand, John Elliott. "The men from the dredge were dazed and injured, and some of the soldiers had been banged up a bit. Mrs. Meyers was a nurse, and she stripped the men down, poured hot coffee and cocoa in them and wrapped them in blankets to keep them warm. They had been in the water so long they were shriveling up," said Pauline.

"During the storm we shoved our big upright piano against the front door to keep the wind from blowing it open," Pauline went on. "The soldiers and the dredge men helped keep everything in place, but most of the windows blew out. Mother had a great big bread box above the refrigerator in the kitchen, and the bread box flew out the window into the pasture." They thought everything else was going out, too. Pauline remembered sitting on the couch as it moved along the floor with the house shaking badly. "The piano kept moving away from the door, and the men kept shoving it back."

After the storm Judge Johnson and Mr. Meyers took their horses to conduct a search on the beach, and they walked back with corpses piled across their saddles. They brought the remains of the dredge men back to the house and put them in the garage underneath. "It was horrible," said Barbara. "That's the first time I ever saw a dead body." [16]

The navy reported that the damage to naval craft and facilities was not as great as had been believed at first. Officials said that no vessels were damaged beyond repair and that a small freighter, a Corps of Engineers dredge, and a tug were sunk. They added that several tankers had gone aground but had been refloated. [17]

Galveston mayor George Fraser asked the Red Cross to put up five hundred tents on school grounds for Galveston construction workers and to let them use the sanitary and cafeteria facilities of the schools. He also requested cots and other tent furnishings for them and announced that a labor force would be organized to begin rebuilding the shattered town. Most people had returned to their homes to begin salvaging their belongings from piles of debris, and only a few homeless were staying at Red Cross centers.

Cleanup progressed as the sun brightened the skies, and thoughts of war were temporarily put aside with repairing and rebuilding. Sodden oleander bushes started to bloom again, and swimmers took to the beaches without much further ado. Galvestonians always made the best of nature's rampages and hoped that the next hurricane would be a long time in coming.

The headquarters of the Eighth Naval District in New Orleans added a hopeful note to the general war situation, announcing that several hundred square miles of fishing grounds in the Gulf of Mexico would now be opened by the navy for commercial night fishing. They warned, however, that the fishing would be done entirely at the fisherman's own risk and that "any damage to a vessel, injury or loss of life would not be the responsibility of the United States government. Whenever a fishing vessel at sea observes or hears any aircraft or surface craft approaching at night, it should turn on all running lights and display its national colors and identify itself beyond a doubt," the navy advised.[18]

By August 5, 1943, the U-boats had sunk nothing in the gulf since March that year, when Adolf Piening downed two ships just north of Cuba. The navy was now cautiously allowing the fishermen to ply their trade close to the shores, but officials still feared more U-boat depredations at Ship Shoal, just west of the Mississippi delta. The German presence was represented by just one U-boat in the summer of 1943—that of Herbert Uhlig in U-527, who patrolled in May, June, and July. In August, there were no U-boats at all. But two more were yet to come.

17

Wissmann and Petersen

BAD LUCK SEEMED TO FOLLOW U-518 from the beginning of her fourth patrol, a trip that began the first week of May, 1943. *Kapitän-leutnant* Friedrich-Wilhelm Wissmann steered his submarine into the Atlantic after leaving Lorient, and shortly afterward a plane zoomed in from nowhere and bombed him, causing extensive damage. Wissmann returned to the Bordeaux bunker for repairs, where his vessel stayed for a month being hammered back into good enough shape to resume its patrol. They left again on July 4, 1943, American Independence Day. U-518's emblem—a lion's head crushing a merchant ship in its jaws—painted on the conning tower symbolized the men's fighting spirit, although they felt somewhat apprehensive about their next mission.

"It was my first patrol," said Peter Petersen, control room operator. "I was stationed at Bordeaux at that time in the personnel pool, and I joined U-518 because another crew member had become ill. It was a last-minute substitution." The flotilla notified Petersen at 7:00 one evening that the crew was to leave the next morning at 7:00 or 8:00. "I didn't have much time to think about it," he said, "and that was really an ungodly busy night trying to get ready." The young sailor ran around getting clothes packed, signing papers, notifying his relatives, and making out his will.

Traditionally, the departure of each German submarine from the French coast was accompanied by great pomp and ceremony, with pretty girls tossing bouquets at the men on board and bands playing jolly marches. A similar scene greeted the boats upon their return, with even more festivities: greetings by Admiral Dönitz, beer, singing, and jubilation. Peter remembered that one of his favorite marches played at the U-boat dockside ceremonies was "Stars and Stripes Forever." He said they had different words for it, but the melody was the same. "When we came home from a patrol, we'd sing funny words to it, like, 'Now we dive into the foaming beer, because U-518's got its ass on the pier.'

"We had a somewhat older skipper named Wissmann, and he was probably in his early thirties," recalled Petersen. "He was very tall, had reddish blond hair, and was somewhat aloof. Our crew members were all young, from about eighteen to twenty-five years old."

When U-518 crossed the Atlantic, the boat traveled at a reduced pace. "We weren't in a hurry—we made slow speed to help fuel consumption, all the while on the lookout for targets. We didn't know what would happen from one day to the next, actually. In those days one didn't buy green bananas," explained Petersen.

The first day out U-518 traveled on the surface. Petersen stayed busy stowing away his gear, learning what his duties were, and becoming familiar with the submarine. There was very little time to worry about what was going to happen. As the day progressed, the U-boat started to wallow and roll in big Atlantic swells, and seasickness struck. "I got deadly sick, and so did many of the crew. We lay in our bunks groaning for hours," he related. At the end of the day the submarine went under, and only then did the crew get relief, for traveling submerged was much smoother. "As soon as the boat started the underwater 'march,' all the guys jumped up and felt fine," said Petersen.

They were constantly driven under by airplanes while crossing the Atlantic and also by radar contacts that they couldn't identify. "You see, we had a device that told us when a radar beam had struck us," he explained. "We didn't know what kind of thing it was coming from, whether it was an airplane, a surface ship or what." When they heard this signal they immediately crash-dived, because radar could not penetrate the water. In the Atlantic, U-518 was the target of many depth charges. "One time we were pinned down by six destroyers for thirty-six hours. It was terrible," Petersen said. "You sat there, and you didn't know whether you were going to be alive the next minute or two, and there was nothing you could do about it."

When an attack came, the immediate orders were for each man to go to his bunk, lie there, and breathe as little as possible to conserve oxygen. They had to whisper if necessary and walk barefoot to keep from making the least sound, which could be picked up by enemy sonar. "Some of us slept, others drummed their fingers, and some of us went to our stations in the control room, because we thought we had a better chance of surviving there," recalled Peter.

"Part of the men were really nervous and some were dead calm, but we all kept looking up at the ceiling. It came from above, you know." Peter said he sat there with the bombs raining down, scared to death. "That was a hell of a problem for a twenty-year-old. But it also taught me something—sometimes when I sat there terrified, I said to myself, 'Man, I've got a *problem* right now and there's nothing I can do about it. I just have to take it.' I swore that if I ever got out of the situation, I would never again bother myself with small things because I could solve them." Peter remarked that afterward, whenever he was having difficulties, he would think of the depth-charge attacks and compare his present troubles to them—they always seemed much less significant.

"We did not hate the Americans, and we did not hate the British," he explained. "We were at war with them, so that was sort of a sporting deal, and we did nothing out of hatred—in fact, we had no animosity at all toward them. They would either kill me, or I better get them first—they were the enemy." Petersen said that the German submarine crews were only indirectly involved in killing their opponents, because the devastation was off at a distance and seemed remote. "We knew when we torpedoed a ship that some people would get hurt and killed—you're aware of that—but never did I see the man that I was going to kill, like the fighter pilots or soldiers did. It was different."

Peter worked in the submarine control room, where the central activities of the vessel went on. "We twisted valves, threw switches, operated the trim and balance of the boat and the oxygen regulation, and generally relayed messages from the bridge whenever needed and communicated with the rest of the boat," said Peter. The men employed in this part of the U-boat enjoyed cooler temperatures than did the rest of the ship. "If you worked in the control room, you had it made," he commented. When the boat was running on the surface the roaring diesel engines emitted terrific heat, which remained in the boat after submerging. To keep the temperature down and conserve electricity, they ate cold food as often as possible in order not to use the stove.[1]

U-518 survived her trip across the Atlantic and on September 23 approached southern Florida, going eight sea miles an hour. It was raining and the visibility was bad. "I intend to go into the Gulf of Mexico tonight through the Providence Canal and the Florida Straits," wrote *Kapitänleutnant* Wissmann. As darkness increased, the commander saw a bright navigation light on Man Island. "All the navigation lights are burning like it is peacetime," he reported. U-518 traveled on, making a slow speed of three sea miles per hour.

The submersible, traveling on the surface at night and underwater during the day, entered the Florida Straits on September 25 and crash-dived when Wissmann observed a small vessel about fifteen hundred meters away. "I guess it's probably an American patrol boat," he commented. That afternoon at 1:15 the hydrophone picked up propeller noises. "Our listening devices were highly effective," said Peter Petersen. "Under good conditions we could detect a ship thirty miles away, because we heard the propeller noise. Not only that, we could identify the type of ship and whether it had diesel engines, steam turbines, or steam pistons, and we could count the propeller revolutions and know whether it was a warship or merchant ship."

Wissmann, after hearing engines nearby, went up to periscope depth to see where his quarry was. A tanker, accompanied by a corvette about five thousand meters away, was fast disappearing. "A shot is not possible . . . and the underwater listening conditions are not very good. We picked up this noise much too late," the commander reported. (At times the salt content, temperature, and layers of water made listening more or less difficult, and the closer to land the submarines were the harder it was to hear propeller noises.)

On September 26 they saw the glow of "very bright lights" and presumed that it was Miami. Wissmann said he saw several navigational lights but could not identify them from his sea charts. "I think that the 'navigational lights' must be coming from the air. From Miami along the coast on both sides I notice air traffic with position lights on, but I'm not going to let them bother me," he stated. He figured they were commercial airline flights. One of the planes came fairly close, and he dove immediately. "You never know," the commander wrote.

As U-518 traveled westward to the middle of the straits, the planes became fewer until finally they saw none at all. Hearing another propeller noise, the captain took his ship up for a look and saw a destroyer, so he submerged as fast as possible. "Then I heard two deep rumbling noises and small vibrations in my boat, like soft blows, almost as if we had touched something," he noted. Perhaps the sub had grazed a shoal or shipwreck, but no further explanation was given.

Wissmann continued through the straits and plotted a course by Havana to get to grid squares DM 18 and 19 (north of western Cuba), where he planned to spend a few days to see what he could see. At that point he mentioned in his log that he was having trouble with his *Wanze* and couldn't seem to get it repaired. The *Wanze* had replaced the Metox, an antenna that rang an alarm when the boat had been hit by radar.

Offshore from Havana, the crew of U-518 could see the city lights but kept on going. "Since the moon is slowly getting fuller, and since I have only seen patrol boats and destroyers in this area, I intend to go from here to DL 61 and 64 [north of the tip of Yucatán]. That will put me at full moon in the middle of the gulf and of the area that has been assigned to me, that is—the steamship routes," the commander noted. The next day, October 4, Wissmann set all the ship's clocks back one hour, because he had changed time zones. (They were still going by German time, and Germany was using daylight savings.)

A message came in from headquarters. Always sent at preset times, the communications were received by the U-boat on the surface with its antenna up. "Wissmann and Schroeter, report your positions." Upon considering his instructions, the commander apparently decided to do nothing for the moment, for there was no mention of a response in his war diary. Hearing propeller noises, he surfaced and saw an Argentine freighter. "Now I'm able to shoot, and I'm not allowed to," he lamented. At that time Argentina was a neutral country, so that sinking one of its ships would have been a disaster.

By October 6 Wissmann had reached his station halfway between Yucatán and the Mississippi Passes. He commented in his log that his "quad" (four-barrel antiaircraft gun) had two nonfunctional barrels on the port side. Then he saw a seven-thousand-ton freighter, but it was speeding off at about fourteen to sixteen knots. There was no way he could catch it. "My position to shoot is quickly deteriorating, and the steamer has zigzagged. A shot is hopeless, and the listening conditions here are very unfavorable because of the differing water layers. Because of this problem, we heard the noise of the steamer much too late," he reported.

Another radio communiqué arrived, telling Wissmann and Schroeter to report their positions that night. "Since I have been undetected so far, I plan for now to keep silent, since I do not want to be detected," the commander wrote. Two days later another dispatch: "Achilles, Schroeter, Wissmann—tonight report your position. See Commanders' Handbook, no. 354." Headquarters needed to keep in touch with all the U-boats for tactical reasons and was quoting them the rule that said: "A submarine may leave its area of attack when under special circumstances or particularly efficient counteraction of the enemy make it impossible for it to stay there. The evacuation of the area must then be reported as soon as possible."

A second message followed a few minutes later, saying, "Becker, Lauzemis, Piening, and Janssen: switch to Amerika II, possibly a radio message relay station for the above-named boats." This could have meant that their radio messages would be forwarded by a German vessel called *Amerika II*. Evidently the home base figured the U-boat commanders were unable to communicate, and the base was beginning to panic because its officers had no way of knowing whether those four submarines were still around.

Wissmann responded to this communication by saying that he was going to give a "short signal," or a fast message, to lessen the chances of being detected. "And then I am going to leave this area at full moon and be in the middle of the gulf at the waning moon," he declared. Just after he wrote this thought, he spotted a steamer going north and started to maneuver to get ahead of it in order to attack. "My radio communication is postponed for the time being," he decided. The ship was zigzagging very little and going medium speed, about twelve sea miles per hour. "I will run with him and attack once the moon gets beyond the horizon," the commander said.

The moon was due to disappear in one hour, and Wissmann ordered all men to battle stations, making ready to fire two shots from the stern tubes. Then, suddenly, the sky darkened and the rain began.

The commander lost sight of his quarry, but he didn't give up, declaring, "I am going to put myself on the attack course and will wait, ready to shoot, because he has to show up again very shortly."

The ship did come into sight, but Wissmann did not like his position, because the distance between them had increased. "Evidently he has just zagged, and again I ran into attack position, and I am 3,000 yards ahead of him. Just as I was ready to turn to port to get ready for the stern shot, the steamer turned toward me," he wrote. The commander ordered his boat turned hard to port in order to fire at the enemy's left bow. "For a moment I thought the ship had spotted me and was trying to ram, but that was not so—he just made another zag," he reported.

The situation seemed perfect. Wissmann shot off two torpedoes from his stern. As he waited for them to cross the water, he noticed that the ship was smaller than he had thought, about three thousand tons, and had a passenger superstructure. When he realized that the two shots had missed, he turned the boat to get positioned to fire another one from the bow. In his log he noted: "My values and numbers were unquestionably right. The distance might have been a little less than I estimated, but however . . . I think the torpedoes ran too deep and went underneath the ship."

Wissmann fired the third torpedo, this time from the bow. Again it missed. "I cannot figure it out," he said. "All the calculations were correct." He again ran up ahead of the ship as it calmly maintained its course. Obviously no one on board had seen him. And again U-518 went into good shooting position and fired an "eel" out of tube 3. Again nothing happened. Four misses. "I am going crazy. I cannot see what I am doing wrong," said Wissmann.

After these four failures, Peter Petersen and his mates discussed the situation, saying they were sad that they had hit nothing but on the other hand were glad that the Americans were still unaware of their presence.

Wissmann and all other U-boat commanders were compelled to spell out their calculations for each torpedo fired so that headquarters could see whether they were making mistakes. On many occasions there were no miscalculations: the torpedoes were merely defective, causing confusion and worry for the captains. Wissmann wrote: "The position of the target was checked by all the watch officers including myself. It is impossible that we were all wrong . . . we all agreed on the values."

"I have given up on this target," he concluded. "And an artillery engagement here in the gulf an hour before daylight is too much of a risk, so I reject that. Endangering the boat that way is in no relation to the worth of the fairly small victory."

U-518 left the elusive steamship, and again the commander checked his figures. Still he could not obtain any different results. "One should have hit. I cannot figure it out," he wrote. He then decided to leave that area and go more toward the center of the gulf. Suddenly he saw a plane in the moonlight and crash-dived. There was no way to tell whether the pilot had spotted him, since his *Wanze* radar detector was not working. "The airplane, especially after the unsuccessful attack, could be a coincidence, but maybe not," Wissmann mused.

On October 12 he proceeded farther north and heard an unconfirmed message that the Azores were now occupied by the enemy. "It is not altogether surprising. However, it is a very disconcerting fact," he wrote. Another message arrived, telling Wissmann and three other captains to start their trip back home. "You cannot be resupplied. Send us a short signal and tell us of your fuel situation."

This came as a surprise, for Wissmann had counted on getting more fuel and food as he was heading home. "It is a very significant signal. . . . I wanted to operate in the middle of the gulf, but that is not possible now," he reflected. He had hoped to stay there until the next new moon and then start his trip back, but that would have taken him just to the refueling point. "Without a rendezvous and without supplies, I have only ninety-eight cubic meters of diesel oil left. If I take into consideration a small reserve for bad weather and so on, with the little remaining [oil] in the bunkers, I must start the homeward journey right away," he decided. The commander said that because things had changed so radically, he had to go through the Florida Straits with a full moon, and that certainly didn't please him. His submarine supply boat had apparently been sunk.

At nightfall on October 15 he saw a light, then another light. Looking closely through his periscope, Wissmann made out a convoy moving slowly on a westerly course. "It consists of six ships and four escorts. I see two flares on the port side," he noted. He weighed his alternatives for a few minutes, then decided that he did not see any possibility for an attack. "It is a very light, full moon, and there is strong sea and air reconnaissance. In the narrow and very well-patrolled straits, I can only run in a northern direction because of the strong currents, and there are American bases nearby, especially at Key West. All these things are running through my head," said the commander. He decided not to pursue the convoy, because he believed he would fail. "I don't have all my antiaircraft guns, the *Wanze* is not working, and my batteries are in very bad shape." So he submerged and left the convoy, continuing his way through the straits.

As he ran along, Wissmann spotted a tanker zigzagging northward. "I'm keeping in touch," he said. But again he could not attack, even though there was no escort with the tanker. "I am in the area of air traffic from Miami and under the eyes of the aircraft, which may be civilian or transport, but I cannot justify attacking the steamer by full moon. If I want to get out of here, I cannot risk being detected, because I need the nights to recharge my weak batteries. . . . It is my personal hard luck that just here, where I am in a good position to shoot, that ships run right under my nose."

The tanker faded away in the distance as the commander said to himself, "I had to make some tough decisions here. These decisions ran contrary to all our teaching about attack, attack, attack." He said he believed he had done the right thing in holding fire because the defenses in the straits were "much more skillful these days and more prevalent." Wissmann noted that the enemy had all the advantages on its side, a fact he could not ignore. "I have to reject any attack plans so I can save the boat for later missions that may be more promising. Since we are expecting new weapons and apparatus, there is a possibility of being much more successful later."

The captain heard propeller noises coming up fast from the stern, went to periscope depth, and saw two destroyers about four thousand meters away, traveling fast. "The destroyers buzzing about give me reassurance that I handled things correctly in the Florida Straits by not attacking," he wrote in his log. Obviously Wissmann was agonizing about his decisions and worried about bringing home reports that showed four misses and no sinkings.

He decided to stay a little farther away from Miami this time, "so that I don't have to contend with those night airplanes doing reconnaissance." As he skirted the coast he observed many planes, but they were mainly patrolling along the shore. Now and then one would cross over the straits going in the direction of the Lesser Antilles. "However, they have reached altitude, so it's not very likely that they can see me," he reasoned.

Wissmann said while leaving the straits that he intended to stay one or two days just east of Florida to watch the outlet, in case he should get one last chance for a sinking. An airplane spotted him, causing a fast dive, so he decided to leave the area. "My intentions are to go home by way of the gulf stream and pass the Azores on the north," he wrote.[2]

On the long voyages across the Atlantic the men, when things were calm, sat around playing cards or chess. Sometimes one of them would bring out a harmonica or accordion and they would sing a few songs. Often they listened to favorite recordings played on the loudspeaker system. They talked a lot, mostly about the females. "Our favorite subject was girls," said Peter Petersen. "We called it *Thema eins*—theme number one." They had no pinup pictures because such things did not exist in Germany at that time, but they had photographs of sweethearts to look at.

Near the end of a four-month patrol, the U-boat began to look far more spacious than it had when it left port. In the beginning, every square inch was crammed with food, tools, ammunition, and supplies. The aft torpedo room, where part of the crew slept, had two torpedoes in the tubes, more on the sides, and a group of them spread over the floor, covered with a wooden deck. The top of the lower bunk was level with the deck, so there was no room to stand upright, and the men had to crouch to move about. Later, when some of the torpedoes had been used, the wooden walkway was thrown away, and the crew could stand up again.

From every ceiling pipe hung bunches of hams and sausages and hammocks of fresh bread. Boxes of vegetables and fruits lined the passageways, and there were so many canned goods in one of the two bathrooms that it couldn't be used for its original purpose. U-boats were definitely not designed for creature comforts. They were simply war machines. "We couldn't walk anywhere—we had to crouch most of the time," recalled Petersen.

The smells inside the compartments grew worse the longer the submarine stayed out at sea. The stench of rotten potatoes, diesel oil, engine smoke, sweat, and other foul odors permeated the stale air. "We got used to it," said Peter, "and they furnished us with bottles of '4711' cologne to freshen up with, but we didn't use it much. We saved it to give away to our girlfriends when we went back home. It was good for one roll in the hay.

"We spent months without seeing the sun, and that caused us to turn slightly yellow. They fed us lemon juice, sugar tablets, and vitamins to keep us healthy, and they probably put saltpeter in our food, because our sex drive was almost nil." When the submarines made it back to France, the men had a hard time walking, and it took a bit of practice to regain their leg strength. "After we had been ashore a day or two, we quickly recovered and started thinking about girls," said Petersen. On the first night at the base there was a huge party for the crew members, and everybody got roaring drunk. The German navy furnished buses to take them to the nearest large town, where they could enjoy the bordellos and beer joints. "We had a lot of money paid to us for the four months at sea—they paid us high wages and gave us lots of bonuses, so we were rich, and we blew it on girls, beer, and presents," said Peter.

Just after U-518 made it to Lorient and Commander Wissmann presented his war diary, the naval high command relieved him of duty as a captain and installed him as an instructor in a U-boat school. This was a common occurrence when the commanders got too old or reached their breaking points. Perhaps Wissmann had been just too cautious—an unacceptable attitude at that time, but he cared very much about his crew and wanted to save his boat. Wissmann's conservatism could have resulted from the fact that eighty-nine U-boats had been sunk in the previous three months, from June to September, 1943. American attacks on submarines were increasing and becoming deadlier—something Wissmann was acutely aware of.

Exuberant at getting back to dry land and having vacationed for a couple of weeks, Peter Petersen and about twenty-five friends decided to escort some buddies, who were traveling back to Germany to visit their families, to the train station. "At that time things in France had deteriorated to a degree that we had to carry arms when we went ashore," recalled Peter. "It could have been a dagger, pistol, or rifle, or whatever we could get hold of, but we had to be armed because partisans were getting pretty bad and we had to protect ourselves."

The crew of celebrating U-boat men, already half buzzed-up with beer and carrying sundry weapons, formed a loose group and started marching down the road toward the train station. Along the way they noticed some pretty flowers in various yards and stopped to pick a few. "I remember one guy in particular who had a rifle slung around his back, and he poked a big fat red rose in his rifle barrel," said Peter. "He was carrying his rifle with a rose sticking out of it."

When they reached the station, the merry-makers saw their friends safely aboard, and within a few minutes the train began to pull out. "I don't know who started it, but somebody said, 'We ought to send them off with a good salute,' and he pulled the rifle off his back and fired. Within seconds everybody had their gun out, banging away. I was looking at this rifle with the rose in the barrel, and the guy didn't bother to aim or anything, he just whipped it off his shoulder, pulled the trigger, and BANG! the rose disintegrated," Peter said.

There was an ungodly amount of firing going on with all the men happily shooting into the air as the train chugged off. When it was out of sight, the comrades were sauntering back down the road when they noticed some German army troops in formation heading right toward them. "Oh, my God," said Peter. "It hit us that they were looking for us. We who had done all the shooting."

The chief petty officer, who was one of the revelers, said, "Hey, guys, line up and we'll go past them in formation, then maybe they won't think anything of it." After a mad scramble they formed several lines and started marching along, singing loudly. "We had almost passed them, and they had their rifles ready, looking for trouble. Later we found out that they had heard all the shooting and thought the French partisans were there to attack a train full of armament and tanks coming in the next day," said Petersen.

The shooters kept innocently marching until they were almost past the army squad when one of squad's lieutenants yelled, "Halt, somebody check this out!" and another ran over and grabbed the heated barrel of a rifle. "The jig was up," said Peter. "They had us."

"We were due to sail the next morning, and the skipper was notified of the incident. Right away he summoned the group and gave us holy hell. And maybe rightly so. We caused a dangerous situation, but everybody's nerves were on edge in those times, and we were letting off steam."

"You drill this crew all night long!" the skipper said to the petty officer. But the commander knew what was going on, and he had a twinkle in his eye when he gave the order. "So they took us out into a cornfield, and the corporals and petty officers, who understood the situation, said, 'Come on, guys, just lie down.' We lay down and waited until night was over," recalled Petersen. "What could happen to us? What could they do to us?" It was imperative that the culprits be available to sail the next day, and the punishment had to be light.

"A lot of those things happened," Peter remarked. "We were young and careless then, and we liked horseplay and fun when we could get it. We never knew how long we had to live. But I'll never forget that rose disintegrating!"[3]

18

Hitler's Weird New Invention

THE YEAR 1943 brought the first major successes for the Allies, beginning in May with Eisenhower's winning campaign in North Africa. The victories continued with Italy's surrender in September and the Allied advance halfway up the Italian boot by mid-October. Meanwhile, American and British planes were hammering away at German war industries and U-boat bases with round-the-clock bombing raids. Germany's big cities came under heavy attack, notably Hamburg, where 77 percent of the buildings lay in smoldering ruins. Berlin was fast becoming a scene of blackened rubble and desolate people.

On September 11 the fuehrer, after six months of silence, delivered a radio address to try to rally the German citizens. Speaking in a grim military manner and without his customary shouting and ranting, Hitler told his countrymen that even though Italy had betrayed them by its capitulation, he considered that to be of little importance. He denounced the "treachery" of Badoglio's government in deserting Germany and vowed he would avenge them by "hard measures." Furthermore, he said that the "ring of steel forged by the German home front will never break." He assured his bomb-weary people that "technical and organizational means are growing that will not only defeat the enemy's air attacks forever but will retaliate with other and more effective means." He did not spell out when or how this was to come about.

At the end of Hitler's sixteen-minute speech he urged his countrymen to believe in victory, but he warned that "every German must know that the fate of many German generations depends on his present attitude." He asked them to bear the Allied bombing attacks with "unwavering heroic resistance." The whole tone of his speech typified the country's new defensive attitude, ignoring the fact that the ramparts of Europe were crumbling under Allied attacks. He mentioned nothing about the great suffering and setbacks of German troops in Russia.[1]

Frank Knox, secretary of the navy, in turn warned the American people that although the German submarine menace seemed to have been checked, there was still great danger that it could strike again. He believed that the Germans were preparing a new offensive.[2]

One week after Knox's announcement, an Allied convoy steaming out of the Mediterranean had just sighted Gibraltar when about fifty German fighter planes zoomed down on the ships. "It was a surprise attack," said Ralph Byers, chief steward of the SS *Anne Bradstreet,* "and the planes came into the convoy low and fast, hedge-hopping over the horizon." He said that in spite of the point-blank fire by the ships' antiaircraft guns, the fighters came in very low over the water in what looked like a suicidal assault. "That's just what it proved to be," he went on.

A big two-engine Junkers-88, roaring in at deck level, banked to launch torpedoes, and as the aft navy gun crew fired, the aircraft seemed to disintegrate in midair, bursting into flames and crashing into the sea. "Meanwhile, the forward gunners were peppering a Heinkel-111, which dove at a Liberty ship next to the *Bradstreet.* Barely clearing the mast, the plane loosed its bombs, but the pilot, apparently distracted by the firing, missed his target, and the smoking plane plunged into the water," continued the steward. At the same time, a Dornier roared in through a wall of gunfire. As it approached, white smoke streamed from the fuselage, but the pilot failed to drop bombs until he was close enough for the gunners to see his goggles.

"Incredibly, these bombs missed, too, and the smoking plane zoomed off so close to the water that the [ship's] crew was certain it also was lost," said Byers. "There were other planes engaged by our gunners in this attack and in another that followed immediately afterward . . . and there can be no doubt that it was the concentrated firepower of the *Bradstreet* that distracted the enemy bombardiers, causing them . . . to overshoot their marks. There is no other explanation for the incredibly poor marksmanship of the Germans, particularly as in two instances the planes were almost resting on the mastheads of the ships."

The twenty-seven men and commanding officer of the Navy Armed Guard crew were all volunteers and mostly in their late teens or early twenties, and only one of them had ever been on the high seas before. "This hectic engagement was their moment, the time for which they had waited," Byers explained. "The score was no ships sunk, two damaged, and ten German planes shot down."[3]

The German navy, suffering grave losses in the submarine fleet, now apparently had turned to new air tactics against the convoys, and the inexperienced pilots could not do the job. Hitler still held out strong hopes for victory, however, banking on the development of secret new weapons.

Prime Minister Winston Churchill, speaking to the House of Commons, described the coming hazards of a new German remote-control bomb. He said that a "parent aircraft" either launched or turned loose a glider that had a "rocket engine of some sort." The parent plane steered the glider by remote control to the vicinity of the target. Churchill did not say how close the glider came to the target, but at some specific height over the target, the glider released the bomb. He explained that the new weapon was being used "at close quarters on ships close to the coast." It was believed that the rocket motors were propelled by one of the more efficient fuels with which German engineers had been experimenting for a dozen years. The last published reports from Germany had described rocket flights of short length, possibly a mile.

Edward Chandler, an engineer and rocket experimenter in Brooklyn, New York, said that the weapon revealed by Churchill was similar to the much-discussed winged bomb or winged torpedo. Instead of a glider carrying a bomb, the bomb would be an integral part of the glider and have wings sufficient to carry it right to the target, driven by rocket propulsion. A remote control could be installed to guide the flying explosive, and its advantage would be a greater speed of impact than was possible with a free-falling bomb.[4]

Two months after Churchill's mysterious comments on the new weapon came the announcement that Germany's rocket bomb was a "weird marvel of ingenuity." According to information gathered by Associated Press reporters in European war zones, the strange self-propelled bomb recently employed against Allied ships was "an engineering and mechanical marvel that flies through the air with the greatest of ease, chases its targets and even behaves as if it had a built-in brain." Newsmen, after interviewing eyewitnesses to the attacks, gave the following details. Apparently there were two types of bombs: one a direct rocket fired from the aircraft simply to give it more accuracy and speed than a regular bomb, and the other a real "Buck Rogers" sort of device. "It is armor-piercing with a delayed-action fuse and is estimated to weigh 3,000 to 3,500 pounds. Its body is like a torpedo, about twenty-five inches in diameter and a dozen feet long, and it has an eight-foot wingspan and tail which make it look like a midget airplane," the reporters explained. They said that in flight it had a fiery glow at its base and emitted whitish smoke. Sailors doing watch duty saw the first ones and identified them as burning aircraft.

The missiles were released from high-flying planes at ten thousand to twenty thousand feet, probably to give them greater protection from antiaircraft fire and to allow the bomb-aimer more time to line up the target. Once released, the bomb glided in the same direction as the parent aircraft at a speed estimated at four hundred miles per hour. The flight path was almost horizontal, having only a slight downward slope. Over the target it suddenly dipped into a vertical dive and hurtled earthward, hitting with "gigantic force and penetrating power."[5]

The new "secret weapon" Hitler had hinted about was the Hs-293, one of a wide variety of rocket-powered guided missiles that reached completion before the end of the war. Next to come was the V-1, a pulse-jet–powered, pilotless aerial bomb; and last of all the V-2, a powerful missile the Germans used against Paris and London in 1944.[6]

As U-boats disappeared by the dozens, Secretary Knox said he thought the Germans were calling in their submarines to install more antiaircraft guns on them (and they were), but he emphatically stated that the battle of the Atlantic had not been won. "It's as sure as sunrise that they will be back in here again," he warned. "There is no reason to believe that we have disposed of the submarine menace."[7]

The news reported that the navy's antisubmarine campaign had "chilled" the fighting spirit of German sailors. "We have information that the Nazis already are being forced to draft the U-boat crews," announced Rear Admiral Francis Low. "Under such conditions, the quality of performance of officers and crews alike is bound to decrease and give unacceptable performance." True enough, experienced submariners were disappearing faster than they could be replaced, and in the latter months of the war, few U-boat commanders were high-ranking officers. Admiral Low warned that even though the German submarine fleet was being hit hard, it was "far from being driven from the seas."[8]

As reports continued of U-boat attacks on convoys with "new and more deadly" torpedoes, colorful stories appeared in U.S. newspapers describing declining morale and mutinous tendencies among German submarine crews in northern Norway. "Discipline is very bad, and the marines seem to neglect their officers completely when they are ashore," reported the Norwegian legation, who supposedly obtained its information from the townspeople of Tromsoe. "In the middle of the night, heavy fighting between U-boat officers and their crews can often be seen in the streets." The legation claimed that six boat crews had refused to go to sea and that two hundred officers and men had been sent to prison at Oslo. Another report said that during the trouble in June at Tromsoe, one crew member threw two pajama-clad officers into a fjord. It may have been true that some of the crewmen went to prison for refusing to go to sea, but the rest of the tales had been greatly exaggerated.[9]

"Axis take note," read the caption of a photograph in the Galveston paper on October 11. The picture, showing an endless line of Liberty ships, gave the reader a grand impression of United States shipping might. In eleven days the California Shipbuilding Corporation had finished ten Liberty ships, a new record for construction speed. The previous record time was thirty-six hours to build a ship, and now the time was down to twenty-six incredible hours.

Following reports that the German submarine war was going downhill, the War and Navy departments, War Production Board (WPB), and Office of Civilian Defense stated that the successful campaign against the enemy U-boats had now made dimouts on the Atlantic and Gulf coasts unnecessary. Two weeks earlier Lieutenant General Emmons, head of the Western Defense Command, had announced the relaxing of dimout regulations along the Pacific Coast. For Galveston and the gulf states, the news came as a big relief. Lights could be brighter starting November 1, but the War Department was requesting that the dimout be followed by a "brownout"—a voluntary semi-dimout to conserve fuel.

The brownout program was part of a nationwide campaign by government and industry to conserve critical resources such as electricity, coal, oil, and gas. Even though the rules were relaxing on extreme darkness, people were urged to eliminate unnecessary lighting on their storefronts and in homes and factories. The WPB and other government agencies warned that unless people cooperated, they would initiate mandatory regulations of night lighting. Further, they said that cities must stay prepared to go back into total darkness if the submarine menace again became serious, and they should remember that the army and navy blackout rules were still in effect.[10]

The Galveston civilian defense chiefs informed island citizens that automobiles would now be allowed to use their full headlights anywhere in the city and county, on Seawall Boulevard, and on the beaches. There would be no more dimout on the beachfront, and all streetlights could be lighted with full candlepower, provided they were shielded at the top and could be turned off in five minutes. All lights and signs on the street floor of buildings could burn at full brightness and lighting on upper floors could be turned on, provided they also could be extinguished in five minutes. Night football and baseball games would be permitted if the stadium lights could be put out quickly. Such things as floodlighting of buildings, illuminated monuments, lighted billboards, and other "unwarranted lighting" would not be allowed.

The local police gave a big sigh of relief at hearing the announcement of dimout curtailment. Patrol cars cruised their districts along Seawall Boulevard with their headlights blazing for the first time in many months. Sergeant W. A. Van Zandt remarked that things looked a lot more pleasant—several beach cafes had switched on their neon signs, Murdoch's Pier glowed brightly, and window lights shone from the Galvez and Buccaneer hotels. Even the moon came up in luminous splendor, reflecting on the shadowy gulf waters. After a year of darkness, the island town once again started to resemble the gay and sparkling Galveston it once was.[11]

As Gulf Coast and other American shipyards produced hundreds of tankers and transport ships, the U-boats were disappearing faster than German shipyards could replace them. Although the German submarines were still scoring a few successes, their end was in sight, and with more and more Allied victories in Europe, the number of Germans taken prisoner increased every month in 1943.

In 1942 German army, navy, and air crews captured from various theaters of war began to arrive in the United States in small numbers. By the end of the year, 512 of them, along with 1,317 Italians and 52 Japanese, were living behind barbed wire. In October, 1943, when U-518 left the Gulf of Mexico, the German POWs numbered 119,401 and were divided among base camps on U.S. military reservations. Every state in the union except Nevada, Montana, North Dakota, and Vermont received these unfortunates, but Texas had almost twice as many camps as any other state. In Texas the fourteen bases included Fort Crockett at Galveston, and other temporary branch camps were set up to provide prisoner labor where there were shortages of men—in forestry and agriculture.[12]

At first the War Department ruled that no camps could exist within one hundred fifty miles of the Gulf Coast, but this order was soon changed. A lack of labor for the rice harvest in Texas and the sugar-cane harvest in Louisiana made extra workers a necessity. The Lone Star State had about thirty-five thousand acres of rice that would go to ruin if not gathered soon, plus timber that was needed for the war. Because of the demand for agricultural workers, the prisoners were transported to Texas army camps and put to work in the woods and fields.

Those lucky enough to be sent to Fort Crockett in Galveston fared better. A group of 165 Germans arrived on November 15, 1943, and were assigned to their compound, which lay within the boundaries of Seawall Boulevard, Fifty-third Street, Avenue Q, and Fifty-seventh Street. It was surrounded by barbed-wire fencing ten feet high with watchtowers and searchlights. The men lived in groups of nineteen, in tar paper–covered barracks hastily thrown up to house them. The buildings looked like all the other army facilities except for the watchtowers and had concrete slab floors, rows of cots and footlockers, and a potbellied stove in the middle. In fall, 1943, the compound contained a kitchen and mess hall, recreation room, offices, canteen, shower house "with all the hot and cold water desired," and a laundry room with washtubs.[13]

German prisoners of war hoeing tomatoes at Alvin, Texas, about 1943–45. Photo courtesy of U.S. National Archives.

In a report written by inspector P. Schnyder on March 15, 1944, he commented that the educational level of the Germans was "very poor." None of them had enough education to teach the others, so they had to study on their own in small groups. "They are trying to learn English, and a class of fifteen is studying agronomy, based on the *Soldatenbriefe*, letters sent to them by the German Red Cross. Anyway, as most of the prisoners perform manual labor, they have little time for study," he noted.[14]

Most of the men worked at various jobs: repairing automobiles used at the camp, hauling loads to the warehouse, helping in the bakery, and cleaning and tending the grounds. For their labors the army paid them eighty cents a day in the form of coupons, which they could spend at the canteen. Galvestonians, driving past the prison yard, were not allowed to stop. Even a motorist with a flat tire was expected to keep on going. MPs marched up and down guarding the place, and passersby could see the German prisoners working. They were constantly mowing and raking, and many Galvestonians commented on the tanned good looks of the young men. "They were just beautiful," said Sara Stubbs, a resident.[15]

One day a group of prisoners, dressed in their faded denim pants and jackets with a big white "P" on the back, were mowing and cleaning the grounds at the army airfield. Across the road at the municipal golf course Dr. Edward Randall and friends were having a game of golf, and the doctor lobbed a ball over the fence into the airfield. "Das ball, das ball, bitte," he yelled at the prisoners, trying to remember a few German words. They looked at him, and one ran to pick up the errant ball. As he threw it back over the fence, the prisoner called, "Here it is, sir."[16]

There was no infirmary inside the stockade, but excellent medical and dental care was given to the prisoners at the post hospital. At the canteen, the prisoners used their coupons to buy cold drinks, cigarettes, and three beers a week. The men could attend a weekly movie, and the camp had a large recreation area for sports, both indoors and outdoors. Because most of them had no way to spend all their coupons at the base, they took up collections and donated $442.00 to the YMCA, who had given them books, and $353.07 to the International Committee of the Red Cross.

At the library, two hundred fifty books in German were in constant use, and the post chaplain conducted religious services once a week. The prisoners formed an orchestra and a drama group, with the promise that the camp commander would buy them some musical instruments. All prisoners said they were "well satisfied with the food and treatment at the camp," according to the Germans' spokesman, *Oberfeldwebel* (top sergeant) Martin Wagner.

Five hundred POWs arrived at Camp Wallace, in nearby Texas City, in October, 1943, just before the first arrivals at Fort Crockett. These were noncommissioned officers and enlisted men who had surrendered in Africa, Sicily, and Russia. Their situation at the camp was similar to the one at Galveston in that the men worked repairing trucks, building furniture, cutting beef, mowing grass, repairing and painting automobiles, making seat covers with discarded tents, and performing other activities in compliance with the Geneva Convention.

A news reporter touring the camp in 1943 said that most of the prisoners were "extremely satisfied" and that the American commander and guards ate with their charges. A later news report commented that the Germans had two pianos to play, and "while they delight in the works of German composers, they also enjoy boogie woogie music and many are now lustily singing 'Pistol Packin' Mama.'"[17]

There was some violence, however. Four Germans carried out a "holy-ghost beating" of five other prisoners and were sent to Fort Crockett for a court-martial. Later, in January, 1945, fourteen violent Nazis attacked five anti-Nazis and attempted to kill them with stools and other makeshift weapons. Some of the troublemakers were to be court-martialed in Galveston and the rest sent to other camps. The political dissention in some of the prison compounds sparked several incidents of brutal beatings and murders, and the violent Nazis had to be separated from the rest. But for the most part, the POW camps at Camp Wallace and Fort Crockett enjoyed a peaceful existence, and Galvestonians curiously watched them at work, playing football and soccer, and swimming in the gulf.[18]

The end of 1943 was near, bringing bright hopes for the end of war in Europe. Admiral Dönitz, however, with typical German persistence, sent one last U-boat into the Gulf of Mexico in November, 1943, just after dimout regulations were lifted. U-193, patrolling off the southeastern Florida coast on December 3, encountered the *Touchet*, a brand-new tanker. She was making her way toward the Yucatán Channel and was headed for New York with one hundred forty thousand barrels of heating oil.

By this time it was assumed that the submarines had been driven off, since no attacks had occurred since March, eight months earlier. With blimps flying out of Hitchcock and Houma, airplanes equipped with radar, and two hunter-killer groups of ships, the commander of the Gulf Sea Frontier had lowered the "A" category of the frontier to "B."

Captain J. T. Bird's tanker had left the port of Houston on December 3 and had reached mid-gulf just after midnight. At 2:30 A.M. Jack

Dodendorf, one of twenty navy armed guards, had just come off duty and was about to lie down when a thunderous roar almost knocked him off his feet. A torpedo had struck. The captain put the engines in reverse to stop the ship and ordered everyone to abandon the vessel.

Dodendorf and Harry Glazebrook, gunner's mate, ran up to the bridge to man the 20-millimeter guns; from there they could see the U-boat on the surface. A second crash came as another torpedo hit, then a third one went off in the engine room. The *Touchet* began to sink rapidly, and there was now only one lifeboat left—the other five had been lowered with the rest of the crew. "It was all tangled up," recalled Dodendorf. He and Glazebrook took out their knives and cut it loose as fast as they could. Clad only in their trousers, the two flipped a coin to decide who should run back to get more clothes. Dodendorf won the toss and dashed back to pick up a few things from their seabags. He then ran back to the deck, where they threw on their jackets, and the two men jumped in the water and climbed into the lifeboat. "We had a hard time rowing away from the sinking ship, because the suction was terrible," Dodendorf said.

That night and all the next day they rowed around, picking up survivors and empty powder cases from the big guns. The water burned for a long time after the *Touchet* had disappeared. Dodendorf and Glazebrook put up the mast and sails in their boat, formed a small convoy with two other lifeboats, and headed north toward Florida. For three days they shivered and looked for help, trying to keep up their spirits. Several ships passed in the distance and they sent up flares, but none of the vessels stopped, fearing a submarine trap.

"It was extremely cold at night and extremely hot in the daytime. We kept sending up flares, and finally a navy plane spotted us and flew off to find a ship," said Dodendorf. The plane located a Norwegian freighter, the SS *Lillemor,* and dropped a message telling the captain to go and rescue the men in the lifeboats. "But he refused," recalled Dodendorf. "So the navy pilot fired a shot across his bow and forced him to come and pick us up. We were finally saved." [19]

Out of eighty crewmen on the *Touchet* three were injured and ten died. They were the last merchantmen to meet a submarine-inflicted death in the Gulf of Mexico during World War II. U-193 went on back to Germany and patrolled for two more years, then disappeared. At the final tally, the German submarines had scored fifty-six sinkings and damaged fourteen merchant ships in the gulf, a major Axis victory that was never known.

Afterword

The U-Boats Scored

THEIR GREATEST VICTORIES in the gulf at the beginning of their surprise visit. Each time a submarine returned to the French bunkers, her commander brought vital information to the German navy about shipping routes and U.S. defenses. Hence the next boats to go over knew more than those before them, and they used the knowledge well. Even after the United States organized convoys and improved offensive maneuvers, the U-boats continued to patrol the gulf looking for targets. The American navy detected them but kept quiet about it because war news censorship had come into play. Galvestonians had no idea that German submarines had roamed the gulf waters almost continually until the end of 1943.

It is interesting to note that the tonnage of ships sunk by the U-boats began with the largest, at ten thousand BRT (Brutto Registered Tons, the net carrying capacity of a ship), and ended with sixteen-ton fishing boats. At the end, there were so few vessels traveling singly that the Germans went after any they could find. Commanders who went home with a score of zero often became submarine training instructors.

Fifty years later, when the great exploits of the German navy in the Gulf of Mexico had been largely forgotten, a reminder appeared. Fuel oil started bubbling to the surface from the wreckage of a World War II victim. "We're 99 percent sure it's from the SS *Heredia*," said a Coastguardsman. The ship, carrying passengers, bananas, and coffee, had been hit by three torpedoes from U-506 and went down about thirty-five miles off the Louisiana coast. The Coast Guard said they would not require the owners, United Fruit Company, to foot the cleanup bill.

The old ghosts are now forgotten, brought to mind only as shipwrecks on the sea charts. Other things have changed, too. In 1991 a group of German and American U-boat–history lovers toured a submarine training school in Wilhelmshaven, Germany. Observing the young trainees in their mock control room, U-boat veteran Peter Petersen asked one of them, "Why are you taking her down so slowly?" "We don't crash-dive any more, sir," came back the answer. "There is no need."

And so the days of dramatic undersea warfare were over. It was a war of men against men, a war of developing technology, a war of personal skill and daring. The stories go on and on, priceless because they happened at the end of an era. Old enemies are reaching out to each other—trading experiences, revelations, and laughs—and finding new appreciation for their days of combat. Something good has come out of it all.

Appendix

Vessels torpedoed or sunk in the Gulf of Mexico. Listed by U-boats, in order of their appearance in the gulf:

U-507 (*Korvettenkapitän* Harro Schacht)

5/4/42 Freighter *Norlindo*, DM 1739 (sunk) 24.57 N, 84.00 W [American].

5/5/42 Tanker *Munger T. Ball*, DM 1467 (sunk) 25.24 N, 83.46 W [American].

5/5/42 Tanker *Joseph M. Cudahy*, DM 1433 (sunk) 25.57 N, 83.57 W [American].

5/6/42 Freighter *Alcoa Puritan*, DA 9393 (sunk) 28.35 N, 88.22 W [American].

5/7/42 Freighter *Ontario*, DB 7426 (sunk) 28.11 N, 87.32 W [Honduran].

5/8/42 Freighter *Torny*, DB 7888 (sunk) 26.40 N, 86.40 W [Norwegian].

5/12/42 Tanker *Virginia*, DA 9347 (sunk) 28.53 N, 89.29 W [American].

5/16/42 Freighter *Amapala*, DL 2211 (sunk) 26.30 N, 89.12 W [Honduran]. Note: U-507 fired some machine-gun salvos to stop *Amapala*. Partially sank her by opening sea valves. Ship later salvaged.

U-506 (*Kapitänleutnant* Erich Würdemann)

5/10/42 Tanker *Aurora*, DA 9288 (sunk) 28.35 N, 90.00 W [American].

5/13/42 Tanker *Gulfpenn*, DA 9546 (sunk) 28.29 N, 89.17 W [American].

5/14/42 Tanker *David McKelvy*, DA 9536 (sunk) 28.30 N, 89.55 W [American].

5/16/42 Tanker *William C. McTarnahan*, DA 9521 (damaged) 28.52 N, 90.20 W [American].

5/16/42 Tanker *Sun*, DA 9521 (damaged) 28.41 N, 90.19 W [American].

5/17/42 Tanker *Gulfoil*, DA 9561 (sunk) 28.08 N, 89.46 W [American].

5/19/42 Freighter *Heredia*, DA 97— (sunk) 28.53 N, 91.03 W [American].

5/20/42 Tanker *Halo*, DA 9553 (sunk) 28.42 N, 90.08 W [American].

U-103 (*Oberleutnant* zur See Werner Winter)

5/19/42 Freighter *Ogontz*, DL 6271 (sunk) 23.30 N, 86.37 W [American].

U-106 (*Kapitänleutnant* Hermann Rasch)

5/21/42 Tanker *Faja de Oro*, DM 4157 (sunk) 23.30 N, 84.24 W [Mexican].

5/26/42 Freighter *Carrabulle*, DL 2168 (sunk) 26.18 N, 89.21 W [American].

5/27/42 Freighter *Atenas*, DL 25— (damaged) 25.50 N, 89.05 W [American]. Note: Only U-106 was in this area, but there was no attack report filed.

5/28/42 Freighter *Mentor*, DL 3746 (sunk) 24.11 N, 87.02 W [British].

6/1/42 Freighter *Hampton Roads*, DL 6538 (sunk) 22.45 N, 85.13 W [American].

U-753 (*Korvettenkapitän* Alfred Manhardt von Mannstein)

5/20/42 Freighter *George Calvert*, DL 6639 (sunk) 22.55 N, 84.26 W [American].

5/20/42 Freighter *E. P. Theriault*, DL 66— (damaged) 24.30 N, 83.55 W [British].

5/25/42 Tanker *Haakon Hauan*, DA 92— (damaged) 28.45 N, 90.03 W [Norwegian].

5/27/42 Tanker *Hamlet*, DA 9423 (sunk) 28.32 N, 91.30 W [Norwegian].

U-158 (*Kapitänleutnant* Erich Rostin)

6/7/42 Freighter *Hermis*, DM 4174 (sunk) 23.08 N, 84.42 W [Panamanian].

6/7/42   Tanker *Sheherazade*, DA 9180 (sunk) 28.41 N, 91.20 W [Panamanian].

6/11/42   Tanker *Cities Service Toledo*, DA 8368 (sunk) 29.02 N, 91.59 W [American].

6/17/42   Freighter *San Blas*, DK 3445 (sunk) 25.26 N, 95.33 W [Panamanian].

6/17/42   Tanker *Moira*, DK 2566 (sunk) 25.35 N, 96.20 W [Norwegian].

6/23/42   Freighter *Henry Gibbons*, DL 2918 (sunk) 24.— N, 89.— W [American].

U-67 (*Kapitänleutnant* Günther Müller-Stockheim)

6/16/42   Freighter *Managua*, DM 5136 (sunk) 24.05 N, 81.40 W [Nicaraguan].

6/20/42   Tanker *Nortind*, DA 9296 (damaged) 28.41 N, 89.34 W [Norwegian].

6/23/42   Tanker *Rawleigh Warner*, DA 9349 (sunk) 28.53 N, 89.15 W [American].

6/29/42   Tanker *Empire Mica*, DB 4987 (sunk) 29.25 N, 85.17 W [British].

7/6/42   Motorship *Bayard*, DA 9326 (sunk) 29.35 N, 88.44 W [Norwegian].

7/7/42   Tanker *Paul H. Harwood*, DA 6997 (damaged) 29.26 N, 88.38 W [American].

7/10/42   Tanker *Benjamin Brewster*, DA 9252 (sunk) 29.05 N, 90.05 W [American].

7/13/42   Tanker *R. W. Gallagher*, DA 9198 (sunk) 28.50 N, 91.05 W [American].

U-129 (*Kapitänleutnant* Hans Witt)

6/27/42   Tanker *Tuxpan*, DK 8259 (sunk) 20.15 N, 96.20 W [Mexican].

6/27/42   Tanker *Las Choapas*, DK 8299 (sunk) 20.15 N, 96.20 W [Mexican].

7/1/42   Freighter *Cadmus*, DK 6636 (sunk) 22.50 N, 92.30 W [Norwegian].

7/2/42   Freighter *Gundersen*, DK 4146 (sunk) 23.33 N, 92.35 W [Norwegian].

7/4/42   Tanker *Tuapse*, DL 6819 (sunk) 22.13 N, 86.06 W [Russian].

7/19/42   Freighter *Port Antonio*, DM 4153 (sunk) 23.39 N, 84.00 W [Norwegian].

U-154 (*Korvettenkapitän* Walther Kölle)

7/6/42   Trawler *Lalita*, DL 6471 (sunk) 21.45 N, 86.40 W [Panamanian].

U-571 (*Kapitänleutnant* Helmut Möhlmann)

7/8/42   Tanker *J. A. Moffett, Jr.*, DM 2824 (sunk) 24.47 N, 80.42 W [American]. (Towed in but a total loss.)

7/9/42   Freighter *Nicholas Cuneo*, DM 4328 (sunk) 23.54 N, 82.33 W [Honduran].

7/15/42   Tanker *Pennsylvania Sun*, DM 1976 (damaged) 24.05 N, 83.42 W [American].

U-84 (*Kapitänleutnant* Horst Uphoff)

7/13/42   Freighter *Andrew Jackson*, DM 5283 (sunk) 23.32 N, 81.02 W [American].

7/16/42   Freighter (no name), DL 6415 (torpedoed and left burning).

7/19/42   Freighter *Baja California*, DM 1651 (sunk) 25.14 N, 82.27 W [Honduran].

7/21/42   Freighter *William Cullen Bryant*, DM 1994 (damaged) 24.08 N, 82.23 W [American].

7/21/42   Tanker (no name), DM 1994 (damaged).

U-171 (*Kapitänleutnant* Günther Pfeffer)

7/26/42   Freighter *Oaxaca*, DA 7625 (sunk) 28.23 N, 96.08 W [Mexican].

8/13/42   Tanker *R. M. Parker*, DA 9192 (sunk) 28.50 N, 90.42 W [American].

9/4/42   Tanker *Amatlan*, DK 5165 (sunk) 23.27 N, 97.30 W [Mexican].

U-508 (*Kapitänleutnant* Georg Staats)

8/6/42   Freighter (no name), DM 4336 (damaged).

8/6/42   Freighter (no name), DM 4336 (damaged).

8/12/42   Freighter *Santiago de Cuba*, DM 2748 (sunk) 24.20 N, 81.50 W [Cuban].

8/12/42   Freighter *Manzanillo*, DM 2748 (sunk) 24.20 N, 81.50 W [Cuban].

8/18/42   Tanker (no name), DM 2747 (damage uncertain).

8/18/42   Freighter (no name), DM 2747 (damage uncertain). (Staats missed both ships, but he heard detonations in the convoy.)

U-166 (*Kapitänleutnant* Hans-Günther Kühlmann)

7/16/42   Trawler *Gertrude*, (sunk) 23.32 N, 82.00 W [American].
7/30/42   Freighter *Robert E. Lee*, (sunk) 28.40 N, 88.42 W [American].

U-183 (*Kapitänleutnant* Heinrich Schäfer)

3/11/43   Freighter *Olancho*, DL 6921 (sunk) 22.08 N, 85.14 W [Honduran].

U-155 (*Kapitänleutnant* Adolf Piening)

4/2/43   Freighter *Lysefjord*, DM 4288 (sunk) 23.09 N, 83.24 W [Norwegian].
4/3/43   Tanker *Gulfstate*, DM 2883 (sunk) 24.26 N, 80.18 W [American].

U-193 (*Korvettenkapitän* Hans Pauckstadt)

12/3/43   Tanker *Touchet*, DL 26—(sunk) 25.50 N, 86.30 W [American].

Months of gulf patrols of all U-boats (asterisk = attacks or sinkings that month):

1942
April (end)   U-507
May   U-506,* 106,* 504, 507,* 753,* 103*
June   U-506, 158,* 504, 753, 67,* 129,* 106*
July   U-134, 154,* 157, 509, 67,* 171,* 129,* 571,* 84,* 166,*
August   U-166,* 508,* 509, 600, 171*
September   U-171*

1943
February   U-183
March   U-183,* 155*
April   U-183, 155
May   U-527
June   U-527, 84
July   U-527
August   None

September   U-518
October   U-518
November   U-193
December   U-193*

List of all U-boats that went into Gulf of Mexico and number of ships attacked or sunk:

U-103	1	U-509	0
U-508	6	U-171	3
U-507	8	U-571	3
U-506	8	U-84	5
U-106	5	U-166	2
U-504	0	U-600	0
U-753	4	U-183	1
U-67	8	U-155	2
U-129	6	U-527	0
U-134	0	U-518	0
U-154	1	U-193	1
U-157	0		
U-158	6	24	70 ships
			(56 sunk, 14 damaged)

Note: Information taken from Jürgen Rohwer, *Axis Submarine Successes: 1939–1945.*

Notes

Chapter 1

1. Emmy Lou Whitridge, interview with author, Houston, Texas, June 14, 1990.

2. Diane Tidemann Hansen, interview with author, Houston, Texas, August 14, 1990.

3. *Galveston Daily News,* May 11, 1940.

4. *Houston Post,* May 25, 1940.

5. *New York Times,* May 2, 1941.

6. Auswärtiges Amt, German Foreign Office, Bonn, Germany.

7. *New Orleans Times-Picayune,* September 12, 1937.

8. Ibid., December 28, 1937.

9. Ibid., January 27, 1938.

10. Ibid., June 15, 1940.

11. Ibid.

12. Ibid., June 17, 1940.

13. Ibid., June 18, 1940.

14. Ibid., June 19, 1940.

15. Ibid., June 23, 1940.

16. Ibid., September 26, 1940.

17. Ibid., November 22, 1940.

18. Ibid.

19. Ibid.

20. Harry Brown, interview with author, Galveston, Texas, July 25, 1990.

21. *New York Times,* June 17, 1941.

22. Erich Gimpel to author, September 2, 1991.

23. William L. Shirer, *The Rise and Fall of the Third Reich,* p. 903.

24. Shirer, *Rise and Fall,* pp. 903, 904.

25. Erich Gimpel in collaboration with Will Berthold, *Spy for Germany,* p. 12; Erich Gimpel, interview with author, Chicago, Illinois, June 5, 1991.

26. *New York Times,* July 16, 1941; Gimpel, *Spy for Germany,* pp. 55, 56.

27. Gimpel, *Spy for Germany,* pp. 55, 56.

28. *New York Times,* June 17, 1941.

29. Ibid.

30. *New York Times,* June 21, 1941; *New Orleans Times-Picayune,* July 2, 1941.

31. Brown interview.

32. *Galveston Daily News,* July 16, 1941.

33. Ibid.; *New York Times,* July 16, 1941.

34. *Galveston Daily News,* July 16, 1941.

Chapter 2

1. *Galveston Daily News,* July 3, 1941.

2. Ibid., July 8, 11, 13, 1941.

3. Lynn Alperin, *Custodians of the Coast: History of the United States Army Engineers at Galveston,* pp. 179, 181.

4. Charles Waldo Hayes, *The Island and City of Galveston,* p. 520.

5. *Galveston Daily News,* July 22, 1941.

6. Ibid.

7. Ibid.

8. Ibid., August 25, 30, 1941.

9. Jim McKaig, interview with author, League City, Texas, May 31, 1991.

10. Justin F. Gleichauf, *Unsung Sailors: The Navy Armed Guard in World War II,* p. 25.

11. *Galveston Daily News,* December 7, 1941.

12. Samuel Eliot Morison, *History of the United States Naval Operations in World War II,* vol. 1, *The Battle of the Atlantic, September 1939–May 1943,* p. 131.

13. V. E. Tarrant, *The U-Boat Offensive, 1914–1945,* p. 104.

14. *Corpus Christi Times,* January 29, 1942.

15. *Galveston Daily News,* January 30, 1942.

16. Ibid., January 29, 1942.

17. Tarrant, *U-Boat Offensive,* p. 104; Jürgen Rohwer,"The German U-Boat War and the United States Atlantic Fleet from June 1941 to May 1942,"

p. 32; John A. Reynolds, "History of the Gulf Sea Frontier, 6 February 1942–14 August 1945," p. 63.

18. Reynolds, "History of Gulf Sea," pp. 9, 10.

19. *Galveston Daily News,* February 14, 1942.

20. Ibid., February 20, 1942.

21. Ibid., February 23, 1942.

22. Ibid., March 11, 1942.

23. Ibid., March 13, 1942.

24. Harris to Nesbitt, Brantly Harris Letters, April 2, 1942, Rosenberg Library, Galveston, Texas.

25. Reynolds, "History of Gulf Sea," pp. 68–70, 227, n. 1.

26. Rohwer, *Axis Submarine Successes, 1939–1945,* pp. 88–92.

27. Morison, *Battle of the Atlantic,* p. 129; Karl Dönitz, *Admiral Dönitz Memoirs: Ten Years and Twenty Days,* p. 202.

28. Morison, *Battle of the Atlantic,* pp. 254, 255.

Chapter 3

1. The primary source for this chapter was the U.S. National Archives and Records Administration (hereafter NARA), Modern Military Division, Record Group (hereafter RG) 242, Records of the German Navy, 1850–1945, received from the United States Naval History Division, *Kriegstagebuch* (KTB) U-507, PG 30545/1–6, 3066, T-6-F, April 30–May, 1942.

Chapter 4

1. Preceding quotes from an article in a German newspaper, probably Hamburg, June 15, 1942, from the U-Boot-Archiv, Cuxhaven, Germany.

2. Naval Historical Center, Operational Archives Branch, Washington Navy Yard (hereafter NHC), Summary of Statements by Survivors, SS *Amapala,* June 2, 1942.

3. NARA, RG 26, box 6, Records of U.S. Coast Guard War Casualty Section; *Galveston Daily News,* May 10, 1942.

4. *Galveston Daily News,* May 10, 1942.

5. *New Orleans Times-Picayune,* May 10, 1942.

6. Preceding quotes from *Galveston Daily News,* May 11, 1942.

7. Ibid., May 14, 1942.

8. Auswärtiges Amt, (German Foreign Office), Bonn, Germany.

9. NARA, RG 242, *Kriegstagebuch* U-506, PG 30544/1–6, 3066, T-6-F, April–May, 1942.

10. Wilhelm Grap to author, November 11, 1991.

11. Previous quotes from NARA, RG 242, *Kriegstagebuch* U-506; Rohwer, *Axis Submarine Successes,* pp. 92–99.

12. Wilhelm Grap to author, November 11, 1991.

13. Monthly Submarine Report, U-506, U-Boot-Archiv, Cuxhaven, Germany.

14. Peter Padfield, *Dönitz: The Last Führer, Portrait of a Nazi War Leader,* p. 255.

Chapter 5

1. NARA, RG 26, Records of U.S. Coast Guard War Casualty Section, Statements by Survivors, SS *Alcoa Puritan,* box 3, NN3-26-80-22, May 12, 1942.

2. NHC, Summary of Statements by Survivors, SS *Alcoa Puritan,* May 12, 1942; NARA, RG 26, Statements from Survivors, box 3, NN3-26-22; Rohwer, *Axis Submarine Successes,* p. 93.

3. Reynolds, "History of the Gulf Sea Frontier," p. 75.

4. Morison, *Battle of the Atlantic,* p. 138.

5. Ibid., pp. 268, 269.

6. NHC, Summary of Statements by Survivors, SS *Aurora,* May 16, 1942.

7. NHC, War Diary, Gulf Sea Frontier Force, May 5, 1942.

8. Reynolds, "History of the Gulf Sea Frontier," p. 80.

9. *Encyclopedia Britannica,* s.v. "Gulf Stream."

10. Reynolds, "History of the Gulf Sea Frontier," p. 79; Rohwer, *Axis Submarine Successes,* pp. 92, 93; NHC, Papers of Headquarters, Gulf Sea Frontier, Key West, Florida. War Diary, May 5, 6, 1942.

11. *Galveston Daily News,* May 20, 1942.

12. NHC, Summary of Statements by Survivors, SS *Gulfpenn,* May 22, 1942.

13. *Galveston Daily News,* May 20, 1942; NARA, RG 26, Records of the U.S. Coast Guard War Casualty Section, Statements from Survivors of Vessel War Casualties, box 3, NN3-26-80-22, May 29, 1942; NARA, RG 26, Report on U.S. Tanker War Action, December 1, 1944.

14. NHC, Summary of Statements by Survivors, SS *David McKelvy,* May 29, 1942.

15. Reynolds, "History of the Gulf Sea Frontier," p. 88.

16. *Galveston Daily News,* May 11, 1942.

17. Ibid., May 12, 1942.

18. Ibid., May 17, 1942.

19. NHC, Summary of Statements by Survivors, SS *Virginia,* May 19, 1942; NARA, RG 26, Reports on U.S. Merchant Tanker War Action.
20. NARA, RG 26, Records of the U.S. Coast Guard War Casualty Section, Statements of Survivors of Vessel War Casualties, box 3, NN3-26-80-22.
21. Dönitz, *Memoirs,* p. 221.
22. *Galveston Daily News,* May 4, 1942.
23. Ibid., May 13, 1942.

Chapter 6

1. Preceding quotes from McKaig interview.
2. Thomas Kessner, *Fiorello H. La Guardia and the Making of Modern New York,* pp. 504, 505; *Galveston Daily News,* May 18, 1942.
3. *Galveston Daily News,* May 18, 1942.
4. Preceding quotes from NARA, RG 242, *Kriegstagebuch* U-106, PG 30102/1–9, 3034, T-304-B, September 24, 1940–February 8, 1943.
5. Preceding quotes from NARA, RG 242, *Kriegstagebuch* U-753, PG 30732–7, 3389, T-21-C, December 12, 1941–May 13, 1943; NHC, Summary of Statements by Survivors, SS *George Calvert,* June 18, 1942.
6. Preceding quotes from NARA, RG 242, *Kriegstagebuch* U-753.
7. Morison, *Battle of the Atlantic,* pp. 144, 413; Rohwer, *Axis Submarine Successes,* pp. 92–99.
8. Harris to Nesbitt, May 25, 1942.

Chapter 7

1. Preceding quotes from *Galveston Daily News,* May 18, 1942.
2. Ibid., May 22, 1942.
3. Ibid., May 18, 1942.
4. NHC, Summary of Statements by Survivors, SS *Halo,* June 19, 1942.
5. Reynolds, "History of the Gulf Sea Frontier," p. 97.
6. *Galveston Daily News,* May 19, 1942.
7. Preceding quotes from H. A. Suhler, interview with author, Galveston, Texas, July 25, 1990.
8. Preceding quotes from *Galveston Daily News,* May 23, 1942.
9. NHC, Summary of Statements by Survivors, SS *Carrabulle,* June 18, 1942; NARA, RG 26, box 6, Records of U.S. Coast Guard War Casualty Section.
10. NHC, Summary of Statements by Survivors, SS *Heredia,* June 5, 1942; NARA, *The Coast Guard at War: Assistance,* 14, vol. 2, pp. 42, 43.

11. NARA, *The Coast Guard at War: Assistance*, 14, vol. 2, p. 41.
12. Morison, *Battle of the Atlantic*, p. 142.

Chapter 8

1. *Galveston Daily News*, June 14, 1942; NHC, Summary of Statements of Survivors, M/T *William C. McTarnahan*, May 24, 1942.
2. *Galveston Daily News*, May 29, 1942.
3. Eberhard Rössler, trans. Harold Erenberg, *The U-Boat: The Evolution and Technical History of German Submarines*, pp. 161, 162.
4. Morison, *Battle of the Atlantic*, p. 129, n. 21.
5. *Galveston Daily News*, May 29, 1942.
6. Ibid., June 1, 1942.
7. Ibid., June 2, 1942.
8. Harris to Nesbitt, June 4, 1942.
9. *Galveston Daily News*, June 2, 1942.
10. Ibid., June 5, 1942.
11. Interview with Galveston woman who wished to remain anonymous.
12. *Galveston Daily News*, June 5, 1942.
13. Ibid.
14. Ibid., June 8, 1942.
15. Official navy reports say two torpedoes struck the first time and two more five minutes later. Handy believes a single torpedo hit, then one more.
16. Preceding quotes from James Handy to author, May 14, 1991.
17. Rohwer, *Axis Submarine Successes*, pp. 104, 105.
18. Preceding quotes from *Galveston Daily News*, June 14, 1942.
19. Ibid., June 16, 1942.
20. Rohwer, *Axis Submarine Successes*, pp. 100–107. Note: Gulf boundaries used for this book are between the southern tip of Florida and Cuba and between western Cuba and the Yucatán.

Chapter 9

1. NARA, RG 242, *Kriegstagebuch* U-67, PG 30064/1–9, 3030, T-300-B, January 22–July 30, 1943; Rohwer, *Axis Submarine Success*, pp. 100–12.
2. Preceding quotes from NARA, RG 242, *Kriegstagebuch* U-67.
3. Rohwer, *Axis Submarine Successes*, pp. 100–107.
4. Homer Hickam, Jr., *Torpedo Junction: U-Boat War off America's East Coast*, pp. 287–89.
5. Morison, *Battle of the Atlantic*, p. 144.
6. Reynolds, "History of the Gulf Sea Frontier," p. 101.

7. Ibid., p. 118.

8. *Galveston Daily News,* July 2, 1942.

9. Dönitz, *Memoirs,* p. 228.

10. *Galveston Daily News,* June 12, 29, 1942.

11. Ibid., July 6, 1942; preceding quotes from NHC, Summary of Statements by Survivors, SS *San Blas,* July 11, 1942.

12. *Galveston Daily News,* July 6, 1942.

13. NARA, RG 242, *Kriegstagebuch* U-171, PG 30158, 4185, October 22, 1941–October 9, 1942.

14. NHC, Summary of Statements by Survivors, SS *R. M. Parker, Jr.,* August 8, 1942; Edward M. Haake to author, May 24, 1991.

15. NARA, RG 242, *Kriegstagebuch* U-171.

Chapter 10

1. Alperin, *Custodians of the Coast,* pp. 195, 196.

2. Adolph Johnson, interview with author, Santa Fe, Texas, May 3, 1990.

3. Records, U.S. Army Corps of Engineers, box 27, file 660.3, "Surface Craft Detector 1941–43."

4. Preceding quotes from Johnson interview.

5. *Congressional Record,* Appendix, vol. 61, 67th Cong., 1st sess., March 4–November 23, 1921, Extension of Remarks, Hon. Charles F. Curry of California, in the House of Representatives, August 23, 1921, 8635.

6. Preceding quotes from Johnson interview.

7. *Galveston Daily News,* July 15, 1942.

8. Ibid., July 17, 1942.

9. Ibid., July 18, 1942.

10. Ibid, July 11, 18, 1942.

11. Preceding quotes from "Swamp Savvy," *Houston Chronicle,* section H, April 15, 1990, p. 1, by Carol Rust.

12. Eleanor C. Bishop, *Prints in the Sand: The U.S. Coast Guard Beach Patrol during World War II,* pp. 1, 2.

13. NARA, *The Coast Guard at War: Beach Patrol,* vol. 17, Washington, D.C.: Historical Section, Public Relations Division, U.S. Coast Guard Headquarters, 1945, p. 9.

14. Malcolm F. Willoughby, *The U.S. Coast Guard in World War II,* p. 47.

15. Bishop, *Prints in the Sand,* p. 43.

16. *Congressional Record,* U.S. House, Appendix, vol. 88, 77th sess.,

April 21–July 24, 1942, Extension of Remarks, Hon. Jared Y. Sanders, Jr. of Louisiana, in the House of Representatives, July 20, 1942, A2859. Elmer Davis headed the Office of War Information, a government agency that regulated the news.

17. Preceding quotes from *Galveston Daily News,* July 20, 1942.

18. Ibid., July 21, 1942.

19. Ibid., July 11, 1942.

20. Ibid.

21. Preceding quotes from *Galveston Daily News,* July 11, 1942.

Chapter 11

1. *Encyclopedia Britannica,* s.v. "Radar"; John Naumczik, interview with author, Beaumont, Texas, February 11, 1992.

2. Alperin, *Custodians of the Coast,* p. 196.

3. *Galveston Daily News,* July 24, 1942.

4. Ibid.

5. Ibid., July 27, 1942.

6. Preceding quotes from Ballinger Mills, interview with author, Galveston, Texas, April 15, 1992. Note: In all U-boat war diaries consulted for this book, no messages were ever received from U.S. shores.

7. Morison, *Battle of the Atlantic,* pp. 257, 259; *Galveston Daily News,* July 30, 1942.

8. NARA, RG 242, *Kriegstagebuch* U-166, PG 30153/1–3, 2884, T-259-A, March 24–August 3, 1942.

9. Capt. Barton M. Holmes and Capt. James E. Wise, Jr., "Here We Go Again!" *Sea Classics* (October, 1990), pp. 24–29.

10. Preceding quotes from NARA, Papers of the War Shipping Administration, "Reports recommending awards for certain personnel of the MS *Arriaga,* SS *Stanvac Palembang,* and SS *Robert E. Lee.*" Typescript.

11. Preceding quotes from NARA, Papers of the United States Fleet, Navy Department, Memorandum of August 1, 1942, to Commander Gulf Sea Frontier.

12. Preceding quotes from Frank Erickson, "David and Goliath."

13. Reynolds, "History of the Gulf Sea Frontier," p. 101.

14. David Kahn, *Seizing the Enigma: The Race to Break the German U-Boat Codes, 1939–1943,* pp. 4, 178 (photo), 215–17.

15. Morison, *Battle of the Atlantic,* p. 257.

16. Reynolds, "History of the Gulf Sea Frontier," pp. 222, 223.

17. Ibid., pp. 222–34; Captain Glenn Tronstad, interview with author, Port Arthur, Texas, April 19, 1991.

18. Tronstad interview.

19. Reynolds, "History of the Gulf Sea Frontier," pp. 121, 122.

Chapter 12

1. *Gladewater Mirror,* May 29, 1991; "Big Inch and Little Inch," from records of the War Emergency Pipelines, Inc.; Charles Morrow Wilson, "Paul Bunyan Underground," *World Petroleum* (June, 1965): 17–21.

2. *Galveston Daily News,* September 3, 1942.

3. Ibid., September 20, 1942.

4. Ibid., July 31, 1942.

5. Ibid., August 3, 1942.

6. Ibid., August 4, 1942.

7. Ibid., August 3, 1942.

8. Ibid., August 2, 1942.

9. Bishop, *Prints in the Sand,* p. 48; George Hamilton, interview with author, Stowell, Texas, October 9, 1990.

10. Hamilton interview.

11. Glenn Cudd, interview with author, Beaumont, Texas, May 30, 1991.

12. Willoughby, *U.S. Coast Guard in World War II,* p. 50.

13. NARA, Coast Guard War Diary Abstracts, New Orleans District, 1942, p. 113.

14. *Galveston Daily News,* August 23, 1942.

15. Ibid., August 4, 1942.

16. *National Cyclopedia of American Biography: Being a History of the United States,* pp. 5, 6; Dwight R. Messimer, *The Merchant U-Boat: Adventures of the Deutschland, 1916–1918,* pp. 59, 60.

17. *Galveston Daily News,* August 13, 1942.

18. Preceding quotes from *Galveston Daily News,* August 23, 1942.

19. Ibid., August 30, 1942.

20. Morison, *Battle of the Atlantic,* pp. 346, 347; NARA, *Guides to the Microfilmed Records of the German Navy,* p. 117.

21. Morison, *Battle of the Atlantic,* p. 347.

22. Reynolds, "History of the Gulf Sea Frontier," p. 121; Morison, *Battle of the Atlantic,* p. 348.

23. *Galveston Daily News,* September 1, 1942.

24. Ibid., September 1, 3, 1942.

25. Ibid, August 14–September 1, 1942.

26. Ibid., September 9, 11, 1942.

Chapter 13

1. Naumczik interview.
2. *Galveston Daily News,* September 4, 1942.
3. Ibid., September 17, 19, 26, 1942.
4. Ibid., September 22, 23, 1942.
5. Ibid., September 27, 1942.
6. Ibid., October 25, 1942.
7. Ibid.
8. Ibid., September 28, 29, 1942.
9. Ibid., September 30, 1942.
10. Ibid., October 4, 1942.
11. Ibid., October 1, 1942.
12. Ibid., October 2, 1942.
13. Ibid.
14. Ibid., October 5, 7, 1942; on display at the Galveston Railroad Museum.
15. *Galveston Daily News,* October 10, 1942.
16. Ibid., October 11, 1942.
17. Ibid., October 6, 1942.
18. Lyda Kempner Quinn, interview with author, Galveston, Texas, July 5, 1990.
19. Lyda Ann Thomas, interview with author, July 5, 1990.
20. Isaac Herbert Kempner to his daughter Cecile, 1942, Rosenberg Library, Galveston, Texas; Ruth Levy Kempner, interview with author, Galveston, Texas, August 22, 1990; Quinn interview.
21. *Galveston Daily News,* October 5, 1942.
22. Ibid., October 12, 1942; *Encyclopedia Britannica,* s.v. "Spanish-American War of 1898."
23. *Galveston Daily News,* October 12, 1942.
24. Ibid.

Chapter 14

1. *Galveston Daily News,* October 30, 1942.
2. Ibid.
3. Ibid., November 2, 1942.
4. Ibid., November 11, 1942.
5. Ibid., November 14, 1942.
6. Peter Petersen, telephone interview with author, November 18, 1991.
7. *Galveston Daily News,* November 12, 1942.
8. Ibid., November 17, 28, 1942.

9. Ibid., November 15, 1942.
10. Preceding quotes from Naumczik interview.
11. *Galveston Daily News,* November 25, 1942.
12. Ibid., December 1, 1942.
13. Ibid.
14. Ibid., December 7, 1942.
15. Preceding quotes from *Galveston Daily News,* December 8, 1942.
16. Ibid., December 22, 1942.
17. Ibid., January 11, 1943.
18. Ibid., January 31, 1943.
19. Ibid., February 8–10, 1943.
20. Dönitz, *Memoirs,* p. 250; Petersen interview.
21. Reynolds, "History of the Gulf Sea Frontier," pp. 141–43.
22. Ibid., pp. 144, 145.
23. Ibid., p. 146; *Dictionary of American Naval Fighting Ships,* p. 116.
24. Preceding quotes from NARA, RG 242, *Kriegstagebuch* U-155, PG 30142/1-12, 2935-36, T-198-D, T-199-D, August 23, 1941–October 21, 1944.
25. Reynolds, "History of the Gulf Sea Frontier," p. 148.

Chapter 15

1. John Kinietz, telephone interview with author, March 25, 1992.
2. No FBI records exist for the Galveston-Houston area from 1941 to 1945; therefore, it is not known whether a radio was found.
3. Reynolds, "History of the Gulf Sea Frontier," pp. 152–53.
4. *Galveston Daily News,* April 28, May 2, 1943.
5. NARA, RG 457 (National Security Agency), German Navy U-Boat Messages Translations and Summaries, SRGN 18643–19199, May, 1943. Box 26, book 18852–19097, SRG 18939.
6. Ibid., SRG 19072.
7. Ibid., SRG 19078.
8. Ibid., SRG 19128.
9. Ibid., SRG 13132; box 27, SRGN 19200–947, June 1–18, 1943.
10. Ibid., SRG 19428.
11. Ibid., SRG 19782.
12. *The U-Boat Commander's Handbook,* pp. 24, 45.
13. Preceding quotes from ibid., pp. 77, 78.
14. *Galveston Daily News,* June 28, 1943; Paolo E. Coletta, ed., *United States Navy and Marine Corps Bases, Domestic,* pp. 229, 230.
15. NHC, "History of U.S. Naval Air Station, Hitchcock, Texas"; Len-

nart Ege, *Balloons and Airships,* pp. 211; *Galveston Daily News,* June 28, 1943.

16. Reynolds, "History of the Gulf Sea Frontier," pp. 164, 165.

17. NARA, *Guides to the Microfilmed Records of the German Navy, 1850–1945: No. 2, Records Relating to U-Boat Warfare, 1939–1945,* p. 52. U-134 was later presumed lost with all hands on September 6, 1943.

18. Ibid., p. 166; Petersen interview.

19. Previous quotes from NARA, RG 242, *Kriegstagebuch* U-527, PG 30565, 2979, T-298, February 9, 1942–December 4, 1943.

20. "U-527," Report of the Commander, U-Boot-Archiv, Cuxhaven, Germany, February 6, 1942; NARA, RG 38, Records of the Chief of Naval Operations, Official Naval Intelligence, Special Activities Branch (OP 16–2), 1941–45, Reports on Interrogations, box 22, file "U-527 Personalia & Prelim."; Herbert Uhlig, interview with Ralph Uhlig, Neuenkirchen/Soltau, Germany, December 24, 1990.

21. Arnold Krammer, *Nazi Prisoners of War in America,* p. 119.

22. Herbert Uhlig interview with Ralph Uhlig.

23. *Galveston Daily News,* May 7, 1943.

24. Ibid., May 8, 1943.

Chapter 16

1. *Galveston Daily News,* May 31, 1943.

2. *Dictionary of American Naval Fighting Ships,* pp. 136, 137.

3. *Galveston Daily News,* June 3, 1943.

4. Preceding quotes from *Galveston Daily News,* June 9, 1943.

5. Ibid., July 10, 1943.

6. Ibid., July 17, 1943.

7. Ibid., July 20, 1943.

8. Ibid., July 25, 26, 1943.

9. Ibid., July 27, 1943.

10. Ibid.

11. Ibid., July 28, 1943.

12. Naumczik interview.

13. *Galveston Daily News,* July 28, 1943.

14. Ibid., July 31, 1943.

15. Ibid., July 29, 1943.

16. Preceding quotes from Melanie Wiggins, *They Made Their Own Law: Stories of Bolivar Peninsula,* pp. 234, 235.

17. Reynolds, "History of the Gulf Sea Frontier," p. 167.

18. *Galveston Daily News,* August 5, 1943.

Chapter 17

1. Peter Petersen, interview with author, May 18, 1992.
2. NARA, RG 242, *Kriegstagebuch* U-518, PG 30556/1–7, 3068, T-8-F, April 25, 1942–October 24, 1944. In October, 1943, Great Britain was given permission by Portugal to build an air base at Lajes Airfield, the Azores.
3. Petersen interview.

Chapter 18

1. *Galveston Daily News,* September 11, 1943.
2. Ibid., September 20, 1943.
3. Preceding quotes from *Galveston Daily News,* September 27, 1943.
4. Ibid., September 22, 1943.
5. Ibid., November 12, 1943.
6. Ibid.; *Encyclopedia Britannica,* s.v. "Rockets."
7. *Galveston Daily News,* September 20, 1943.
8. Ibid., September 29, 1943.
9. Ibid., October 4, 1943.
10. Ibid., October 11, 28, 1943.
11. Ibid., October 28, November 3, 1943.
12. Krammer, *Nazi Prisoners of War,* appendix 271; Robert Tissing, "Stalag Texas, 1943–1945: Detention and Use of Prisoners of War in Texas during World War II," *Military History of Texas and the Southwest* 13 (1976): 23, 24.
13. Ida M. Blanchett, "POWs in Galveston County," *In Between* 105 (July, 1981): 13–15; Arnold P. Krammer, "When the Afrika Korps Came to Texas," *Southwestern Historical Quarterly* 80 (January, 1977): 247–82.
14. NARA, RG 389 (Provost Marshall General), Enemy POW Information, Bureau Reporting Branch, Subject File 1942–46, Inspection and Field Reports, Concordia to Custer, box 2659.
15. Blanchette, "POWs in Galveston County"; Sara Stubbs, interview with author, Galveston, Texas, October 16, 1991.
16. Risher Randall, interview with author, Galveston, Texas, December 13, 1991.
17. *Galveston Daily News,* October 17, November 26, 1943.
18. *Galveston Daily News,* October 17, 1943; Ida M. Blanchette, "POWs In Galveston County, Part II: Camp Wallace–Hitchcock," *In Between* 106 (July, 1981): 13–15.
19. Jack Dodendorf to author, August 17, 1990.

Bibliography

Published Sources

Alperin, Lynn M. *Custodians of the Coast: History of the United States Army Engineers at Galveston.* Washington, D.C.: U.S. Government Printing Office, 1977.

Bishop, Eleanor C. *Prints in the Sand: The U.S. Coast Guard Beach Patrol during World War II.* Prairie View: Texas A&M University at Prairie View, 1989.

Blanchette, Ida M. "POWs in Galveston County, Part II: Camp Wallace–Hitchcock." *In Between* 106 (July, 1981): 13–15.

———. "POW's in Galveston County." *In Between* 105 (July, 1981): 13–15.

Coletta, Paolo, ed. *United States Navy and Marine Corps Bases, Domestic.* Westport, Conn.: Greenwood Press, 1985.

Dictionary of American Naval Fighting Ships. Vol. 2. Washington, D.C.: Navy Department, Office of the Chief of Naval Operations, Naval History Division, 1963.

Dönitz, Karl. *Admiral Dönitz Memoirs: Ten Years and Twenty Days.* Translated by R. H. Stevens, in collaboration with David Woodward. Cleveland: World Pub. Co., 1959.

Ege, Lennart. *Balloons and Airships.* New York: Macmillan Co., 1974. *Encyclopedia Britannica,* 1963 edition.

Erickson, Frank. "David and Goliath." N.p., n.d.

Gimpel, Erich, in collaboration with Will Berthold. *Spy for Germany.* London: Robert Hale Ltd., 1957.

Gleichauf, Justin. *Unsung Sailors: The Navy Armed Guard in World War II.* Annapolis: Naval Institute Press, 1990.

Guides to the Microfilmed Records of the German Navy, 1850–1945. No.

2: *Records Relating to U-Boat Warfare, 1939–1945.* Washington: National Archives and Records Administration, 1985.

Hayes, Charles Waldo. *The Island and City of Galveston.* Vol. 1. 1879. Reprint. Austin: Jenkins Garrett Press, 1974.

Hickam, Homer, Jr. *Torpedo Junction: U-Boat War off America's East Coast.* Annapolis: Naval Institute Press, 1989.

Holmes, Capt. Barton M. and Capt. James E. Wise. "Here We Go Again!" *Sea Classics* (October, 1990), 24–29.

Kahn, David. *Seizing the Enigma: The Race to Break the German U-Boat Codes, 1939–1943.* Boston: Houghton Mifflin Co., 1991.

Kessner, Thomas. *Fiorello H. La Guardia and the Making of Modern New York.* New York: McGraw-Hill Pub. Co., 1989.

Krammer, Arnold. *Nazi Prisoners of War in America.* New York: Stern and Day Pub., 1979.

———. "When the Afrika Korps Came to Texas." *Southwestern Historical Quarterly* 80 (January, 1977): 247–82.

Messimer, Dwight R. *The Merchant U-Boat: Adventures of the Deutschland, 1916–1918.* Annapolis: Naval Institute Press, 1988.

Morison, Samuel Eliot. *History of the United States Naval Operations in World War II.* Vol. 1, *The Battle of the Atlantic, September 1939–May 1943.* Boston: Little, Brown & Co., 1954.

National Archives and Records Administration (NARA), *Guides to the Microfilmed Records of the German Navy, 1850–1945: No. 2, Records Relating to U-Boat Warfare, 1939–1945.* Compiled by Timothy Mulligan. Washington, D.C.: U.S. National Archives, 1985.

National Cyclopedia of American Biography: Being a History of the United States. Vol. 15. New York: James T. White & Co., 1916.

Padfield, Peter. *Dönitz: The Last Führer, Portrait of a Nazi War Leader.* New York: Harper & Row, 1984.

Rohwer, Jürgen. *Axis Submarine Successes: 1939–1945.* Annapolis: Naval Institute Press, 1983.

Rössler, Eberhard. Translated by Harold Erenberg. *The U-Boat: The Evolution and Technical History of German Submarines.* Annapolis: Naval Institute Press, 1989.

Rust, Carol. "Swamp Savvy." *Houston Chronicle,* section H, April 15, 1990.

Shirer, William L. *The Rise and Fall of the Third Reich.* New York: Fawcett Crest by arrangement with Simon & Schuster, 1989.

Tarrant, V. E. *The U-Boat Offensive, 1914–1945.* Annapolis: Naval Institute Press, 1989.

Thomas, Lowell. *Raiders of the Deep.* Garden City, N.Y.: Garden City Pub. Co., 1928.

Tissing, Robert. "Stalag Texas, 1943–1945: Detention and Use of Prisoners of War in Texas during World War II." *Military History of Texas and the Southwest* 13 (1975): 23–34.

The U-Boat Commander's Handbook. Gettysburg, Penn.: Thomas Pub., 1989.

Wiggins, Melanie. *They Made Their Own Law: Stories of Bolivar Peninsula.* Houston: Rice University Press, 1991.

Willoughby, Malcolm F. *The U.S. Coast Guard in World War II.* Annapolis: Naval Institute Press, 1957.

Wilson, Charles Morrow. "Paul Bunyan Underground." *World Petroleum* (June, 1965): 17–21.

Unpublished Sources

Auswärtiges Amt (Foreign Office), Bonn, Germany.

Bundesarchiv, Koblenz, Germany.

National Archives and Records Administration (NARA), Naval Historical Center, Washington, D.C.

Reynolds, Lt. John A. "History of the Gulf Sea Frontier, 6 February–14 August 1945," U.S. Naval Administration in World War II, Naval Historical Center, Washington, D.C. Typescript.

Rohwer, Jürgen. "The German U-Boat War and the United States Atlantic Fleet from June 1941 to May 1942." Paper written for the conference, Battle of the Atlantic: The Eastern Sea Frontier Campaign. February 22–23, 1991, Virginia Beach, Virginia.

Rosenberg Library, Galveston, Texas.

U-Boot-Archiv, Cuxhaven, Germany.

United States Army Corps of Engineers, Galveston, Texas.

Index

NOTE: **Boldface** page numbers indicate photos.

CPSIA information can be obtained at www.ICGtesting.com
Printed in the USA
LVOW10s2131140715

446077LV00003B/12/P